Gulf Politics and Economics in a Changing World

Gulf Politics and Economics in a Changing World

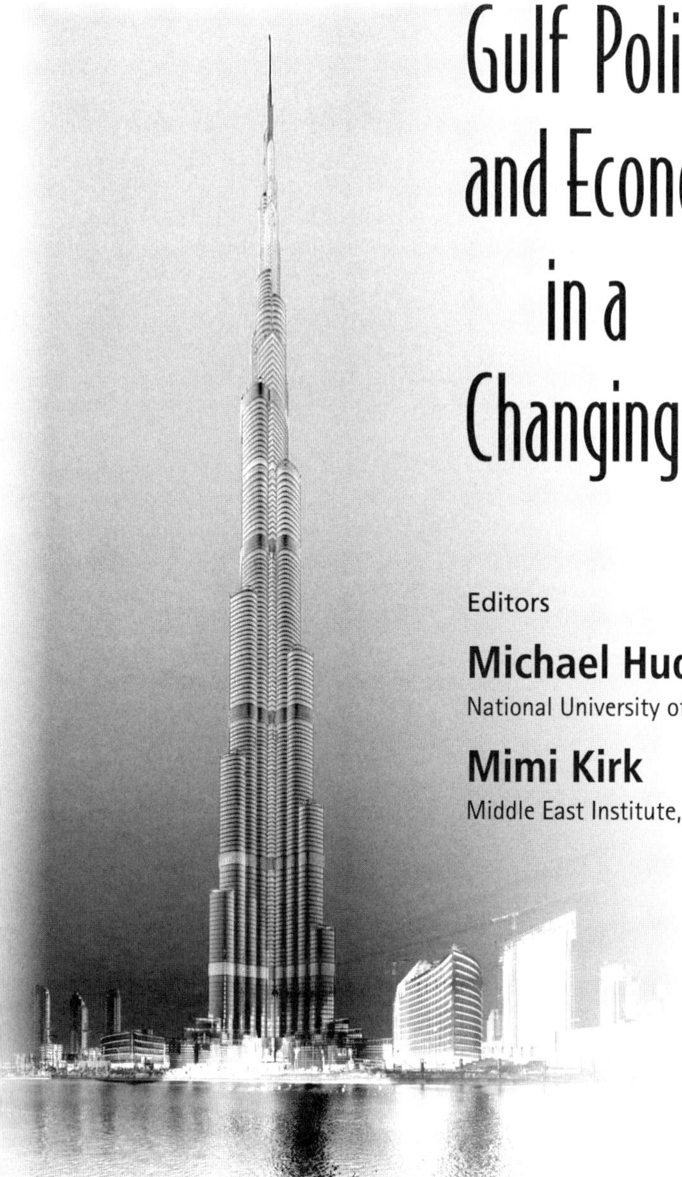

Editors

Michael Hudson
National University of Singapore, Singapore

Mimi Kirk
Middle East Institute, USA

NEW JERSEY · LONDON · SINGAPORE · BEIJING · SHANGHAI · HONG KONG · TAIPEI · CHENNAI

Published by

World Scientific Publishing Co. Pte. Ltd.
5 Toh Tuck Link, Singapore 596224
USA office: 27 Warren Street, Suite 401-402, Hackensack, NJ 07601
UK office: 57 Shelton Street, Covent Garden, London WC2H 9HE

Library of Congress Cataloging-in-Publication Data
Gulf politics and economics in a changing world / edited by Michael Hudson (Middle East Institute, National University of Singapore) and Mimi Kirk (Middle East Institute, Washington DC).
 pages cm
 ISBN 978-9814566193 (hardcover : alk. paper)
 1. Persian Gulf Region--Politics and government--21st century. 2. Persian Gulf Region--Foreign relations--21st century. 3. Persian Gulf Region--Economic conditions--21st century. 4. Persian Gulf Region--Strategic aspects. 5. Persian Gulf Region--Foreign relations--United States. 6. United States--Foreign relations--Persian Gulf Region. I. Hudson, Michael, 1939– , editor of compilation. II. Kirk, Mimi, editor of compilation.
 JQ1840.G85 2014
 320.9536--dc23
                                                                                                2013034298

British Library Cataloguing-in-Publication Data
A catalogue record for this book is available from the British Library.

Cover image © Nicolas Lannuzel

Copyright © 2014 by World Scientific Publishing Co. Pte. Ltd.

All rights reserved. This book, or parts thereof, may not be reproduced in any form or by any means, electronic or mechanical, including photocopying, recording or any information storage and retrieval system now known or to be invented, without written permission from the publisher.

For photocopying of material in this volume, please pay a copying fee through the Copyright Clearance Center, Inc., 222 Rosewood Drive, Danvers, MA 01923, USA. In this case permission to photocopy is not required from the publisher.

In-house Editor: Chye Shu Wen

Typeset by Stallion Press
Email: enquiries@stallionpress.com

Printed in Singapore by World Scientific Printers.

Contents

About the Editors vii
About the Contributors ix

Introduction: The Gulf Enigma 1
Michael Hudson

The Gulf States and the Economy 9

Chapter 1: The Development Trajectory of the GCC States: An Analysis of Aims and Visions in Current Development Plans 11
Martin Hvidt

Chapter 2: Redesigning the Distributional Bargain in the GCC 29
Steffen Hertog

Chapter 3: State-Business Relations in the Gulf: The Role of Business Actors in the Decision-Making Process in Bahrain and Oman 55
Marc Valeri

Gulf Governance 77

Chapter 4: The Rule of Law and Political Liberalization in the Arab Gulf 79
David M. Mednicoff and Joanna E. Springer

Chapter 5:	The Dynamics of Distribution in the Gulf: Selective Allocations, Agency, and Bureaucratic Accessibility in Kuwait	109
	James C. A. Redman	

The Gulf and Beyond: Relations and Tensions   139

Chapter 6:	Rethinking Regional Organization in the Gulf and the Greater Middle East	141
	Malik R. Dahlan	
Chapter 7:	Sources of Continuity in Iran's Foreign Policy	161
	Mahmood Sariolghalam	

The United States and the Gulf   179

Chapter 8:	American Policy in the Persian Gulf: From Balance of Power to Failed Hegemony	181
	F. Gregory Gause, III	
Chapter 9:	Neither East Nor West? The Gulf in a Post-American World	197
	Alain Gresh	
Chapter 10:	U.S. Military Bases in the Gulf and the Dynamics of Redeployment	207
	Degang Sun	

Index	223

About the Editors

Michael Hudson is Director of the Middle East Institute and Professor of Political Science at the National University of Singapore. He is also Professor Emeritus at Georgetown University, where he served as Director of the Center for Contemporary Arab Studies for many years. He has edited and contributed to numerous books, including *Middle East Dilemma: The Politics and Economics of Arab Integration* (Columbia University Press/CCAS, 1999); *The Palestinians: New Directions* (CCAS, 1990); and *Alternative Approaches to the Arab-Israeli Conflict* (CCAS, 1984). His other works include *The Precarious Republic: Political Modernization in Lebanon* (Random House, 1968, 1985); *Arab Politics: The Search for Legitimacy* (Yale University Press, 1977), and numerous chapters and articles appearing in such journals as *The Middle East Journal, Middle East Policy, International Affairs, Comparative Politics*, and *al-Mustaqbil al-'Arabi*. Hudson was awarded the 2011 Jere L. Bacharach Service Award from the Middle East Studies Association (MESA), of which he is a past president.

Mimi Kirk, Research Director at the Middle East Institute in Washington, D. C., was formerly editor for the Center for Contemporary Arab Studies at Georgetown University and for the Middle East Institute at the National University of Singapore. Her publications include *Palestine and the Palestinians in the Twenty-First Century* (edited with Rochelle Davis, Indiana University Press, 2013); *Modern Middle East Authoritarianism: Roots, Ramifications, and Crisis* (edited with Noureddine Jebnoun and Mehrdad Kia, Routledge, 2013);

and *Uncovering Iraq: Trajectories of Disintegration and Transformation* (edited with Chris Toensing, CCAS Georgetown, 2011). She holds an M.A. in cultural studies from Emory University and an M.A. in creative nonfiction writing from Johns Hopkins University. Her writing has appeared in *Middle East Report*, *Jadaliyya*, and *The Atlantic*.

About the Contributors

Malik R. Dahlan, a lawyer trained in both the Middle East and the West, is the Founder and President of the law and policy reform organization iPlatform for Global Change, Chief Lawyer at the Middle East law firm MBR Legal, and principal of Institution Quraysh. He also serves as the Vice President International of the Harvard Law School Association and is the founding president of the Harvard Law School Association of Arabia.

F. Gregory Gause, III is Professor of Political Science at the University of Vermont and a Non-Resident Senior Fellow at the Brookings Doha Center. He was previously on the faculty of Columbia University (1987–1995) and was Fellow for Arab and Islamic Studies at the Council on Foreign Relations in New York (1993–1994). During the 2009–2010 academic year he was Kuwait Foundation Visiting Professor of International Affairs at the Kennedy School of Government, Harvard University. In the spring of 2009 he was a Fulbright scholar at the American University of Kuwait. In the spring of 2010 he served as a research fellow at the King Faisal Center for Islamic Studies and Research in Riyadh, Saudi Arabia. He has published three books, the most recent of which is *The International Relations of the Persian Gulf* (Cambridge University Press, 2010). His articles have appeared in *Foreign Affairs*, *Foreign Policy*, *The Middle East Journal*, *Security Studies*, the *Washington Quarterly*, *National Interest*, and in other journals and edited volumes. He received his Ph.D. in political science from Harvard University in 1987 and his B.A. (summa cum laude) from St. Joseph's University in Philadelphia in 1980. He studied Arabic at the American University in Cairo (1982–1983) and Middlebury College (1984).

Alain Gresh was Editor of *Le Monde Diplomatique* from 1995 to 2005 and has been the paper's Deputy Director since 2008. He is the president of the Association of French Journalists Specialized on the Maghreb and the Middle East (AJMO). He is also the author of *De quoi la Palestine est-elle le nom?* (Actes Sud, 2012); *L'Islam, la République et le monde* (Fayard, 2004); and *Israël-Palestine, vérités sur un conflit* (Fayard, 2001). With Françoise Germain-Robin and Tariq Ramadan, he is author of *L'Islam en questions* (Actes-Sud/Sindbad, 2000 and 2002) and, with Dominique Vidal, *An A to Z of the Middle East* (Zed, 1990; I. B. Tauris, 2004).

Steffen Hertog is Associate Professor in Comparative Politics at the London School of Economics. He was previously Kuwait Professor at Sciences Po in Paris and holds a Ph.D. from the University of Oxford. He has been traveling and working in the Middle East extensively since 2000, both as an academic and as a public policy consultant. Hertog's main interest lies in Gulf and Middle East political economy, specifically Arab bureaucracies, state-business relations, and labor markets. He has a subsidiary interest in issues of political violence in the Islamic world. His academic publications have appeared in leading political science and area studies journals, including *World Politics*, *International Journal of Middle East Studies*, *Review of International Political Economy*, and *Comparative Studies in Society and History*. His book on the politics of economic reform in Saudi Arabia, *Princes, Brokers and Bureaucrats: Oil and the State in Saudi Arabia*, was published by Cornell University Press in 2010. He is the editor of *Labour Market, Unemployment and Migration in the GCC* (Gerlach Press, 2012) and co-editor, with Giacomo Luciani and Marc Valeri for *Business Politics in the Middle East* (Hurst, 2013). His book about Islamic radicalism and higher education, co-authored with Diego Gambetta, is forthcoming from Princeton University Press.

Martin Hvidt is Professor at Zayed University, Dubai, United Arab Emirates and formerly Associate Professor at the Centre for Contemporary Middle East Studies, University of Southern Denmark. Educated as a geographer and economist, he teaches courses in political economy and development economics related to the Middle East. His current research focuses on the (economic) development of the Gulf countries, and he is the author of a range of articles and book chapters on the Gulf, among them "Economic Diversification in GCC Countries" (London School of Economic and Political Science, 2013); "Planning for Development in the GCC States: A Content Analysis of Current Development Plans" (*Journal of Arabian Studies*, 2012); "Economic and Institutional Reforms in the Arab Gulf Countries" (*The Middle East Journal*, 2011); "The Dubai Model: An Outline of Key Development-process Elements in Dubai" (*International Journal of Middle East Studies*, 2009); and "Public-Private Ties and Their Contribution to Development: The Case of Dubai" (*Middle Eastern Studies*, 2007).

David M. Mednicoff directs the Master's in Public Policy and Middle Eastern Studies programs at the University of Massachusetts, Amherst. His areas of expertise include Middle Eastern law and politics, international law, human rights, globalization studies, and comparative public policy. He holds a J.D. as well as a Ph.D. (in Political Science) from Harvard University. Mednicoff's publications and ongoing research deal broadly with interdisciplinary connections between legal and political ideas, and institutions at the national and transnational levels, particularly as they relate to current policy issues in the Middle East. He is currently completing two book manuscripts on the politics of the rule of law, democratization, and U.S. foreign policy in five Arab societies. He has also written on Arab constitutional politics and Islam before and after the events of 2011, the legal regulation of migrant workers in the Arab Gulf, human rights in the Middle East, and humanitarian intervention. He has been invited to present his work at the Carnegie Endowment for International Peace, the U.S. Department of State, the Saudi Arabia Institute of Diplomatic Studies, and Georgetown, Harvard, Stanford, and Yale Universities, among other places.

James C. A. Redman is a cultural anthropologist whose research focuses on the primacy of social connections in the Middle East and the ways that these interpersonal ties can provide economic and political rewards as well as access to state resources. His current projects are based on his ethnographic fieldwork conducted in Kuwait between 2005 and 2010 that included in-depth, longitudinal interviews and participant observation with citizens and expatriates in both the public and private sectors. Particularly, he is concerned with the occurrences of informality in state structures and the means through which bureaucratic channels can be approached or circumvented outside of official avenues. By developing these examples of the junctures where state and society intersect, he hopes to better illustrate what "working the system" means in terms of local capital, as defined in the broadest sense possible, for both supplicants and their benefactors.

Mahmood Sariolghalam is Professor of International Relations at the National University of Iran in Tehran (Shahid Beheshti). He completed his B.A. in political science at California State University and earned his M.A. and Ph.D. in international relations at the University of Southern California. Sariolghalam pursued a postdoctorate at the Ohio State University. He specializes in international politics of the Middle East, Iranian foreign policy and political culture, and has written extensively in Farsi, Arabic, and English. He has made presentations in more than 100 countries. His recent publications include *Iranian Authoritarianism During the Qajar Period* (5th edition) (in Farsi) (Farzan Rooz Publishing House, 2013); "Transition in the Middle East: New Arab Realities and Iran" (*Middle East Policy*, Spring 2013); "The Evolution of State in Iran: A Political Culture Perspective" (Strategic Studies Center of Kuwait University, 2010); "International Relations in Iran: Achievements and Limitations" (in *International Relations Scholarship Around the World*, Routledge, 2009); and "Iran in Search of Itself" (*Current History*, 2008). Sariolghalam spent the 2009–2010 academic year at Kuwait University. He is a member of the International Studies Association (United States) and the Global Agenda Council of the World Economic Forum (Switzerland), and serves as a Non-Resident Scholar at ASERI (Italy). Sariolghalam was a Visiting Fellow at the Brookings Institution in Washington, D.C. in early 2012.

Joanna E. Springer is a Master's candidate in the Public Policy and Administration Program at the University of Massachusetts, Amherst. She holds a B.A. from Hampshire College in political sociology. She worked as a project developer for two years for the Middle Eastern Languages and Cultures program at the Five Colleges in Amherst, Massachusetts. During the summers of 2011 and 2013, she interned as a grant writer at the Episcopal Technological and Vocational Training Center in Ramallah, West Bank. In 2013, she also interned as Outreach Coordinator at Dalia Association, a community development organization in Ramallah. Her research interests focus on economic policy and government accountability in the Middle East. She is fluent in French, reads Modern Standard Arabic, and is conversant in the Levantine dialect.

Degang Sun is Associate Professor of Political Science and Assistant Director of the Middle East Studies Institute, Shanghai International Studies University, China. He received his Ph.D. in 2006 and spent two years in a post-doctoral research program at the School of International Relations and Public Affairs at Fudan University (2010–2012). He has been an academic visitor at the University of Hong Kong (2004–2005), Denver University (2007–2008), and the Middle East Centre at the University of Oxford and the Oxford Centre for Islamic Studies (2012–2013). He serves on the editorial board of the *Journal of Mediterranean and Balkan Intelligence* and the *Journal of Middle Eastern and Islamic Studies* (*in Asia*). In 2012, he was named one of the "New Century Excellent Talents in Universities" for his research project, "Western Powers' Military Base Deployment in the Middle East and Its Implications for China," granted by China's Ministry of Education. He has published more than a dozen articles in key academic journals in China and abroad and has published three books, the most recent titled *Quasi-alliance in Theory and Practice: An Empirical Study of Big Powers' Relations with Middle East Countries*.

Marc Valeri is Senior Lecturer in Political Economy of the Middle East and Director of the Centre for Gulf Studies at the University of Exeter. His main research interests are the social, political, and economic transformations in the Gulf monarchies. He is currently conducting an ESRC-funded research project on state-business relations in the GCC states. He is the author of *Oman: Politics and Society in the Qaboos State* (Hurst and Oxford University Press, 2009).

Introduction: The Gulf Enigma

Michael Hudson

There was a time — less than half a century ago — when the principalities on the Arab side of the Persian Gulf were known outside of the Middle East mainly for their colorful postage stamps. A bare subsistence economy was sustained by pearling, fishing, and smuggling. Life spans were short. British officials advised and manipulated a cluster of ruling tribal families. Around 1970 a visiting American researcher was invited to watch a polo match between Brits and Pakistanis of the Trucial Oman Scouts and then taken to the officer's mess for the customary gin and tonic, where old hands reminisced about their adventures in Aden, Iraq, and Palestine. A British ambassador in Muscat told the American visitor that "this will someday be yours." On the other side of the Gulf, the Shah was campaigning to modernize Iran to the level of Germany by the end of the twentieth century and become the regional hegemon, while in the Arab world to the west, populist, anti-imperialist, and nationalist elements were casting their eyes on the Gulf's rising oil riches. Further behind the scenes the United States was beginning to worry about "Gulf security" as Britain loosened its grip and the Soviet Union sought to expand its influence in and around the Arabian Peninsula.

What happened subsequently is well known. Fueled by immense oil revenues the Gulf states embarked on a development binge. But with their small populations, meager skilled human resources, and almost no hard power, they turned mainly to Western advisors to guide them on their steep upward trajectory. How would they cope with the challenges and dangers of intense growth in a volatile regional environment?

They needed, first of all, to fashion an economy driven by exogenous oil rents that would enhance the growth of their "states" without diluting the traditional rulers' authority. The strategy involved encouraging a capitalist private sector capable of modernizing the socioeconomic infrastructure but always dependent on the ruling elites. Whether this model could also handle issues involving redistribution and equity, an enormous expatriate labor force, and voluntary or involuntary unemployment of the growing indigenous youth cohort remained to be seen.

Secondly, they needed to confront the problem of governance in a fast-modernizing environment. In particular they sought to avoid what political scientists had described as "the king's dilemma" — how to expand governmental and administrative capabilities and yet maintain personal and family rule through clientelism and *wasta* (connections). The diminutive size of most of the shaykhdoms eased the dilemma, and in the case of Saudi Arabia — by far the largest of them — the existence of a royal family numbering in the thousands of male princes provided almost the functional equivalent of a caste or a single party to further strengthen tribal control mechanisms. But could such a system accommodate growing regional ideological forces for democratization and political Islam?

The third challenge arose out of the turbulent environment of the larger Middle East by the 1970s. Britain's withdrawal as "protector" of the Gulf Arab states in 1971 was met, it is said, with dismay by many of the ruling shaykhs, and with good reason. Iran was left as the dominant regional power and lost no time in reasserting a claim to sovereignty over Bahrain. Although the Shah accepted the results of a Bahraini referendum that strongly favored independence, the Islamist regime in Tehran adapted a more menacing approach, after his overthrow and also seized three small islands belonging to the United Arab Emirates — Abu Musa and the Greater and Lesser Tunbs. Only Oman retained good relations with Iran, and even solicited Iranian military support against the Arab nationalist-inspired revolt in Dhofar in the 1970s. The year 1979 marked a new era of Gulf insecurity, with the Soviet invasion of Afghanistan, the siege of the Grand Mosque of Mecca and, of course, the Islamic Revolution in Iran.

Enter the United States as the new great power protector of the Gulf. The fourth challenge of the Arab Gulf states was to promote and ensure an American security umbrella after the fading of British power, continued probing by the Soviet Union, and the Iranian Revolution. Saudi Arabia remained the main pillar of America's security architecture. The Kingdom and the United States cooperated to contain the ideological threat of Arab nationalism led by Egypt's Gamal Abdel Nasser, and were greatly aided by Israel's defeat of the Egyptian army in 1967. Subsequently Saudi Arabia and the United States worked together to contain the two big Gulf states, Iran and Iraq, and also teamed up to engage militant Islamist factions in Afghanistan against the Soviet Union. They then worked together in the early 2000s to contain those same Islamist forces that had turned against their erstwhile sponsors. Even as the Gulf states were modernizing economically and administratively, they could not guarantee their own security without massive American protection.

The Gulf Today: Powerhouse or Power Vacuum?

No one would deny that the Gulf has undergone extraordinary changes over the past decades. But how stable, how durable, and how "developed" is it? There has been a sufficient transformation such that we can speak of a "Gulf model" appropriate to the conditions and challenges of the twenty-first century? To be sure, oil and gas revenues now sustain one of the world's major markets and investment centers. Notwithstanding their modest population base, the economies of the Gulf Cooperation Council (GCC) states easily compare with those of the much larger, older, and established countries like Egypt. In terms of physical infrastructure the region is so far advanced that it hardly seems to be part of the Middle East.

Its political order, seemingly anachronistic, has proven to be remarkably stable so far, with its ruling families apparently secure and its small indigenous populations comfortable and complacent in their general affluence. With the qualified exception of Kuwait, the Gulf Arab states have eschewed the democratic model for an "enlightened family despotism" — what political scientists would call the "rentier model" in which populations, in a putative pact with their rulers, give up political rights for social and economic welfare. And behind the "carrot" of welfare is the "stick" of the discreet but pervasive security forces, which discourage political expression beyond the limits set by the ruling families.

And what of the Gulf's position in the region and the world? Long regarded as peripheral and dependent, we now see the Gulf states acting like major powers despite their paucity of "hard power." For most of the post-World War II period, the Arab state system was dominated first by Egypt and then by a quartet of medium powers — Egypt, Saudi Arabia, Syria, and Iraq. Today it is Saudi Arabia and its small GCC satellites that seem to comprise a new pole, if not center, of the Middle East state system. Tiny Qatar indeed acts like a great power, mediating disputes here and there, influencing public opinion via its vastly successful Al Jazeera media empire, and deploying its riches and even symbolic military capability to faraway conflicts from Libya to Syria. Gulf intellectuals deliver stern lectures to India, China, Russia, and Europe about respecting the new Gulf power. Speaking at a conference in Singapore in 2013, a prominent Saudi prince joked that he wished the Arabian Peninsula could be detached from the rest of the Middle East and float toward Asia.

As for relations with the United States, a new assertiveness on the part of Gulf rulers and elites is also evident. They warn Washington not to take the traditional "special relationship" for granted, and that Washington must stand tough against what they see as the Iranian threat and the populist, Islamist dangers of the so-called "Arab Spring." If an American military security umbrella remains essential, it is also true that Gulf riches can help ease the economic distress of Arab countries in the throes of revolutionary upheavals, thus further securing Gulf influence regionally and internationally. In addition, some Gulf intellectuals see a rising China as a useful counterweight to the troublesome Americans.

But there is another side to this coin. Successful as they have been economically, the Gulf states are still vulnerable to global trends, as the near collapse of Dubai after the 2008 international economic crisis revealed. How well does the "rentier bargain" hold up in the larger countries, like Saudi Arabia, where youth unemployment can lead to social and political problems? How long can the Gulf economies run on mostly expatriate labor without giving these foreigners more civil and political rights? What of the subordination of an increasingly educated female population? And what happens if and when new sources of energy, fossil and non-fossil, begin to lower the price of oil and gas?

The perceived threat of the "Arab Spring" has led Gulf states in a repressive political direction, exposing rulers' anxiety about the durability of their traditional systems. Broadly speaking, the Gulf political systems are gerontocracies. While they have had more than their share of wise leaders, the chain of succession in some countries is opaque and fragile. As succession issues loom, the question of factional rivalries within ruling families becomes a more serious matter.

Those who contend that the Gulf countries have become a new force in regional and international affairs assume that these countries act as a coherent bloc. True, the GCC has scored some modest successes in functional cooperation, but it has failed to develop a common military capability, and it certainly lacks political unity. Quarrels among the ruling families dilute collective power. Qatar will pursue policies that the Saudis oppose. Oman will go its own way. For its part, Iran — the sole remaining regional hegemon — stands as the major security threat to the Arab Gulf states. Indeed, for all their new power and influence, the Gulf states remain deeply insecure and always in need of an outside protector.

Gulf elites worry, however, that the protector — the United States — could begin to lose interest in their region as they develop significant new energy supplies from fracking in North America. And there are no new protectors immediately in sight. In the decades ahead, China and India, far more dependent on Middle East oil than the United States or Europe, might come to play such a role but that seems to be a long way off.

In short, there are two competing narratives about the Gulf in a changing world. The first (which we might describe as the "glass half full" narrative) depicts growth, modernization, and the institutionalization of a "Gulf model" that stands as a dynamic force in the Middle East. Economically robust, politically stable, regionally powerful, and globally protected, the Gulf in this reading is now a major player in world affairs. The competing narrative, however, tells a different story. It depicts a distorted rent-driven economy suffering from the "oil curse" and unable to diversify, saddled with a bloated and occasionally restive expatriate labor force. The legitimizing principle of benign tribal patriarchy is being eroded by youth and marginalized social sectors demanding meaningful participation in governance. Inter-family rivalries impede a unified approach to regional security threats, and riches alone cannot substitute for hard power. As ideological storms sweep across the greater Middle East, can the Gulf monarchies be truly secure in their bubble? And when a fatigued superpower protector begins to lose interest, what will transpire?

About This Book

This book does not purport to choose sides. Nor does it attempt to catalogue the latest twists and turns in the region's economic, political, and security situation. Rather, the Chapters presented here seek to illuminate the underlying trends in the economic, governmental, regional, and global environments. The strength in the Chapters lies in their ability to look deeply into the issues and demonstrate their complexity; thus few take a fully "glass half full" or "glass half empty" stance. We therefore leave it to the reader to draw his or her own conclusions from these multilayered studies.

The first Section, "The Gulf States and the Economy," features three Chapters on the Gulf's prevalent system of state capitalism and the rentier model. **Martin Hvidt**, through a study of state development plans, points out the entrenched nature of state capitalism in the GCC, even if Bahrain and Oman lean more toward a neoliberal free market economy. **Steffen Hertog**'s Chapter argues that the state capitalism model, particularly the distribution of rents to citizens, should be re-engineered. For Hertog, such an arrangement drives too many citizens out of the private labor market and ultimately hinders economic growth. **Marc Valeri** demonstrates the machinations of state capitalism through an examination of business elites' relationship with their respective governments. He shows that in Oman, the government has granted priority to the private sector, whereas in Bahrain, prominent business families are more restrained in terms of latitude of action. In all cases, however, the threat of the spread of the Arab uprisings to the Gulf has meant that GCC governments have poured millions of dollars into subsidies and other offerings for their populations in order to stem unrest. Thus, if there ever was movement toward relinquishing the rentier model, the "Arab Spring" has driven anxious Gulf governments back to a system of subsidies and *wasta*.

The second Section, on "Gulf Governance," features two Chapters, one by **David M. Mednicoff** and **Joanna E. Springer** from a top-down approach, and one by **James C. A. Redman** from a bottom-up, anthropological approach. Mednicoff and Springer argue that a merging of global international law and shari'a law in the Gulf could generate liberalization. Such a hybridized system, he asserts, may bring about "the politically liberalizing potential of law." Redman looks at governmental rent distribution in Kuwait, questioning assumptions that it is either equitable or that rent seeking by the populace is uniform. In contrast, he finds that individual actors pursue "personalized connections to successfully navigate labyrinthine [government] agencies." Hence, while Mednicoff and Springer prescribe an improved legal system for the Arab Gulf to bring about transparency and openness, Redman examines how individuals living in the current, opaque system negotiate its often corrupt constraints.

The following Section, "The Gulf and Beyond: Relations and Tensions," examines the regional dynamics of the Gulf with a focus on the GCC and Iran. **Malik R. Dahlan** calls for further integration of the GCC to bring about the rule of law, economic opportunity, and social justice. Dahlan contests that Western-imposed regulation and liberalization may bring the Gulf as well as the greater Middle East further violence and instability, thus implicitly questioning the wisdom of the United States as protector of first resort. **Mahmood Sariolghalam** also looks at the idea of turning inward, but in the Iranian context and with a different viewpoint. He asserts that Iranian foreign policy, with its anti-West fixation, is dictated by ideological rather than economic interests. Such a fixation, he notes, has not fostered consensus among Iranians about their national identity, and as such must be overcome in order to forge a social contract in the Islamic Republic. Thus while Dahlan cautions against a hegemony of Western influence, Sariolghalam examines how taking an anti-Western standpoint has created divisions within one society.

The final Section, "The United States and the Gulf," features three Chapters that address the changing nature of relations between the players. F. **Gregory Gause III** gives a history of American policy in the Gulf, noting that George W. Bush sought to reform the region via the Iraq War. While the venture failed, it demonstrated the Bush Administration's emphasis on the region. The Obama Administration, on the contrary, has returned to more of a concern with the status quo and stability. **Alain Gresh**'s Chapter argues for the emergence of a multi-polar world in which American influence is waning and China, for instance, is now much more involved in the Gulf. Though the United States remains a major actor, "its capacity to shape the evolution of other countries has diminished." The third Chapter, by **Degang Sun**, offers a different interpretation of events. Sun tracks the changing nature of U.S. military bases in the Gulf and concludes that a redeployment rather than a decrease in power is occurring. "A more strategic plan is actually underway," he writes. Together, the Chapters offer timely and somewhat divergent takes on what role the United States currently plays — and may ultimately play — in the Gulf. While Gause and Gresh explore a certain lessening in American influence, Sun suggests that, at least in the case of U.S. military bases, power is only shifting, not diminishing.

The Gulf States and the Economy

Chapter 1

The Development Trajectory of the GCC States: An Analysis of Aims and Visions in Current Development Plans

Martin Hvidt

Introduction

The GCC states—Bahrain, Kuwait, Oman, Qatar, Saudi Arabia, and the United Arab Emirates—have earned and are earning by far the largest share of their incomes from mining their oil and gas resources.[1] This has fostered an economic model that emphasizes state-led development and wealth distribution with a limited emphasis on creating real economic assets.

Applying Luciani's distinction between "allocation states" and "production states," the GCC states may be viewed as typical "allocation states"[2] in that their governments are largely distinct from their national economies. With the large income from exports of oil, gas, and other rents, the state is not forced to tax the local economy to finance its activities. This situation results in a lack of

---

[1] Between 62 percent and 80 percent of state incomes originate from oil in the GCC countries. Martin Hvidt, "Economic Reforms in the Arab Gulf Countries: Lip Service or Actual Implementation?," in *Shifting Geo-Economic Power of the Gulf: Oil, Finance and Institutions*, ed. Matteo Legrenzi and Bessma Momani (Surrey and London: Ashgate, 2011), p. 43.
[2] See Giacomo Luciani, "Allocation vs. Production States: A Theoretical Framework," in *The Arab State*, ed. Giacomo Luciani (Berkeley and Los Angeles: The University of California Press, 1990), see p. 71 onwards for an in-depth discussion of the concepts of allocation and production states.

incentive or pressure to develop an efficient economic basis within society. In the "production state," the situation is reversed. In such states, the creation of a solid economic base for society determines the state's ability, through taxation, to strengthen its power nationally and internationally. As such, allocation and production states must be understood as opposite extremes on a continuum.

From a neoliberal economist's point of view, the development of allocation states in the GCC, which followed the rising incomes from oil and gas, encompasses problems both obvious and fundamental. First, this economic model does not create much employment. Oil and gas production are capital intensive and employ few people relative to the profits they create. Furthermore, a combination of foreign experts and imported blue collar workers undertake oil production in the Gulf states and hence a limited numbers of locals are involved. Essentially, oil wealth is created without significant inclusion of the skills and manpower of the local population.

Second, because the rulers, in an effort to legitimize their rule,[3] have adopted the practice of distributing oil wealth within society through what Christopher Davidson calls a "rentier pact," such societies have been co-opted into a neo-patrimonial state structure.[4] In the rentier pact, rulers distribute a package of wealth to both locals and expatriates, a policy that enables them to secure political acquiescence and considerable popularity. In the Gulf countries, the rentier pact usually includes distribution of land to loyal supporters and important families, highly subsidized electricity, water, and housing facilities, free welfare services such as education and health care, well-paid jobs in the public sector, cash handouts, and forgiveness of debt.[5]

These factors are outcomes of the allocation state model, which diminishes incentives for the state to create jobs and not least for citizens to engage in productive activities. As such, a vicious circle exists in these states that leads

---

[3] See Michael C. Hudson, *Arab Politics: The Search for Legitimacy* (New Haven, CT: Yale University Press, 1977), pp. 4–5 and p. 165 onwards. This publication represents a dated but still competent and relevant discussion of the basic questions of legitimacy in the Gulf states.
[4] Christopher M. Davidson, *The United Arab Emirates: A Study in Survival* (Boulder, CO: Lynne Rienner, 2005), p. 104.
[5] Interviews conducted by the author in the Gulf region. See also Roger Owen, *State, Power and Politics in the Making of the Modern Middle East* (London: Routledge, 2004), p. 52.

to both undiversified sources of income and a high cost of welfare services provided through the rentier pact. When we add a demographic component, namely that more than 11 million people (approximately 25 percent of the GCC's population) are below 15 years of age,[6] with high unemployment figures and large numbers of progressively better educated young people entering the job market, it becomes apparent that these countries are in a serious need of job creation. The Arab uprisings of 2011 are testimony to the forces that can be set in motion by youth with unfulfilled expectations.[7] One way to counter the dual problems of unemployment and the lack of incentive to engage in productive activities would be to implement a more production-oriented developmental model.

This Chapter addresses the question of whether the GCC states express a desire to shift their economic model from that of the allocation state toward a more production-oriented state. A neoclassical economic framework is applied, which emphasizes incentives, the role of the private sector, and the market. Current development plans are analyzed to present a systematic overview of the future goals and visions of the Gulf states. The following three questions guide the reading of the development plans: What sectors and activities should be stimulated in order to create future income streams and employment in industry, trade, finance, tourism, oil, gas, and knowledge;[8] whether the public sector or the private sector will drive the economy; and what role the market and the states should play in determining what and how much is to be produced. It must be emphasized that this Chapter is limited to analyzing what each government claims to desire, not what it actually accomplishes.[9]

---

[6] United Nations Population Division, *Source: Population Division of the Department of Economic and Social Affairs of the United Nations Secretariat, World Population Prospects: The 2008 Revision*, 2009.
[7] Yasser Abdih, "Closing the Jobs Gap," *Finance and Development* 48, 2 (2011). Available online at www.imf.org/external/pubs/ft/fandd/2011/06/abdih.htm.
[8] See Peter B. Evans, *Embedded Autonomy: States and Industrial Transformation* (Princeton, NJ: Princeton University Press, 1995), Chapter 1 for further discussion of the concept of "created comparative advantages."
[9] An attempt to answer the latter question can be found in a recent work by this author. Martin Hvidt, "Economic Reforms in the Arab Gulf Countries."

The distinction between private and public economic activities is blurred in these economies, since they are dominated by vast governmental spending and dense neo-patrimonial ties between rulers and the business elite. Thus, one must be cautious when speaking of the private sector in the traditional sense.[10] Nonetheless, Timothy Niblock suggests that the term "private sector" can be used, even though it should be more accurately termed the "corporate sector" or the "business sector." As he points out, the important factor is whether or not a publicly-owned company operates its business as a private company.[11]

Methodology and Data

The framework developed for this Chapter uses qualitative content analysis[12] and takes into account neoliberal economic thought, as such thought dominates the international agenda despite its exposed weakness, particularly since the 2008 economic crisis. Development plans are therefore read within this framework. It must also be stated that development plans are not representations of physical events but are written documents — images and models created to be seen, read, interpreted, and acted upon. As a result, the reading of these plans result in a subjective interpretation of their content. Admittedly, the data is somewhat weak. The GCC countries vary in planning history, quality of planning, degree of detail, and, not least of all, in their policies governing publishing these plans. Some states publish their plans in full while others only make the highlights available.[13] Therefore, this study is exploratory and an attempt to chart unknown territory rather than test a hypothesis. It should be read as a review of the future growth trajectory for the region.

---

[10] See Martin Hvidt, "Public-Private Ties and Their Contribution to Development: The Case of Dubai," *Middle Eastern Studies* 43, 4 (2007): 557–577.
[11] Timothy Niblock and Monica Malik, *The Political Economy of Saudi Arabia* (London: Routledge, 2007), p. 27.
[12] See Klaus Krippendorff, *Content Analysis: An Introduction to Its Methodology* (Thousand Oaks, CA: Sage, 2004), for an in-depth account of qualitative content analysis.
[13] It is recognized that planning can and does take place even without a written plan. This Chapter, however, limits itself to the analysis of written plans.

Planning: What and Why

In its heyday in the 1960s and 1970s, national planning was widely believed to offer the essential and perhaps the only institutional and organizational mechanism for overcoming the major obstacles to development and for ensuring a sustained high rate of economic growth. To catch up with their former rulers, poor nations were persuaded that they required a comprehensive national plan.[14] Davidoff and Reiner define planning as a process for determining appropriate future action through a sequence of choices.[15] Martinussen defines development planning broadly as an effort to identify the most appropriate means and measures for achieving specific development objectives.[16] Todaro and Smith seem to incorporate both definitions by stating that planning is

> a deliberate governmental attempt to coordinate economic decision making over the long run and to influence, direct, and in some cases even control the level and growth of a nation's principal economic variables (income, consumption, employment, investment, saving, exports, imports, etc.) to achieve a predetermined set of development objectives.[17]

There are four general reasons for planning in developing countries:[18] Firstly, market failure. The market mechanisms do not always function properly, and individual investment decisions might not promote or lead to development — thus making coordination of, for instance, investments through a broader national plan necessary. Secondly, planning might facilitate mobilization and an optimal allocation of resources in countries with limited financial and skilled human resources. Thirdly, planning might have an

---

[14] Michael P. Todaro and Stephen C. Smith, *Economic Development* (Harlow, UK: Pearson/Addison Wesly, 2009), p. 531.
[15] Paul Davidoff and Thomas A. Reiner, "A Choice Theory of Planning," in *A Reader in Planning Theory*, ed. Andreas Faludi (Oxford: Pergamon Press, 1973 [1962]), p. 11.
[16] John Degnbol-Martinussen, *Society, State & Market: A Guide to Competing Theories of Development* (London: Zed Books, 1997), p. 228.
[17] Todaro and Smith, *Economic Development*, p. 532.
[18] Todaro and Smith, *Economic Development*, p. 533 onwards; Degnbol-Martinussen, *Society, State & Market*, p. 229.

attitudinal or psychological impact in fragmented societies, creating nationwide adherence to developmental aims. Furthermore, plans might include a "feel good" element, signaling that the ruler or the government understands the problems facing the society and is determined to solve them. Lastly, detailed plans have often been a necessary precondition to receiving foreign aid. However, this issue is of little relevance for the capital rich Gulf countries.[19] As Thirlwall points out, almost all developing countries, whether socialist or capitalist, have made and still make development plans.[20]

Planning as a tool for development was, however, brought into disrepute by the so-called neoclassical counterrevolution and its corollary, the Washington Consensus, which conservative politicians such as Ronald Reagan, Margaret Thatcher, and Helmut Kohl swept through the political agenda when they came to power in the early1980s. They brought a return to neoclassical economic theory and policy, which emphasized dismantling state planning, public ownership, and government regulation of economic activities. Excessive state intervention was seen as the primary hindrance to development in Third World countries. Their policy was therefore to promote free markets and laissez-faire economics within the context of permissive governments that would allow the "magic of the marketplace" and the "invisible hand" to guide resource allocation and stimulate economic development.[21] This shift to neoliberal policies in the Western world and its developmental institutions was so significant that Gore has described it as a paradigm shift.[22]

However, during the late 1990s and especially after the turn of the millennium, a renewed emphasis on the role of the state in development has

---

[19] Martin Hvidt, "Limited Success of the IMF and the World Bank in Middle Eastern Reforms," *Journal of Social Affairs* 21, 81 (2004): 77–103.
[20] A. P. Thirlwall, *Growth & Development: With Special Reference to Developing Economies* (Houndsmills, UK: Palgrave Macmillan, 2006), p. 299.
[21] Todaro and Smith, *Economic Development*, p. 127. For further information on the Washington Consensus, see Hvidt, "Limited Success;" John Williamson, "From Reform Agenda to Damaged Brand Name: A Short History of the Washington Consensus and Suggestions for What to Do Next," *Finance and Development* 40, 3 (2003); Charles Gore, "The Rise and Fall of the Washington Consensus as a Paradigm for Developing Countries," *World Development* 28, 5 (2000): 790.
[22] Gore, "The Rise and Fall of the Washington Consensus," p. 790.

emerged.[23] This move was first and foremost a result of the numerous problems experienced with the neoclassical free market approach to development.[24] The realization that the East Asian economic miracle occurred as a result of active and well-planned government intervention rather than the workings of the free market also fostered this renewed interest in the state.[25] Indeed, a balance between a state-led and free market economy was the case for most countries that succeeded in their industrialization efforts in the twentieth century, not least the European countries. Most recently, Lauridsen has pointed out that the current financial crisis, which began in 2008, has "led to a rethinking on the relative roles of state and markets. Public investments and industrial policies are no longer seen as interventions that inevitably lead to inefficient, uncompetitive, and rent-extracting forms of industrialization."[26]

In other words, after more than 20 years in disrepute, planning — understood as deliberate state intervention in the economy — seems to be back on the agenda. It is important to note, however, that the focus of planning has shifted from comprehensive planning to plans of a more limited scope, that is, partial plans such as sector plans or project plans. More importantly, the process has shifted from rational planning to more vision-based planning, which involves stating long-term developmental goals for a society or a sector without specifying the exact means of achieving these long-term goals.

---

[23] However, the Washington Consensus still dominates the agenda of large financial institutions such as the IMF and the World Bank. See Hvidt, "Limited Success."
[24] See, for instance, Charles F. Sabel, "Bootstrapping Development: Rethinking the Role of Public Intervention in Promoting Growth," paper presented at the Protestant Ethic and Spirit of Capitalism Conference, Cornell University, Ithaca, New York, 8–10 October 2004, published November 2005; Joseph E. Stiglitz, *Globalization and Its Discontents* (London: Penguin, 2002), Chapters 4–6.
[25] Mario Cimoli *et al.*, "Institutions and Policies Shaping Industrial Development: An Introductory Note," in *Industrial Policy and Development: A Political Economy of Capabilities Accumulation*, ed. Mario Cimoli, Giovanni Dosi, and Joseph E. Stiglitz (Oxford: Oxford University Press, 2009), p. 25; Laurids S. Lauridsen, "The Developmental State and the Asian Miracles: An Introduction to the Debate," *Institutions and Industrial Development: Asian Experiences*, ed. Laurids S. Lauridsen (Roskilde: IDS Roskilde University, 1995), p. 24 onwards.
[26] Laurids S. Lauridsen, "Strategic Industrial Policy and Latecomer Development: The What, the Why and the How," *Forum for Development Studies* 37, 1 (2010): 7.

One could say that where "old-style" planning was built on a rational approach, higher levels of flexibility characterize "new-style" planning.[27] Old-style planning, in its attempt to factor in all relevant economic and societal factors, usually involved a long list of specific actions that had to be seen through simultaneously in order to reach the targets. If one or more of these items for any reason did not materialize, then the overall plan was compromised. New-style planning, for its part, establishes visions, sets goals, identifies priorities, and leaves room for the actors — both within the public and the private sector — to pursue developmental aims in a flexible manner.[28] The idea is to promote cumulative change in the direction chosen.[29] This type of planning is less vulnerable because the overall approach does not collapse if one or more individual targets are not met.

As Rodrik pointed out, we should depart from the image of omniscient planners and instead perceive planning as an "interactive process of strategic cooperation between the private and the public sectors which, on the one hand, serves to elicit information on business opportunities and constraints and, on the other hand, generates policy initiatives in response."[30] Planning in the GCC states is mostly of the new-style type. However, Oman and Saudi Arabia, which have the longest planning histories, adhere to old-style planning.

Development Planning in the GCC Countries

What follows is an analysis of the current plans, with special reference to economic development, for the six GCC countries. Planning, understood as economic planning, is a rather recent phenomenon in the GCC countries with the exception of Oman and Saudi Arabia. Physical planning has been undertaken in these countries to various degrees, especially in the booming

---

[27] I have adopted the expressions "old-style" and "new-style" from Lauridsen, "Strategic Industrial Policy," 10.
[28] Dani Rodrik, "Industrial Policy for the Twenty-First Century," CEPR Discussion Paper No. 4767, November 2004, p. 18.
[29] Lauridsen, "Strategic Industrial Policy," p. 10.
[30] Lauridsen, "Strategic Industrial Policy," p. 38. For a similar view see also Sabel, "Bootstrapping Development," p. 28 onwards.

years of the 1970s, with the purpose of coordinating the physical build-up of cities and major infrastructural projects.

Plans reflect the historical context in which they are made. Two contextual factors seem relevant to the frame of these planning efforts, namely the neoliberal economic view, which continues to dominate the understanding of economic issues but has softened since its advent in the 1980s, and the optimism created by a decade of record high oil and gas prices. Starting the decade with modest oil prices of between $20 and $30 per barrel for the OPEC price basket, the average yearly oil price rose to above $50 per barrel in 2005. In 2008, the previous record year, the average yearly oil price reached $94.45, but after a dip to $66.06 in 2009 and $71.45 in 2010, the average oil price for 2011 stood at $107.46 and ended at $109.45 for 2012.[31] The IMF expects this price level to continue in the medium term.[32] In other words, the Gulf has been making excellent money over the past decades, the profits from which they plan to use for development. As pointed out by the Institute of International Finance (IIF) in 2008:

> An ambitious investment program is currently underway to expand capacity in real estate, tourism, transportation, manufacturing, and hydrocarbon sectors. These investments exceed $1 trillion for the next five years (about the combined size of the GCC economies) even after assuming that half of the planned projects will be cancelled or postponed due to the current global credit crunch.[33]

Analysis of the Plans

The table below shows an overview of the plans, according to sets of predetermined issues.

---

[31] OPEC, *OPEC Basket Price*, available online at http://www.opec.org/opec_web/en/data_graphs/40.htm (visited 3 January 2013).
[32] International Monetary Fund (IMF), *World Economic Outlook April 2011* (Washington, D.C.: International Monetary Fund, 2011), p. 5 and p. 196.
[33] Institute of International Finance (IIF), *Summary Appraisal: Gulf Cooperation Council Countries* (Washington, D.C.: Institute of International Finance, 2008), p. 13.

Table 1.1: Summary of Current Development Plans.

	Bahrain[34]	Kuwait[35]	Oman[36]	Qatar[37]	Saudi Arabia[38]	The UAE[39]
Planning History	No previous economic development plans	Poor planning record, current plan first in 16 years	Long planning history, first plan in 1976. National Work Program from 2005	No previous economic development plans[40]	Long planning history, first plan in 1970	Preceded by the National Work Program from 2005 and the UAE government strategy 2008–2010
Name of Current Plan	*Vision 2030* (published 2008)	*State Vision Kuwait 2030* and the *Blair Report* (both published 2010)	*Vision 2020* (published 1995)	*National Vision 2030* (published 2008)	*Ninth Development Plan (2010–2014)* (published 2009) and *Long-term Strategy (2005–2024)* (published 2004)	*Vision 2021*[41] (published 2010)

(*Continued*)

[34] Dominic Dudley, "Bahrain Economy," *MEED* (www.meed.com), 29 October 2009; Government of Bahrain, *Our Vision: The Economic Vision 2030 for Bahrain*, 2008.

Table 1.1: (Continued)

35 Peter Salisbury, "Kuwait: Testing Private-Sector Reform," *MEED* (www.meed.com), 25 June–1 July 2010; Tony Blair Associates, *Vision Kuwait 2030: Final Report*, 2010; State of Kuwait, *Five-Year Development Plan of the State of Kuwait 2009/2010–2013/2014: A Draft General Framework*, 2009.
36 Sultanate of Oman, Ministry of National Economy, *Vision 2020: Human Resources Development Strategy, Social Sector*, 2011, available online at http://www.moneoman.gov.om/loader.aspx?view=planning-hrds-social&type=plan; Verity Ratcliffe, "Oman Sets Out a Vision for Economic Growth," *MEED Middle East Economic Digest* 54, 26 (2010); Sultanate of Oman, Ministry of National Economy, *Development Strategy: Second Long Term Development Strategy (1996–2020)*, 1995, available online at http://www.moneoman.gov.om/loader.aspx?view= planning-dsslrds&type=plan.
37 Elizabeth Bains, "Controlling Qatar's Pace of Change: Special Report Qatar," *MEED* (www.meed.com), 2 April 2009; General Secretariat for Development Planning, *Qatar National Vision 2030*, July 2008.
38 Kingdom of Saudi Arabia, *Brief Report on the Ninth Development Plan (2010–2014)*, 2010, available online at http://www.mep.gov.sa/index.jsp;jsessionid=15729754528E874E14D282C6D3AA0B8D.beta?event=ArticleView&Article.ObjectID=80 (visited 3 September 2010); Europa Publications, "Saudi Arabia," *The Middle East and North Africa Handbook 2010*; Kingdom of Saudi Arabia, *Long-Term Strategy for the Saudi Economy*, 2004.
39 Government of the UAE, *Highlights of the UAE Government Strategy (2008–2010)*, 2007; Government of the UAE, *UAE Vision 2021: United in Ambition and Determination*, 2010, availble online at http://www.vision2021.ae/downloads/UAE-Vision2021-Brochure-English.pdf.
40 The Urban Planning and Development Authority is also drawing up a master plan to guide development of infrastructure, mega-projects, housing, and industrial activities.
41 The target year 2021 was chosen because in that year the UAE will celebrate its 50-year anniversary as a federation. Both Dubai and Abu Dhabi have already published their own development plans.

Table 1.1: (Continued)

	Bahrain	Kuwait	Oman	Qatar	Saudi Arabia	The UAE
Aims	Double household income before 2030, secure employment, make Bahraini workforce the preferred choice of labor, establish a knowledge-based society	Improve the economic system to counter three challenges: demographic, fiscal, and future oil incomes[42]	Economic diversification via investment in such areas as industry and ports	Foster sound economic management, responsible exploitation of oil and gas, and suitable economic diversification; establish a knowledge-based society	Create productive employment for Saudi nationals, improve quality of life, double per capita income, diversify the economy, expand the economic base of society	Become one of the best places in the world to do business, diversify away from oil by expanding new strategic sectors
Leading Sectors	Finance, tourism, business services, manufacturing, logistics	Regional trade and finance	Tourism and gas-based industries	Oil and gas,[43] education	Oil and gas	Financial services, aviation, trade and commerce

(Continued)

[42]The plan discusses three so-called time bombs: demographic (the population is set to double by 2030, and 50 percent of the current population is under 20 years of age); fiscal, which relates to the fact that expenditure for employment (83 percent of the Kuwaiti workforce is employed by the state) and the vast welfare system cannot be sustained in the long term; and oil, in that oil production and thus income will decrease in the future.
[43]Estimated reserves of gas will last 200 years. Elizabeth Bains, "Qatar Implementing National Vision," *MEED* (www.meed.com), 9 September 2009.

Table 1.1: (Continued)

	Bahrain	Kuwait	Oman	Qatar	Saudi Arabia	The UAE
Means (To Achieve Goals)	Investment in human capital	Investment in the oil and gas sector, infrastructure, and a new port, plus economic reforms	Investment in such areas as industrialization and human resources, privatization, economic reforms to attract FDI, "Omanization"	Investment in education, particularly universities	Private sector participation in the economy	Economic reform, innovation, research, encouragement of high value-added sectors
Driver of the Economy (Private vs. Public)	Increased role of the private sector	Private sector to finance new investments	Increased role of the private sector	The state, until the private sector is ready to play a prominent role	The state (through spending), yet an increasing role for private sector	The state, with a very limited role for the private sector
State vs. Market	Market-based development	State-led development	State-led development	State-led development	State-led development	Market-based (but state-owned) development

(Continued)

Table 1.1: (Continued)

	Bahrain	Kuwait	Oman	Qatar	Saudi Arabia	The UAE
Allocation vs. Production State	Production-based	Moving toward a production state	Already well underway as a production state	Continues to be an allocation state	Moving toward a production state	Moving toward a production state
Comment	Frontal attack on the allocation state approach and the boldest of the GCC strategic plans; there is an urgency to diversify due to limited oil reserves	Attempts to reinvigorate the economy by involving the private sector and instituting broad reforms	Dwindling oil reserves, urgency to diversify	Planning in a "situation of plenty"	Sufficient oil, but significant problems with youth unemployment	Diversification without privatization

Conclusion

Every development plan mirrors the historical epoch in which it was created, and it therefore reflects dominating ideas and ideologies, perceived continuities, and the global financial situation, among other elements. As noted earlier, plans are political documents that signal leadership intentions to citizens, potential investors, financial analysts, and the international community. Thus, plans serve other purposes than mere implementation. The foregoing content analysis has identified the aims of the GCC states.

Generally, the GCC states share the intention of diversifying their economies away from a dependence on oil and gas. There are various reasons for this. Oman and Bahrain signal urgency in wanting to accomplish the diversification process due to their small and rapidly dwindling oil reserves. Kuwait, Qatar, and the UAE, on the other hand, show little of such urgency.[44] Qatar deliberately aims for a slow diversification process. Saudi Arabia falls between these two groups.

Two main concerns are listed as the reasons for diversification. First, with fast growing populations and the prospect of dwindling oil incomes, to various degrees the states can no longer act as the sole sponsor of vast welfare societies established over the last half a century. Second, diversification is motivated by the aim of creating appropriate jobs, both in content and in income, for the increasing youth population. Both concerns necessitate GCC citizens to become economically active.

Furthermore, all six GCC countries emphasize providing excellent education and health care for their citizens. They are seen as an end in themselves, but also a precondition for transforming the economies from low value-added to high value-added industrial and service activities. The aimed-for "knowledge economy" promises to provide jobs with a higher knowledge content. Such jobs should result in higher pay and thus are seen as a prerequisite for a suitable monetary income for citizens.

---

[44] Concerning Kuwait, I did not include the statements of the report by Tony Blair Associates, since it is unclear whether or not this report is an expression of the official standpoint of the government.

All the plans also aim to create "comparative advantages." That is, current oil and gas revenues are to be invested in economic assets such as infrastructure, production facilities, housing, education, and health within each country, which will generate future income. A typical example is the current expansion within aviation, in which significant investments in new planes, airports, and cargo handling facilities are being undertaken in each of the six Gulf countries.[45]

It is thus possible from the review of the development plans to conclude that significant emphasis is being placed on adopting a more production oriented developmental model, and that this model could facilitate a shift from an allocation state model to a production state model in the longer run. In each of the GCC states there is a distinct focus on erecting real and productive assets that can secure future income streams, not least to create employment for the rapidly growing national workforce. Development, therefore, seems to be back on the agenda for the GCC states.[46]

However, the countries differ significantly in the role they envision for the market and the private sector to play in their economies. Bahrain and Oman explicitly aim to create a neoliberal free market economy, in which the private sector (as opposed to the state) is the driver of the economy, and where meritocracy is to be re-introduced into the public sector through a competitive job market. Oman is currently the only country among the six that holds specific plans to privatize state-owned firms.

Kuwait, Qatar, and Saudi Arabia, however, signal a continuation of the state-led developmental model, with a mention of a future role for the private sector. For them, the state remains the driver of the economy through its significant development budget and ownership of firms, while the private sector

---

[45] Qatar General Secretariat for Development Planning, *Qatar National Development Strategy 2011–2016*, 2011, p. 102.
[46] The emphasis on development has been facilitated by the high income from oil and gas over the last decade, which has continued despite the financial crisis. High levels of governmental spending have continued as well. IMF, *IMF Sees Spending by Middle Eastern Oil Exporters Softening Global Financial Crisis Impact*, 2009; Institute of International Finance (IIF), *Record Oil Prices Fuel Major Expansion of Gulf Economies and Large Gains in Surplus Funds — Foreign Assets Reach $1.8 Trillion*, 16 January 2008.

operates in a niche market in which the state has chosen not to invest, such as in trading, retail, and construction. Yet Kuwait and Saudi Arabia aim to encourage further investments by the private sector in their economies by both local and foreign firms through a series of substantial economic reform programs that should make investment in the country attractive. The UAE is the only country that does not aim to increase either the role of the free market or the private sector.

This analysis leads to the second conclusion, namely that it is not possible from these development plans to identify a distinct turn toward a neoliberal, private sector-oriented policy among the GCC countries. Bahrain and Oman envision such policies in their development plans in the medium to long term. For the remaining countries, the state-led model — state capitalism — which has proven successful in Asian countries, seems to be the preferred choice.[47] The private sector, which in the first place is dependent on the state budget, will continue to operate in niches left open by the government sector. This situation, however, does not imply that the presumed virtues of market mechanisms are completely neglected. The public-owned companies and service providers will continue to operate under competitive market conditions, as has long been the tradition in the Gulf countries.[48]

Hence the overall conclusion is that dominant neoclassical thought has made very little imprint on the development plans produced by the GCC countries. It can be hypothesized that the strong financial situation of this group of countries over the last decade, both before and after the commencement of the financial crisis in 2008, has not made it necessary to introduce significant change to the state-led economic model. On the contrary, the financial crisis that originated in the United States as a result of international macroeconomic issues and, in particular, weak regulation of the financial sector[49] vindicated

---

[47] "Special Report: The Rise of State Capitalism: The Emerging World's New Model," *The Economist*, 21–27 January 2012, pp. 11–12 and in Special Section, pp. 1–18.

[48] Steffen Hertog, "Lean and Mean: The New Breed of State-Owned Enterprises in the Gulf Monarchies," in *Industrialization in the Gulf: A Socioeconomic Revolution*, eds. Jean-François Seznec and Mimi Kirk (London: Routledge, 2011), pp. 17–29.

[49] Adrian Blundell-Wignall, Paul Atkinson, and Se Hoon Lee, *The Current Financial Crisis: Causes and Policy Issues* (Paris: OECD, 2008).

the idea of increased state involvement. Indeed, the crisis prompted governments around the world to intervene to save more or less dysfunctional private businesses, notably banks. In some cases governments actually overtook manufacturing firms, such as in the United States, where the government ended up owning significant parts of both Chrysler and General Motors.[50] As a result, because of the GCC countries' strong financial standing, we expect to see no significant changes in their economic policies in the medium term.

In addition, the "Arab Spring" that commenced in early 2011 is not likely to strengthen the incentives of the governments to reform their policies toward a more neoliberal orientation. The responses of the governments of the GCC countries to the uprisings has been a return to the traditional way of keeping the "ruling bargain," namely appeasing the population by pampering it with economic gifts. Such gifts have included cash handouts, increased wages in the public sector, and the introduction of unemployment benefits. Furthermore, in most of these countries and in direct contradiction to their stated aims of emphasizing job creation in the private sector, the governments have created new jobs in the public sector — e.g., in Saudi Arabia 60,000, in Bahrain 20,000, and in Oman 41,000.[51] Thus, the likely result of the Arab Spring is a slower pace of reform, simply because the governments are uneasy at the prospect of placing increased burdens on their populations. In other words, the most probable scenario for the medium term is that the Gulf countries will continue to apply the state capitalist development model.

---

[50] Paul Kiel, "Biggest Financial Crisis Bailout Fails," *The Huffington Post*, 6 September 2012, available online at http://www.huffingtonpost.com/2012/09/06/financial-bailout-wallstreet_n_1861853.html 2013.
[51] IMF, *Regional Economic Outlook: Middle East and Central Asia*, October 2011, p. 16; Suzanne Fenton, "Oman Spends to Quell Unrest," *MEED* (www.meed.com), 29 July–4 August 2011.

Chapter 2

Redesigning the Distributional Bargain in the GCC

Steffen Hertog

Introduction

In the face of revolutions in the wider Arab world, the Gulf Cooperation Council (GCC) countries have shown that they truly are "oil monarchies."[1] Although political systems in the GCC differ quite substantially, when faced with oppositional stirrings all of them have instinctively reacted to the crisis with stepped-up patronage spending, financed through greatly augmented oil revenues. Together with more or less measured security crackdowns, rentier largesse seems to have done the trick. For the time being, the regimes are stable and the opposition, where it exists, is subdued.

At the same time, however, increased levels of spending raise questions of long-term sustainability — not only in political but also in purely economic terms. The oil prices needed to sustain current systems of patronage in the GCC are several times higher than they were just a decade ago. And even if the richer of the GCC countries do not run out of money any time soon, the way in which patronage is organized arguably reinforces problematic socioeconomic cleavages within society.

As this Chapter will argue, stepped-up distribution ironically means more economic exclusion for the majority of GCC citizens, as it tends to drive them out of the private labor market, deepening the cleavage between the

---

[1] F. Gregory Gause, *Oil Monarchies* (New York: Council on Foreign Relations Press, 1994).

citizenry at large and the local private sector. As long as distribution of rents in the GCC is not fundamentally re-engineered, it will entrench structures of entitlement that are both costly and exclusionary, and that give the vast majority of nationals a rational interest in policies that are deleterious to long-term economic development. This is true under both authoritarian and semi-democratic conditions, although it is a more acute problem in the latter case, in which citizens have a stronger say in economic policy.

This Chapter will both analyze the socioeconomic incentives and interests created by the current distributional regimes and outline a number of potential alternatives that would serve to integrate the citizenry into the private economy. It will start with an empirical overview of existing distributional systems in the GCC and of the efficiency, equity, and fiscal sustainability issues they create. It will then discuss a number of potential scenarios for redesigning distribution regimes in a more incentive-neutral and sustainable way, with a particular focus on the idea of a general "citizens' income." The final section will then discuss how such re-engineered distribution would need to combine with targeted labor market reforms in order to integrate citizens in the private labor market and generate common interests between business and citizenry.

The Chapter's theoretical ambition is the revision and refinement of the classical fiscal sociology of rentier states.[2] Similar to work recently done by Michael Herb,[3] I aim to disaggregate the political effects of rentier distribution on different groups in society, moving beyond the (often implicit) assumption that state and society in rentier states are, for political purposes, coherent

---

[2]Jacques Delacroix, "The Distributive State in the World System," *Studies in Comparative International Development* 15, 3 (1980): 3–21; Mick Moore, "Revenues, State Formation, and the Quality of Governance in Developing Countries," *International Political Science Review* 25, 3 (2004): 297–319; Hootan Shambayati, "The Rentier State, Interest Groups, and the Paradox of Autonomy: State and Business in Turkey and Iran," *Comparative Politics* 26, 3 (1994): 307–331; Hazem Beblawi and Giacomo Luciani, eds. *The Rentier State* (London; New York: Croom Helm, 1987); Hussein Mahdavy, "Patterns and Problems of Economic Development in Rentier States," *Studies in the Economic History of the Middle East: From the Rise of Islam to the Present Day*, ed. M.A. Cook (Oxford: Oxford University Press, 1970).
[3]Michael Herb, "A Nation of Bureaucrats: Political Participation and Economic Diversification in Kuwait and the United Arab Emirates," *International Journal of Middle East Studies* 41, 3 (2009): 375–395.

aggregates. As in previous, more state-centric work,[4] I aim to trace more closely what rentier states actually do when they distribute resources — a process that has too often been dealt with in pure macro-terms.

An Overview of GCC Distributional Systems and the Incentives They Create

The GCC's reaction to the "Arab Spring" has uniformly deepened existing structures of rentier patronage. Measures announced include more than 300,000 new public jobs in Saudi Arabia, 35,000 new public sector positions in Oman, and 20,000 new positions in Bahrain.[5] All of the latter are to be created in the country's Ministry of Interior; the number is equivalent to more than half of the existing (official) public sector labor force of 35,000.[6]

Increased public sector wages, new food subsidies, and reduced fees for a variety of public services, as well as a plethora of new welfare payments and public housing initiatives, have also been announced. The total spending package declared in Saudi Arabia in February and March 2011 amounts to an estimated $130 billion — equivalent to twice the size of the total national budget as recently as 2003.[7]

None of the measures is revolutionary or even original; for the most part, they deepen existing structures of patronage. They do this at a time, however, when the GCC countries are striving to develop a modern, or even "post-oil," economy and when they are trying to increasingly integrate their growing national populations into the productive workforce. All of these objectives have become harder to obtain after the recent bonanza of giveaways. Some of the generosity is fairly incentive-neutral, such as the one-off payments to families of nationals in Kuwait and Bahrain, and the "damage" done is limited to the

---

[4] Steffen Hertog, *Princes, Brokers, and Bureaucrats: Oil and the State in Saudi Arabia* (Ithaca, NY: Cornell University Press, 2010).
[5] *Gulf News*, 6 March 2011; *Emirates 24/7 Business*, 31 May 2011; *Reuters*, 18 March 2011; *Arab News*, 5 June 2011.
[6] Central Bank of Bahrain, Economic Indicators, September 2009.
[7] For details see John Sfakianakis, Daliah Merzaban, and Turki A. Al Hugail, *Strategy Shift: Saudi Spending Swells, Oil Price Jump Evens Out Fiscal Balance*, Banque Saudi Fransi report, April 2011.

immediate fiscal cost. Other forms of patronage, however, distort economic behavior in ways that either undermine fiscal sustainability through overconsumption of precious goods and services with valuable alternative uses, or push nationals out of private employment. The following section will analyze these types of distribution, focusing on the provision of cheap domestic energy and public job creation.[8]

Free or subsidized public services and goods[9]

The provision of cheap energy in the shape of free or low tariff electricity and water as well as very cheap transport fuels has a long tradition in the GCC. Low prices lead to high levels of consumption per capita and, very likely, even higher levels of consumption per citizen.

The GCC is the world region with the lowest gasoline prices; the UAE is the only GCC country that provides gasoline at a price that is close to the production cost based on international oil prices. Consumption levels are accordingly high. Per capita gasoline consumption in the GCC has risen by a third since 1986, and total consumption has risen by 158 percent.[10] In the same period, U.S. consumption per capita has stayed constant, while total consumption has increased only by 28 percent.

The provision of very cheap gas and oil products to utility companies, most of which are still publicly owned, allows the provision of cheap or free electricity and desalinated water for national consumers.[11] Low prices lead to very high energy consumption. For example, Kuwaiti, Emirati, and Qatari electricity consumption is about twice as high per capita as in the EU, despite the presence of a large and for the most part poor expatriate population whose

---

[8]Other significant forms of distribution that are relatively less distortionary include government provision of housing and land, subsidized public services that are not energy-based, food subsidies, and pensions and other welfare payments.
[9]In significant parts, the following section draws on a working paper by Nathan Hodson on distributional systems in the Gulf. See Nathan Hodson, "Distributional Structures in the Arab Gulf: Public Employment, Subsidies, and Potential Reform," Kuwait Program at Sciences Po, Paris, 2010.
[10]Hodson, "Distributional Structures in the Arab Gulf."
[11]Natural gas in the GCC is made available to electricity producers at prices below $1 per million Btu, compared to Henry Hub prices of $4–5 in the United States in 2011.

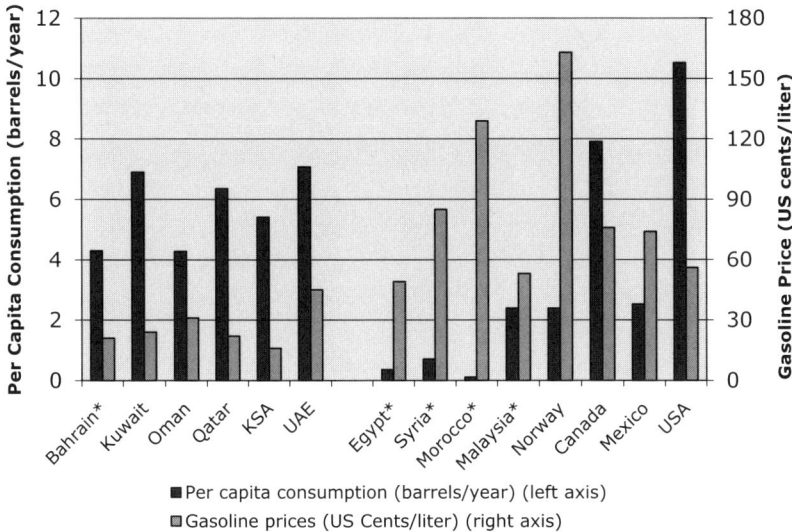

Figure 2.1: Gasoline Prices and Consumption in International Comparison.
Source: Taken from Hodson (2011). Sources cited there: GTZ International Fuel Prices (2009); OPEC Statistical Bulletin (2009); U.S. Department of Energy's Energy Information Administration (EIA) (2009).
Note: *Figures from 2006.

consumption needs are modest. Annual growth rates are between 6 and 10 percent, that is, significantly above population growth. A disproportionate share of electricity is used in the residential sector: 42.5 percent of the 2007 total in the whole GCC, compared to an OECD average of 26.8 percent and a non-OECD average of 17.5 percent.[12]

In the 1980s, when populations were smaller, the international market for oil was saturated, and associated gas from local oil production was available in relative abundance, provision of cheap fuels and energy was a fairly rational thing to do in the GCC. Nowadays, however, populations are much larger, oil can be sold internationally at much higher prices, spare capacity is scarce, and the region is short of gas for either electricity generation or industrial use. Low tariff policies hence impose a much larger opportunity cost, forcing states to

---
[12] For details see Hodson, "Distributional Structures in the Arab Gulf."

Table 2.1: Dry Natural Gas Consumption (billion cf, EIA).

	2000	2009	Growth
Bahrain	303	444	47%
Algeria	726	1016	40%
Kuwait	339	437	29%
Oman	221	520	135%
Qatar	532	745	40%
Saudi Arabia	1759	2770	57%
The UAE	1110	2086	88%

Table 2.2: Petroleum Consumption ('000 bpd, EIA).

	2000	2009	Growth
Bahrain	23	45	93%
Egypt	553	716	30%
Kuwait	264	372	41%
Libya	210	264	26%
Oman	53	115	119%
Qatar	48	147	205%
Saudi Arabia	1537	2438	59%
The UAE	330	492	49%

build and maintain expensive spare production capacity and forego significant export revenue.[13] The below tables show the rapid pace at which gas and oil consumption has grown in the GCC.

The volumes of consumption have become very significant in macro-economic and fiscal terms. Electricity subsidies in the GCC as measured by the difference between *de facto* production costs (based on international input

---

[13] Giacomo Luciani, "Domestic Pricing of Energy and Industrial Competitiveness," in *Resource Blessed*, ed. Giacomo Luciani (Geneva: Gulf Research Center, 2011).

prices) and retail revenue are estimated between 0.6 percent (Bahrain) and 3 percent (Saudi Arabia) of GDP.[14]

The implicit costs of cheap gasoline and diesel can be even higher. In Saudi Arabia, the GCC country with the lowest fuel prices, the subsidy for premium gasoline was $10.4 billion in 2008, representing 2.2 percent of GDP, while the subsidy for diesel fuel was $22.6 billion, or 4.8 percent of GDP. The total subsidy hence amounted to 7 percent of GDP, corresponding to 23.8 percent of total government spending.[15] In Kuwait and Qatar, the total subsidy is estimated at 1.5 and 1.2 percent of GDP, respectively.

Saudi Arabia's total energy demand in 2010 amounted to 3.4 million barrels of oil equivalent per day.[16] The previous year, the country produced an average of 9.8 million bpd of oil, but only exported 7.3 million. It thus consumed as much oil domestically as Germany, a much richer country with three times the population.[17] If current trends continue, national oil company Saudi Aramco expects the number of barrels per day needed domestically to reach 8.3 million by 2028, leaving little energy for export.[18]

It is doubtful that the utility that consumers derive from cheap energy is anywhere near its implicit cost. A good deal of the near-costless consumption of energy in the GCC is frivolous. Some Qataris, who as citizens receive electricity for free, are reported to run air conditioners in their homes for weeks during summer vacation just to have a cool house on return from their holiday. There are no incentives for buying more fuel efficient cars and appliances, insulating houses, or turning off the lights — all of which would only modestly inconvenience most consumers but could drastically improve the long-term fiscal position of the government and liberate funds for more productive uses.

The benefits of cheap electricity, water, and fuel accrue disproportionately to wealthy households and are hence equivalent to a regressive tax. This becomes an issue especially when there are insufficient funds for rival fiscal purposes. This is not currently a problem, but it was a significant issue in the 1990s when

---

[14,15] See Hodson, "Distributional Structures in the Arab Gulf," Table 6.
[16] *Saudi Gazette*, 25 January 2011.
[17] This is according to data from the U.S. Energy Information Administration.
[18] *Arab News*, 23 March 2010.

GCC governments were running out of money and responded by curtailing infrastructure and other public service investment while in several cases being politically unable to increase utility prices.[19]

Public employment

While implicit energy and fuel subsidies are huge, the largest mechanism of patronage in the GCC is arguably that of public employment. Although for different reasons, it is as inequitable as the provision of cheap energy and it creates its own set of perverse incentives. In the less wealthy GCC countries — Bahrain, Oman, and Saudi Arabia — an unusually large share of budgets is used for public salaries.[20] The officially allocated share in Saudi Arabia in 2008 was around 45 percent,[21] far above OECD levels, which lie between 20 and 30 percent.

The GCC public sector is notoriously overstaffed and is dominated by nationals enjoying high wages, short working hours, and generous fringe benefits.[22] The wage gap between the public and the private sector, which is predominantly staffed by expatriates, is enormous. The average salary of Saudi civil servants is about 9,000 Saudi riyals (SR) per month, while the average wage for Saudis in the private sector has been fluctuating around 3,000 SR.[23] The average wage of the private sector in general is closer to 1,000 SR, reflecting the large presence of low-wage foreign labor[24] — itself a significant source of rent for the local private sector, although a rent not directly derived from government resource allocation.

The segmentation of wages and work conditions between public and private sectors is similar or worse in other GCC countries and pushes nationals into unproductive public employment, even if that means they sometimes

---

[19] See Hertog, *Princes, Brokers, and Bureaucrats*, Chapter 4, for the Saudi case.
[20] Hodson, "Distributional Structures in the Arab Gulf."
[21] Kingdom of Saudi Arabia, "Statistical Yearbook 2008," 2009.
[22] Ingo Forstenlechner and Emilie Rutledge, "Unemployment in the Gulf: Time to Update the 'Social Contract,'" *Middle East Policy* 17, 2 (2010): 38–51.
[23] Ministry of Labor, various yearbooks; John Sfakianakis *et al.*, *Quota Counting: New Saudi Employment Rules to Shake up Private Sector*, Banque Saudi Fransi report, June 2011.
[24] *Saudi Gazette*, 11 October 2010.

spend years waiting for a job. It also deters nationals from acquiring skills that would be relevant in private employment; instead, they enroll in low-effort higher education programs that put them into the pipeline for higher-level civil service jobs. Private sector representatives frequently complain about the irrelevance of nationals' education.[25]

Recent bureaucratic wage increases and promises of additional public employment have further deterred nationals from orienting themselves toward the private economy and have increased their reservation wages. The agenda of "nationalizing" private job markets that GCC governments have been pursuing since at least the 1990s has been dealt a heavy blow. If unreported employment in the security sector is counted, even the poorer GCC countries are very likely to have more nationals working for the state than in the private sector. This contrasts with public employment shares in the rest of the world that are closer to 20 percent.[26] Of course, the total volume of public salaries dwarves that of (lower) private salaries.

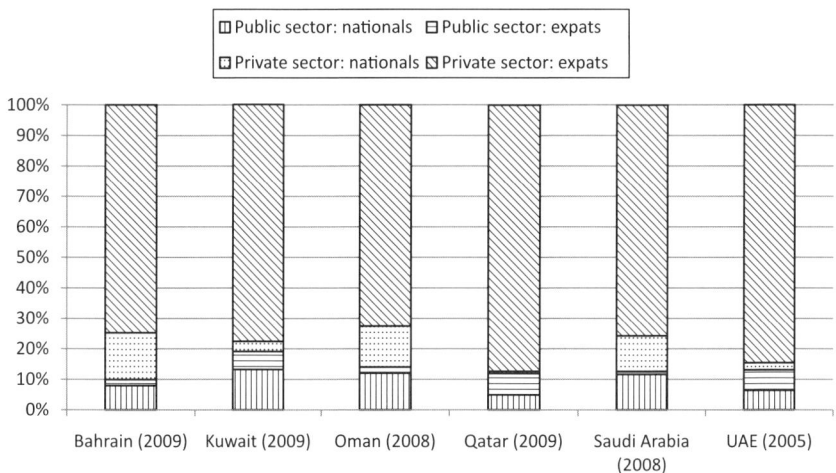

Figure 2.2: Employment Patterns in the GCC.
Source: Based on Hodson (2011).

---

[25]Various research interviews in Saudi Arabia, Bahrain, Saudi Arabia and Kuwait, 2003 to 2011.
[26]Messaoud Hammouya, *Statistics on Public Sector Employment: Methodology, Structures, and Trends* (Geneva: International Labor Organization, 1999).

Overstaffing of bureaucracies tends to be bad for quality and responsiveness of the administration, especially if jobs are seen as entitlements and there is no competitive entry. Public employment as a distributional tool is also deeply unfair, at least in the states where not every national can be supplied with a low-effort bureaucratic job due to insufficient rents per capita, namely Saudi Arabia, Bahrain, and Oman.

Most GCC nationals are effectively excluded from productive economic activities in their own countries. Even those who are active in business often do so as access brokers rather than as real entrepreneurs. The stipulation of part or full national ownership of businesses in many sectors has led to the emergence of "cover-up" businesses across the GCC that are formally owned by nationals but are in fact financed and operated by expatriates who pay an informal "rent" to the official owner. Privilege again serves to keep nationals out of their national economy.[27]

Sustainability Issues

We have seen that energy consumption grows faster than the population. The structural need for public employment grows somewhat less quickly, but still at a significant pace. Cohorts of nationals entering the labor market now were born 20 years ago, when demographic growth was still considerably above 2 percent in most GCC countries. With private job creation for nationals stagnant, all other things equal the need for public jobs will increase. The recent knee-jerk patronage decrees stepping up job creation and increasing civil service benefits have added considerably to public employment costs in the lower-rent countries.

Expenditure trends over the last decade paint an alarming picture. In Saudi Arabia, the official budgetary allocation for wages and benefits increased from 116 billion to 181 billion SR between 2003 and 2008.[28] In 2010, it reached 248 billion SR.[29] This allocation nominally doubled in just seven

---

[27] Steffen Hertog, "The Sociology of the Gulf Rentier Systems: Societies of Intermediaries," *Comparative Studies in Society and History* 52, 2 (2010): 282–318.
[28] Kingdom of Saudi Arabia, "Statistical Yearbook 2008."
[29] Sfakianakis *et al.*, *Strategy Shift: Saudi Spending Swells*.

years, and these figures do not take into account the issuance of recent patronage decrees, which will significantly inflate the (yet unpublished) 2011 and 2012 wage bills.

Saudi Arabia is now spending more than four times as much as in the late 1990s.[30] The Institute of International Finance estimates that its 2011 breakeven oil price is $85 per barrel and will increase to $110 by 2015. Bahrain's and Oman's breakeven oil prices are already around $100. Among the higher-rent GCC countries, the UAE has also reached a breakeven oil price of around $85. Kuwait's and Qatar's breakeven prices are still estimated to lie below $50, but here, too, the figures have at least doubled since 2003.[31]

Spending is unlikely to continue growing as rapidly as it has during the last decade. Yet unless there is a fundamental reform to GCC distributional systems, spending will have to increase at least somewhat due to the above structural factors that will both demand increased domestic outlays and put a squeeze on oil exports. In the past, it has proven impossible to shrink public

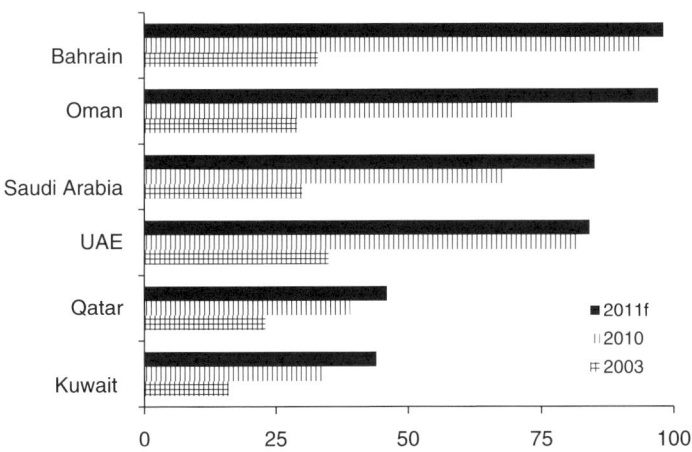

Figure 2.3: GCC Breakeven Oil Prices (USD per Barrel).
Source: Institute of International Finance, 2011.

---

[30] SAMA annual reports, various issues.
[31] Institute of International Finance, *The Arab World in Transition: Assessing the Economic Impact*, IIF Regional Overview, May 2011.

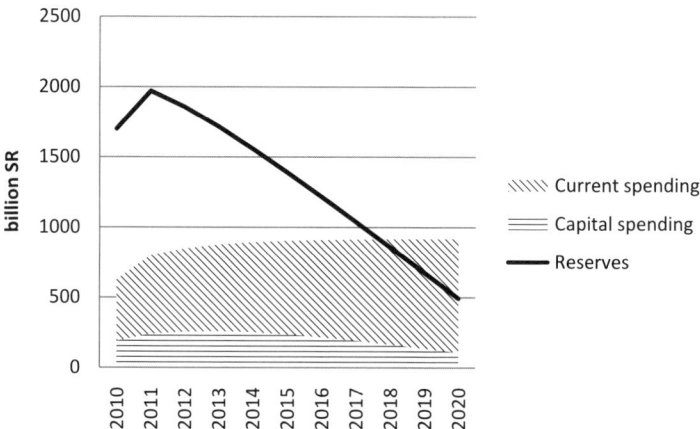

Figure 2.4: Saudi Fiscal Scenarios for Saudi Arabia under $80/Barrel.

sectors and most attempts at tariff reform have faltered.[32] In the long run, however, current systems of distribution are not sustainable.

The time at which the situation will become critical depends most on oil price developments. The figures below show three different scenarios for Saudi fiscal policy under three different oil prices. Based on past experience, they assume that current spending — which includes wages — will see minimum growth of 4 percent even if the government runs a deficit. Capital spending, by contrast, is likely to be the first victim of austerity, as it was in the 1980s and 1990s. For all oil prices below $80 per barrel, Saudi Arabia is likely to run down its overseas capital reserves by the end of the decade. Once reserves are used up, the government still has the option to incur domestic debt as it did in the 1990s, but this would likely postpone the reckoning only by a few years.

The situation in Oman and Bahrain is more dramatic, as fiscal needs measured in terms of oil prices are larger and overseas reserves are much smaller because the savings the two countries made during the recent oil boom are negligible. Both have pledged extensive patronage spending during the recent unrest, putting them on an unsustainable fiscal path. It remains to be seen how

---

[32] Hertog, *Princes, Brokers, and Bureaucrats*, Chapter 4.

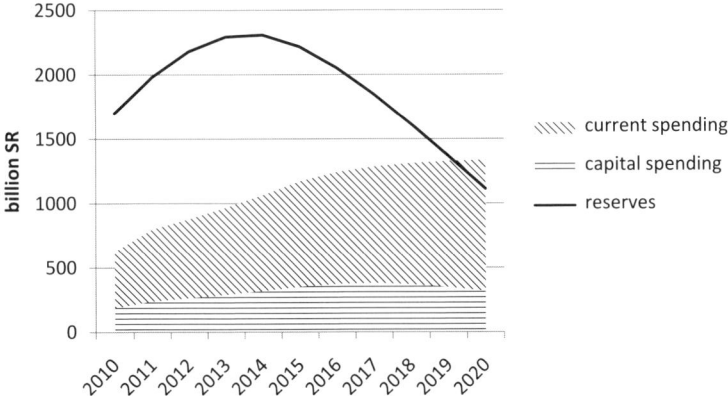

Figure 2.5:   Saudi Fiscal Scenarios for Saudi Arabia under $120/Barrel.

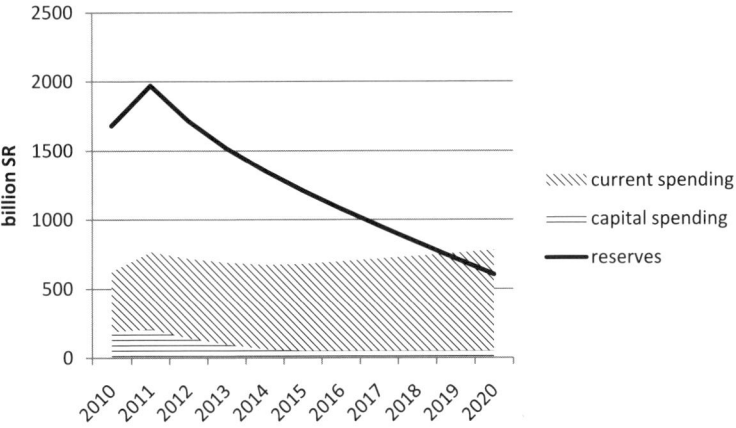

Figure 2.6:   Saudi Fiscal Scenarios for Saudi Arabia under $50/Barrel.

long the budgetary support pledged by their richer GCC neighbors can stave off a fiscal crisis.

Potential Policies

Although time horizons differ significantly from one country to the next, current regimes of distribution in the GCC all appear fiscally unsustainable in the long run. Their socioeconomic sustainability is also in question, as they exclude nationals from their own economies, all regime efforts of forcible integration notwithstanding. Economic exclusion in turn feeds into fiscal unsustainability, as the absence of private incomes for nationals heightens pressure for public employment and other direct or indirect transfer schemes.

Distribution in the GCC is a political fact; even the most authoritarian Gulf ruler would find it difficult to rescind his obligation of care toward his subjects. In the fiscal crisis of the 1990s, public employment and cheap public services were the very last budget items that regimes dared to touch. Most of the modest price increases in utility prices or public transport that have occurred across the region were subsequently reversed. Entitlements, once created, are very hard to rescind.

Large-scale distribution cannot and arguably should not be abandoned. But if abolition is not an option, are there ways of making it less destructive and unsustainable? There is a growing, if still inchoate, debate about this issue among GCC technocrats. Dramatic steps are unlikely in the coming years, but a growing understanding of the challenges could lead to more creative thinking than the region has witnessed to date. Even if ideal solutions may never be implemented in practice, it is important to develop them as a theoretical benchmark, if only to deepen our understanding of the fiscal sociology of GCC rentier states.

How would distribution be reorganized in an ideal world? Three basic criteria appear to be relevant:

- The fiscal basis of the state should be protected.
- The citizenry should play a substantial role in the private economy.
- Local private sector and citizenry should develop a shared interest in growth-oriented economic policy.

The importance of the last point will emerge later in the Chapter. For now, let us note that the challenge of re-engineering distribution is the same in authoritarian and semi-democratic GCC rentier states, even if the political conditions for re-engineering differ between them. Even a fully democratic GCC regime would face the same problem set, although it might find it harder to deal with.

Overconsumption of Energy

A more equitable and incentive-neutral distribution system would avoid overconsumption of costly state-provided services and goods and direct nationals toward private rather than state employment. Addressing the overconsumption issue is the relatively easier bit. The challenge is to create marginal consumption costs for electricity and fuel that are in line with the value of these goods, while maintaining the income gains inherent in the lower prices.

One option of achieving this would be a system of free minimal consumption allotments in which every citizen is entitled to a certain level of reasonable consumption for free, above which tariffs apply that reflect the actual opportunity costs of energy. Overall consumption levels would be considerably lower, conservation efforts would be encouraged, and the implicit subsidy to the larger, wealthier consumers would be removed. Reimbursing citizens for consumption below their allotted level could be considered, a measure that could have both an additional conservation and a stronger poverty alleviation effect.

A stacked tariff system in which marginal prices rise with rising consumption would be a second-best option that has already been implemented to some (quite modest) extent in the GCC.[33] The introduction of a steeper stacked tariff regime by itself, however, would simply mean taking away existing entitlements, which would be politically difficult. It would also incentivize savings only above a certain level.

Both consumption allotment and stacked tariff schemes would be harder to organize for transport fuels than for water and electricity. A more easily administered alternative would be a direct cash grant to every adult citizen that would buy a reasonable amount of fuel at market rates. Such cash grants could potentially be subsumed under a broader citizens' income scheme, an idea that will be discussed in the following section.

An issue that is politically and socially much more complex than overconsumption of energy is large-scale overemployment in the public sector. While cheap energy is merely a nice perk of GCC citizenship, the livelihood of

---

[33] Saudi Arabia, for example, has stacked electricity tariffs for both residential and business consumers. See http://www.se.com.sa/SEC/English/Menu/Customers/Consumption+bills/TarifAndTax.htm.

the majority of GCC nationals depends directly or indirectly on public sector employment. The volume of salaries accruing to Saudis through the public sector is more than four times as large as that derived from the private sector. The ratios in Bahrain and Oman are somewhat lower, while they are even higher in Kuwait, Qatar, and the UAE.

Public employment reform and citizens' income

I have argued above that overemployment in the public sector is an inequitable form of distribution that tends to undermine the quality of bureaucracies and, more importantly, undermines incentives for nationals to seek gainful private employment and the skills required for it. To alleviate these problems, GCC rentier states should move from public sector overemployment to a modern welfare system in which distributional entitlements are based on citizenship rather than holding a public sector job.

A substantial trimming down of the civil service would free resources for policies such as the introduction of general unemployment insurance and an unemployment assistance scheme for first-time job seekers. Such measures would be politically insufficient as a quid pro quo for reduced public employment, however. Given the low salary levels prevalent on the private GCC labor market, they would also disincentivize private job-seeking unless set at an unacceptably low amount.

There is a politically more palatable and less economically distortionary, if unconventional, alternative: A general citizens' income that is not means-tested but is simply paid to all passport holders. Such a distribution mechanism could meet broader political support, particularly among those excluded from public employment, and could make the gradual slimming down of the civil service less of a zero-sum game.

Economists in the OECD countries originally proposed such basic income schemes for tax-based economies, but the idea appears uniquely apposite in the GCC rentier context.[34] They entail unconditional cash grants for all

---

[34] Alaska is the only oil-producing entity that has a *de facto* citizens' income, although it is only starting to be analyzed in these terms now. A "citizens' income policy" is under discussion in Iraq and is about to be introduced in Iran. Karl Widerquist, "A Day-Long Discussion

citizens above a certain age, usually paid on a regular basis but potentially also paid as a one-off lump sum transfer.[35] The one GCC-specific modification to the standard model should be that public servants — who already are *de facto* rent recipients — should be excluded from the scheme.

Rent recycling through a GCC citizens' income would make distribution broader, less exclusive, less discretionary, and much less distortionary in terms of labor market incentives. The level of a citizens' income would have to lie considerably below current civil service salaries, but could be set above the average wage in the private sector at large. It might be difficult to convince significant numbers of incumbent civil servants to leave their jobs for a citizens' income, but it should be easier to persuade future labor market entrants to exchange the more or less vague hope of future public employment for a concrete, life-long entitlement.

In the richer countries where public employment is a more certain prospect for young nationals, namely Kuwait, Qatar, and the UAE, a citizens' income would have to be set at a relatively higher level — luckily, these are the countries where this would be less fiscally burdensome.

The delinking of public employment and rent distribution would orient nationals toward private employment. Prospects of an easy public job would be more remote, requiring them to seek other sources of work income. In this context, the citizens' income would function somewhat analogous to a wage subsidy.[36] Nationals could achieve acceptable total income levels even if

---

of 'the Alaska Model' at the University of Alaska-Anchorage," May 2011, available online at http://works.bepress.com/cgi/viewcontent.cgi?article=1024&context=widerquist. For a General argument in favor of a "resource dividend," especially for poorer rentier states, see Paul Segal, "Resource Rents, Redistribution, and Halving Global Poverty: The Resource Dividend," *World Development* 39, 4 (2011): 475–489. On Iran, see Tabatabai Hamid, "The Basic Income Road to Reforming Iran's Price Subsidies," *Basic Income Studies* 6, 1 (2011): 1–24.

[35] Giacomo Corneo, "Stakeholding as a New Development Strategy for Saudi Arabia," *Review of Middle East Economics and Finance* 7, 1 (2011), available online at http://www.bepress.com/rmeef/vol7/iss1/art1.

[36] This is not strictly analogous, as wage subsidies are only paid when an individual is in paid employment. Such a policy in the GCC context would appear less equitable, however, and be more prone to abuse through "phantom" employment — as has already happened in the case of Kuwait, where many women hold "paper jobs" in collusion with employers only to collect wage subsidies.

holding less well paying jobs than currently, as their citizens' income would top up their private sector wages without penalty. This might by itself be insufficient to integrate the majority of young GCC job-seekers into the private labor market, but it would be an important step in that direction.

A citizens' income would be less damaging to bureaucratic efficiency and more equitable than the status quo. Of all options to distribute wealth, it would be the least distortive of labor market incentives for citizens. In combination with more restrictive public sector hiring, it would strongly reduce nationals' reservation wages, allowing them to compete more effectively with expatriate labor than to date — but without exposing them to net income levels that are socially and politically unacceptable.

Economist James Meade has made the argument that a citizens' income in Western economies would allow full employment without exposing low earners to unacceptably low total incomes.[37] It is noteworthy that he argued for such a policy in a context in which implementation would be fiscally vastly more complex — and a context in which the need for income supplement policies for private employees is much less urgent, as most private sector wages in the West are much higher than in the GCC, despite similar levels of overall wealth.

Most of the conventional arguments against basic income regarding effects on tax rates, labor market incentives, and redistribution do not apply in the GCC.[38] The system would not require taxing higher earners, would not create any more "free riding" than the current system, and relative to the status quo would increase rather than decrease work incentives.

None of the above is to say that a citizens' income combined with stricter public sector recruitment will solve all GCC labor market problems. I will argue below that by themselves the measures are likely insufficient. It should be clear by now, however, that the outlined policy options are far superior to the status quo and to conventional "welfare state" alternatives.

---

[37] James Edward Meade, *Full Employment Regained?* (Cambridge: Cambridge University Press, 1996).
[38] For an overview see Philippe Van Parijs, "Basic Income: A Simple and Powerful Idea for the Twenty-First Century," *Politics & Society* 32, 1 (2004): 7–39.

Costs and feasibility

In a rentier state context, the costs of citizens' income schemes are very easy to calculate. Let us take Saudi Arabia as example. A citizens' income of SR1,200 for Saudis age 20 and over who are not employed by the state would cost less than SR100 billion per year. This is perhaps a third of current salary expenditure and about 11 percent of the total government spending expected for 2012.[39]

It was noted above that cheap domestic energy in Saudi Arabia imposes an estimated cost of about 10 percent of GDP, which on the basis of estimated numbers for 2012 corresponds to almost 30 percent of the government budget. So eliminating only half of the implicit gasoline, diesel, and electricity subsidies could potentially pay for a full-fledged citizens' income scheme.[40] The potential for a large quid *pro quo* with many winners and few losers seems obvious; it appears the most elegant way of addressing energy overconsumption and labor market disincentives at the same time.

Cheap energy imposes less dramatic costs in the rest of the GCC, but savings potential is nonetheless substantial. And even if a citizens' income should impose short-term cost, it offers long-term saving through a leaner, and quite likely more efficient, civil service. Creating a citizens' income would be easier in the smaller, richer GCC countries than in Saudi Arabia, and would not be much harder in Bahrain and Oman.

Including the Private Sector in the Distributional Bargain

I have outlined steps that could solve overconsumption problems and increase incentives to seek more productive private sector employment. While the various tariff reform options mentioned above would be sufficient to address

---

[39] Sfakianakis, *Strategy Shift: Saudi Spending Swells*.
[40] This is a simplified statement. As outlined above, higher domestic prices would lead to reduced consumption, resulting in potentially larger exports of oil and oil products (though not of gas, which Saudi Arabia does not export and which could instead be put to more productive industrial uses). However, not all of the additional oil will necessarily find a market, and increased exports could put pressure on international prices. The effect is likely to be modest, however, given that consumption patterns will not change drastically overnight and only concern international sales, not local sales at higher prices.

energy overconsumption issues, it is not clear whether the combination of citizens' income and civil service reform would suffice to integrate the majority of the national population of working age into the private labor market — an aim that GCC governments have long pursued under the banner of such programs as "Kuwaitization," "Saudization," and "Bahrainization," and an aim that has become increasingly pressing with growing populations.

The impact of the policies outlined above would no doubt increase participation in the private labor market, but given the current structure of wages and competition in GCC labor markets it is not clear that the effect would be sufficient to involve the majority of adult nationals in the private economy — an outcome that is desirable not only in its own right, but would also serve to defuse socioeconomic tensions that threaten to undermine rational economic policy-making in the GCC.

For many GCC nationals, a citizens' income could result in a "no-effort" result in which an individual would prefer to not work at all and simply live off the citizens' income. The risk of this happening is smaller than under conventional welfare mechanisms, but given the very low private salaries in the GCC it is still considerable.

In many segments of GCC labor markets, available wages are a small fraction of the household expenditure of average national families. One can imagine that many young Saudis would refuse a job paying 1,000 or 1,500 SR/month, preferring to live off their citizens' income combined with parental or other private support — and possibly waiting for a government job after all, despite the longer odds of getting one.

The situation is even more problematic in the richer GCC countries, where average private sector salaries are comparable to those in Saudi Arabia, but living standards for national households are much higher. Against the background of expatriate-dominated labor markets with low salaries, governments could find themselves exposed to residual pressure to provide surplus public jobs despite the availability of a citizens' income. In many ways, a combination of the citizens' income and continuing surplus recruitment in the public sector would still be better than the status quo, but it would be less than ideal. How could pressures leading to this scenario be reduced?

There seems to be one simple answer: Wages in the private sector need to increase to reach a level that makes full-time employment, in combination with the citizens' income, attractive for the bulk of nationals.

The easiest way to increase wages in the GCC private sectors is by making expatriate labor more expensive, either by reducing its inflow, hence making it scarcer, or by taxing it. In either case, the opportunity costs of employing nationals at higher wages would be reduced. Both approaches would obviously impose at least a short-term burden on the local private sector.[41]

The private sector's privileges in GCC distributional systems are a crucial factor in the segmentation of labor markets. The almost unrestricted imports of low-wage labor allow local business to extract considerable surpluses, but at the same time this practice contributes to the exclusion of nationals from private employment, which in turn increases the pressure to create surplus public sector jobs that further cement segmentation.

How could the local private sector be integrated in a new distributional bargain that would allow a gradual increase in the price of foreign labor? To answer this question, we need to understand how existing structures of rent recycling shape the fiscal sociology of state-business relations in the GCC.

It is generally known that business profits strongly from state spending in the GCC, be it directly through contracts or indirectly through consumption generated through state salaries. Econometric tests show that the short-term link of state spending growth and business growth is less tight than in the 1970s and 1980s, but that in the long run the size of business activity is still closely correlated with the size of state spending, as Figures 2.7 and 2.8 (see next page) illustrate for the Saudi and Kuwaiti cases.[42]

---

[41] Blanket taxes and total quantitative caps will probably not do the trick, as they would remove many (very) low-cost expatriates from the market who could not be replaced by nationals in the short run. For details on more targeted taxation and supply mechanisms aimed at sectors and jobs in which the wage gap is relatively narrower, see Eberhard Feess, "Minimum Wages in Gulf States — An Economic Analysis," in *Labour Market, Unemployment, and Migration in the GCC*, ed. Steffen Hertog (Geneva: Gulf Research Center, 2011).

[42] While in tax economies, the causal link can run in both directions — more business activity leading to higher tax revenue and hence higher spending — the linkage in the GCC can almost by definition only be one way.

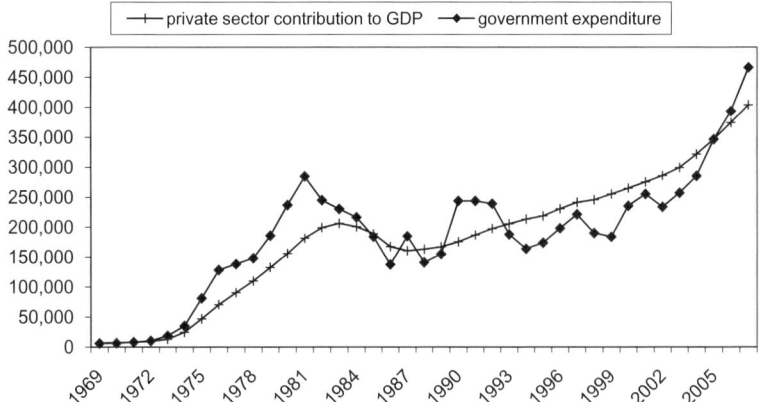

Figure 2.7: Private Sector Contribution to Saudi GDP vs. Government Expenditure (Million SR).
Source: SAMA.

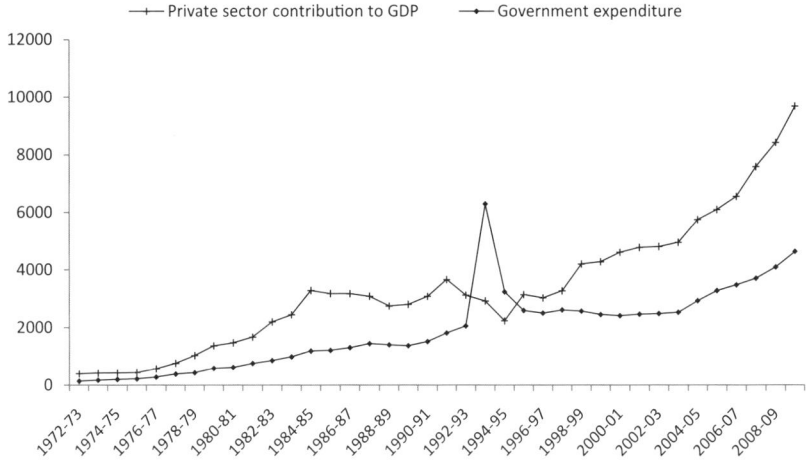

Figure 2.8: Private Sector Contribution to Kuwaiti GDP vs. Total Government Expenditure (Million KD).[43]
Source: Central Statistical Office.

---

[43] The spike in spending in the early 1990s is due to reconstruction expenditures after the 1990–1991 Gulf War.

What is less well understood is that the rentier nature of GCC economies leads to an unusually direct opposition between the fiscal interests of the citizenry at large and those of the business class. As business growth leads neither to a larger tax base nor to significant employment of nationals, the latter have little rational interest in pro-business spending or indeed any pro-business economic policy. To the extent that voters have a say in economic policy, which is the case notably in Kuwait, they vote for populist distributional policies that are deleterious to private sector development but in their own rational interest — including excess employment in the public sector and a variety of other subsidization schemes.[44]

In the absence of national employment and taxation effects, state spending on business and other pro-business policies only benefit a relatively small group of private investors. Different from conventional tax economies, expansionary fiscal policy is only beneficial to the bulk of the citizenry if it puts money directly into its pockets. If money is spent on, say, public works, in income terms this benefits only the contractors and sub-contractors involved and their predominantly foreign employees, who remit a large share of their salaries to their home countries.

There is a certain asymmetry of interests here, as business still benefits somewhat from spending on public sector salaries, as the salaries subsequently get spent in the local economy, while pro-business spending bypasses most citizens and leads to a seepage of resources abroad. Business benefits at least from citizens' role as consumers, while business conversely does nothing to generate income for most of the citizenry.[45]

In conventional tax states, linkages of taxation, employment, and demand generation create interdependence and a potential for class compromise between citizenry and business.[46] Citizens in private sector employment should have some interest in pro-growth spending and regulatory policies; democratic participation allows them to articulate these balanced interests.

---

[44] See Herb, "A Nation of Bureaucrats," for the general argument as well as two case studies.
[45] This is perhaps a subsidiary reason why broad salary spending has always been privileged over project spending in times of economic crisis.
[46] Adam Przeworski, *Capitalism and Social Democracy* (Cambridge: Cambridge University Press, 1986).

In rentier states, by contrast, there is a near zero-sum conflict between most citizens and the private sector; the two simply want to maximize patronage policies and pro-growth policies, respectively. The citizenry is particularly disinterested in pro-growth measures and does not get to feel the negative economic externalities of patronage spending that act as a deterrent to populist policies in tax states.

There are numerous fields in which policy interests of citizens and business can be at odds:

- Distributional spending (public jobs and subsidized services) vs. spending on industrial and trade infrastructure, technology acquisition.
- Cheap (if potentially low quality) services vs. privatization.
- Bureaucracy as a distributional tool vs. government streamlining, building of specialized agencies and regulatory capacity.
- Consumer loans and subsidies vs. industrial loans and subsidies.

The conflicts involve the question of what the state should spend money on, but they also highlight a more fundamental struggle over whether a government should primarily be an efficient regulator and enabler or a tool of distribution. Even policy issues that most voters don't care about much, such as the creation of a capital markets authority or the planning of new ports infrastructure in Kuwait, can become bargaining chips in distributional haggling. Many fiscally neutral initiatives of diversification and regulatory modernization in Kuwait have become collateral damage in parliamentary fights that are primarily concerned with distributional conflicts, as these initiatives are the least costly to give up.

Elected bodies in the GCC appear to be systematically more populist and oriented toward the politics of distribution, while appointed bodies have a more technocratic and development-oriented bent broadly in line with business interests. Populist inclinations are visible even in very tame (semi-) elected institutions such as the Federal National Council in the UAE or the Majlis al-Shura in Oman. Even the unelected Majlis al-Shura in Saudi Arabia seems to have become more populist after the ruling family started to choose its membership along regional and tribal rather than purely technocratic criteria.[47]

---

[47] Author's discussion with Majlis al-Shura members, May 2011.

It is against this background that labor market reforms aimed at increased private wage levels become relevant. An increase in the cost of foreign labor could indirectly reduce the tension between the fiscal interests of citizenry and business at the same time that it would relieve the distributional pressures on the government budget.

As outlined above, higher wages would imply a shift toward national employment, as nationals would become more competitive on the private labor market — ideally while at the same time having less easy access to guaranteed state employment and drawing on a citizens' income as a least distortionary rent entitlement. Jobs for nationals in turn would help to link the fiscal interests of business and citizenry, as pro-business policies and the resulting private sector growth would benefit a growing class of national employees.

In the case of the semi-representative rentier system in Kuwait, development has been falling behind that of its neighbors for decades precisely because the citizenry has a voice in economic policy. The potential link of private Kuwaiti employment and popular support for pro-business policies, however, might also reduce business resistance against policies that aim to narrow the local-expatriate wage gap. Based on a proper understanding of these linkages, Kuwait could once again become the spearhead of policy reform, as it is the only GCC country where all actors — government, business, and citizenry — have at least some incentives for a grand distributional bargain. In the long run, higher labor costs would be likely to force stronger investment in national labor skills and productivity, as has historically happened in successful exporters like Germany or Singapore.

At least in the short run, higher private sector salaries — even if induced by quantitative restrictions on foreign labor rather than fees — would be the political and in many ways fiscal equivalent of a tax on local business or a transfer from business to government. While business expenses on labor would increase, government expenditure on state employment would be allowed to shrink, liberating funds for pro-growth investment. This shift of the cost burden would bring the GCC more in line with conventional tax states, even in the absence of formal taxes.

Business has benefited from state spending and open migration for decades without paying back to society through either taxes or employment. A more mature local business class should arguably step up to the plate and start contributing to the local economy in a way that includes nationals and relieves some of the excessive burden on governments that have been expected to be the singular providers of full employment. While this might impose short-term costs for business, it reduces the long-term threat of severe distributional conflicts and anti-growth populist policies. It would allow for the gradual downscaling of the very distributional policies that have led to skewed labor markets in the first place.

In practical terms, it is unlikely that business can be "sold" on such a class compromise easily, even in a state like Kuwait where populist pressures are severe, as the potential benefits are long-term and not certain. There is therefore a potential need for a wider pro-employment coalition in society, mobilizing popular support for migration reform and against a business class that is structurally parasitic. This particular type of populism would be developmental in the long run, although it would require substantial efforts to educate national job seekers about their own rational interest in more expensive and scarce expatriate labor. In an ideal world, authoritarian leaders' fiscal and developmental interest in labor reform would lead them to increase political participation in order to be able to pressure business more effectively.

Chapter 3

State-Business Relations in the Gulf: The Role of Business Actors in the Decision-Making Process in Bahrain and Oman[1]

Marc Valeri

The last ten years have seen an unprecedented awareness by Gulf Cooperation Council (GCC) elites of the need to rethink the socioeconomic structures of their states, with the goal of addressing the challenges of sociopolitical and economic sustainability. While high oil prices arguably reduced the pressure to transform and diversify in the 1970s, the latest period of high oil prices (2004–2009) coincided with sustained economic liberalizing reforms, including changes in the role of the state, economic diversification policies, and reforms in labor markets, health, and education. These changes have had major implications for the social contract in these states, particularly in regard to the relationship between the business sector and the political authority. This Chapter argues that internal power politics within the ruling elite in Bahrain and Oman largely explain the manner in which social and economic reforms have been implemented. More precisely, one key variable whose effects will be examined is the degree of closeness or independence of the business elite to the ruling elite. By understanding the relationship between business and political

---

[1] This research was supported by the UK Economic and Social Research Council (grant number ES/J012696/1).

elites as a crucial factor in comprehending social and economic reform, the approach adopted here aims to offer a new means of assessing challenges to political legitimacy induced by the current transformations.

Before undertaking a brief overview of the similar dilemmas Bahrain and Oman have faced since the 1970s and 1980s (when they first tried to diversify their revenues) and their common objective of an alternative model of economic development, this Chapter first highlights the differences between the two states in the organization of their respective business communities and in the sociology of these communities' relations with the political authority. In Bahrain, where the political elite and the economic elite are historically distinct, and in Oman, where the bourgeoisie has been directly involved in the decision-making sphere since the 1970s, the varying power of the private sector has had a major impact on what direction economic reforms have taken during the last ten years. The impact of the business elite in both states on the economic diversification policies and the privatization process during the last decade will be examined. In particular, this Chapter pays special attention to the perceptions and views of influential members of the business community *vis-à-vis* labor market reforms as well as to the actual effects of these members' actions and decisions.

State-Business Relationship: A Different Historical Background

Jill Crystal explains that the development of oil production in Kuwait and Qatar led to the merchants' withdrawal from political life.[2] The merchants constituted the group that historically pressed its claims on the state. Before oil, a tacit arrangement linked Qatari and Kuwaiti rulers to the local merchant families; in exchange for the merchant families' financial support, the former granted the latter wide influence in political decision-making so that the merchants could preserve their interests. The unexpected material self-sufficiency of the rulers after oil was discovered disrupted this historical alliance. The

---

[2] Jill Crystal, *Oil and Politics in the Gulf: Rulers and Merchants in Kuwait and Qatar* (Cambridge: Cambridge University Press, 1995).

rulers were freed from their economic dependence on the merchants, while the merchants were forced to renounce their historical claim to participate in decision-making; in exchange, the rulers granted them a large share of oil revenues. A subtle but major difference emerged nonetheless between the two countries: While in Kuwait the ruler was forced to promise to keep royal family members out of business, in Qatar, because the merchant community was weaker and smaller, the ruler allowed his relatives into the merchants' economic territory.

In Oman, merchants were not "forced to choose money over formal political influence" until the late 1990s.[3] This situation finds its roots in the alliance developed between Sultan Said bin Taimur (r.1932–1970) and the merchants from Muscat and Muttrah who held monopoly over export and import trade in Oman from the end of the nineteenth century onward. Politically harmless, the merchants showed skill in proving indispensable to the ruler's political survival; not only were they the only ones able to provide the sultan's growing need for liquid assets, but the sultan deducted huge taxes from their resources, which represented one of the major sources of the sultanate's revenue. Unknown among his subjects in 1970, and denounced by opponents as the last card played by the British who were about to leave the "Gulf game," the new sultan — Qaboos — had no other choice than to maintain this alliance with merchant elites. He gave guarantees to the merchants' networks, ensuring his non-interference in the business sphere and the merchants' privileged access to the oil godsend through public contracts. Moreover, Qaboos granted the merchants positions in government with decision-making power so that they could secure these public contracts and control the distribution of the oil wealth.

The al-Sultan family is an example of one of these merchant dynasties. The family acted as representatives in Oman for the British India shipping line and Lloyds in the first half of the twentieth century. The leading al-Sultan family company is W.J. Towell, which is involved in more than 40 sectors, such as motors, telecommunications, construction, computer engineering, and insurance. Maqbul Ali Sultan, a former chairman (1987–1991) of the

---

[3]Crystal, *Oil and Politics*, p. 195.

Omani Chamber of Commerce, held the post of Minister for Commerce and Industry from 1991 to February 2011. His brother Jamil was vice president of the Chamber of Commerce until 2011.

Another example of the direct participation of business families in Oman's decision-making process is the al-Zawawi family. A native of Hejaz, Yusif al-Zawawi came to Muscat at the end of the nineteenth century to establish a trading company. He became one of the unofficial advisors to Sultan Faisal (r.1888–1913), Qaboos' great-grandfather. Qais al-Zawawi, Yusif's grandson, held the position of Foreign Minister between 1973 and 1982, and then became Deputy Prime Minister for Finance and Economy until his death in 1995. His brother Umar currently holds the position of Special Advisor to the Sultan for External Affairs. Economically speaking, the Umar Zawawi Establishment has become one of the leading Omani holding companies.

The Zubair family also owes much of its economic success to its historic connections with the sultans of Muscat. Zubair al-Hutti acted as governor of Dhofar in the 1930s, and Sultan Said entrusted him with running his personal real estate projects. Muhammad bin Zubair, who was the first chairman of the Omani Chamber of Commerce in 1972, was appointed to the post of Minister for Commerce and Industry in November 1974. He left in 1982 to become Personal Advisor to the Sultan for Economic Affairs, his current position. Muhammad bin Zubair's son, Khalid, is currently member of the board of the Chamber of Commerce. The nephew of Muhammad bin Zubair, Juma bin Ali, was Minister for Manpower until 2008.

At the same time, oil revenues profoundly changed the boundaries between politics and the economy, as many ministers whose families were previously not active in the economy become personally rich. Qaboos did not question this process, as it both increased the dependency of the elites on the state and the stability of his rule. The symbolic debts owed by Qaboos at the beginning of his rule to these key players who supported him after 1970 thus gradually turned into a weapon in his hands, forestalling any challenges to his reign by turning the most powerful societal forces into unfailing allies.

On the eve of the 2011 Arab Spring, few members of the Omani Council of Ministers had not personally derived material profit from oil revenue. One of the most illustrative cases is the noble branch of the Khalili family — heirs to a prestigious lineage of Ibadi imams who opposed the sultans of Muscat until the 1950s. Saud al-Khalili, the nephew of the imam of Oman Muhammad al-Khalili (1920–1954), became one of the four members of Qaboos' first cabinet appointed in August 1970. He is also the founder (1973) and owner of the powerful business group al-Taher, which is active in construction contracting (Caterpillar), food and drink (Sprite and Coke), and the distribution of Shell products. His nephew, Salim bin Hilal, Minister for Agriculture until 2011, was formerly chairman of the Chamber of Commerce, while another of his nephews, Abd al-Malik bin Abdallah, who had previously held successively the positions of executive chairman of the Royal Court Pension Fund, of chairman of the first Omani banking group, Bank Muscat, and of Minister for Tourism (2011–2012), is currently Minister of Justice.

The situation in Bahrain, in which the important and most sensitive ministries are monopolized by the al-Khalifas,[4] cannot be compared with the situation in Oman, in which only two members of the Cabinet belong to the al-Said royal family[5] and where businessmen hold prominent decision-making positions. Even more, if a number of Bahrani[6] merchant families were historical allies of the al-Khalifas (such as the al-Baharna, al-Urayyid, and Rajab families), the Bahraini business elite is mainly composed of Sunni families, either of Najdi background or Hawala.[7] Given that this merchant elite view themselves as a

---

[4] 11 (out of 24) ministerial portfolios are held by members of the al-Khalifa royal family, including Defense, Interior, Foreign Affairs, Justice, and Finances.
[5] Sayyid Haitham bin Tariq al-Said is Minister of Heritage and Culture, while Sayyid Fahad bin Mahmud al-Said has been the Deputy Prime Minister for Cabinet Affairs since 1994. Several other ministers belong to collateral branches of the al-Busaidi tribe but not to the royal family.
[6] The Baharina (sing. Bahrani) are the indigenous Shi'i Arabs in Bahrain. All Shi'a — both indigenous and of Persian origin — are considered to be 65 percent of the national population.
[7] The Hawala are Sunnis that migrated to Bahrain starting in the nineteenth century from the Iranian coast but claim Arab origins. An example of one of these merchant families historically close to the al-Khalifas is the Kanoo family, who moved to Bahrain from southern Persia in the mid-nineteenth century. Yusif Kanoo, who began as a small merchant in 1890 trading with India, became in the 1920s and 1930s the largest banker on the island and the Bahrain agent of companies such as the Anglo-Persian Oil Company and Ford. In the 1950s and 1960s, the House of Kanoo evolved into a conglomerate of companies, with headquarters in Bahrain, Dammam, and Dubai. The Kanoo group of companies is currently one of the largest family-owned groups of companies in the Gulf, and in 2012 the family was estimated to rank 14th on the Arab fortune list

minority and that their influence is not based on deep social networks, they have never been powerful enough to force the ruling family to stay out of business — as is the case in Kuwait. As a result, the al-Khalifa family has never been forced to grant a substantial number of leading positions in the decision-making field to the economic elite, and it retains extensive political room for maneuver *vis-à-vis* the merchants. Moreover, the al-Khalifas themselves have always been substantially involved in business. Indeed, the al-Khalifa family was the first beneficiary of the oil wealth:

> The wealth of the state has been the Al Khalifas' to distribute as largesse to grateful citizens.... Most of the land on the island belongs to the Al Khalifa family and there has been no institutional accountability of the family to the public... since the suspension of the parliament [in 1975].[8]

In the 1990s, Prime Minister Shaykh Khalifa "allegedly became the richest person in Bahrain with extensive holdings in land, hotels, commercial property, and profits on government contracts"[9] while it was well known that "you can't get permission for any project without giving a percentage to the al-Khalifas."[10] In November 2013, only three members of the business elite held positions in the cabinet. Jawad al-Urayyid, a former Minister of State for Cabinet Affairs (1973–1982) who is the grandson of Mansur al-Urayyid, a leading Bahrani pearl merchant in the 1930s, has held the position of Deputy Prime Minister Without Portfolio since December 2006. Hassan Fakhro, who belongs to a wealthy Hawala merchant family,[11] is currently Minister of Industry and Commerce. His brother Isam, chairman of Fakhro Group, succeeded

---

("Arabian Business Rich List 2012," available online at http://richlist.arabianbusiness.com/richlist-2012/profile/17698/#.Un91--L5PIU). Khalid Kanoo, the current managing director of the Kanoo Group in Bahrain, was chairman of the Bahrain Chamber of Commerce until 2005.
[8] Graham E. Fuller and Rend Rahim Francke, *The Arab Shi'a: The Forgotten Muslims* (New York: St. Martin's Press, 1999), p. 125.
[9] John E. Peterson, "Bahrain: Reform, Promise and Reality," in *Political Liberalization in the Persian Gulf*, ed. Joshua Teitelbaum (London: Hurst, 2009), p. 158.
[10] *The Wall Street Journal*, 12 June 1995.
[11] The Fakhro Group was founded in 1888 by Abdul Rahman Fakhro. Yusif bin Abdul Rahman (the current minister's grandfather) and his five sons expanded the family business from the 1930s into a trade and economic empire spreading from Bahrain to India and Iraq.

Khalid Kanoo at the top of the Chamber of Commerce in 2005 and was reelected its chairman in 2009. Samira Rajab was appointed Minister of State for Information Affairs in April 2012.

Thus, even if the Bahraini situation seems to show similarities with Oman, the background of the state-business relationship is very different. The Bahraini private sector has been therefore heavily dependent both on the balance of power within the royal family and on its good relationship with the most influential individuals among the royal family. In Oman, on the contrary, as a legacy of twentieth-century history, Sultan Qaboos has been more dependent on the business elite for the stability of the regime than the merchants have been on the ruler to develop their economic assets.

Economic Diversification and Labor Market Reform: A Shared Must in Bahrain and Oman

Political debates in Bahrain and Oman over the necessity to rethink the economic model of development based on oil revenue are not new, as early diversification plans and nationalization policies of employment can testify. In the 1970s, Bahrain became the first oil producing state in the Gulf to implement a large-scale policy of diversification of state revenues, focusing on major industrial projects such as ALBA (Aluminium Bahrain), which was the first non-oil industry venture in Bahrain. ALBA opened in 1971, and is now the third largest smelter in the world. In addition, ASRY (Arab Shipbuilding and Repair Yard Co.) started operations in September 1977. The decline in oil reserves in the late 1970s coincided with the second phase of diversification in Bahrain and the al-Khalifas' attempt to position their country as a banking hub for the Persian Gulf.

In Oman, the trend of economic reform started much later. The economic slowdown in the 1980s, combined with the emergence of endemic unemployment among the younger generations, led to the implementation of Omanization policies favoring nationals in employment. The sultan then called for a committee chaired by the Deputy Prime Minister for Financial and Economic Affairs and composed of 14 ministers. In June 1995, the committee formulated a long-term program entitled "Oman 2020: Vision for Oman's Economy," later approved by Qaboos himself after making a number of amendments to the text. Two series of objectives were set out. The first was economic diversification: The oil sector's share of GDP had to fall from 41 percent in 1996 to nine percent by 2020, while that of non-oil industries was to increase from 7.5 to 29 percent. The second objective had to do with human resources and employment. It planned to raise the proportion of nationals in the public and private sectors from 68 to 95 percent and from 7.5 to 75 percent, respectively, while the share of expatriates in the whole population would be reduced from 25 percent in 1995 to 15 percent by 2020. Moreover, a royal decree in May 1996 established the practical modalities for implementing privatization through an inter-ministerial committee in charge of determining with which sectors and projects to contend.

Nevertheless, the real turning point in economic policies came concomitantly in Bahrain and Oman at the beginning of the 2000s, for both peculiar and common structural reasons. In Oman, oil revenue in 2000 represented 70 percent of total state resources. The all-time peak of the country's production came in August of that year, with more than one million barrels produced daily. National oil production was to experience a drop of 26 percent between 2001 and 2007. Furthermore, in 2000, 55 percent of nationals were less than 20 years old. From this perspective, the sixth (2001–2005) and the seventh (2006–2010) five-year plans of the sultanate called for a wide array of economic diversification projects via the development of the gas sector, tourism, and non-oil industries.

To promote the use of gas resources and heavy industries especially, Oman launched several large-scale projects. The most important was the Sohar industrial port, under development since 1998. On the site, various endeavors, including an oil refinery and an aluminium smelter, were scheduled to generate more than 8,000 stable jobs and 30,000 other jobs indirectly in the Batinah region. The total investment was $12 billion.

In addition, in order to widen the state's financial resources, all companies registered in Oman have been subject to the same rules since September 2003: For those with 5,000 Omani rial (OR)[12] or less profit, no tax is collected;

---

[12] OR 1 = $2.6 (as of 11 November 2013).

beyond this threshold, profits are taxed at 12 percent. In the case of the branches of non-GCC foreign companies established in Oman, profits beyond OR 5,000 can attract taxes of up to 30 percent.

The diversification policy was supported by a strong desire to promote the private sector, as explained by then Minister of Commerce and Industry Maqbul Ali Sultan:

> Oman's industrial strategy up to the year 2020 envisages that [...] sustainable development will be attained by using private sector as the primary engine of growth.[13]

In 2001, the percentage of foreign shares allowed in an Omani company was extended to 70 percent in all sectors; in 2003, 100 percent began to be allowed in banking and insurance, while in 2005 telecommunications followed suit. In July 2004, two privatization laws were promulgated, one dealing with water and electricity that involved a plan to divide the responsibilities of the Ministry of Electricity and Water among several entities before its dissolution. The second law dealt with an important axis of the Oman privatization process — the telecommunications sector. In March 2002, a law established the Telecommunications Regulation Authority, which is in charge of competition regulation in the sector, privatization of the sole operator Omantel, and the granting of licenses and implementation of tariffs.

In Bahrain, Shaykh Hamad's accession to the throne in 1999 marked the beginning of a series of political and economic reforms intended to renew social cohesion in the aftermath of the Shi'i unrest of 1994–1999 and to strengthen the legitimacy of al-Khalifa rule. In the economic sector, Shaykh Hamad declared his intention to adopt a more interventionist approach to economic decision-making. A Supreme Council for Economic Development was created in April 2000 by royal decree, and it transformed into an Economic Development Board (Majlis al-Tanmia al-Iqtisadiyya), or EDB, in 2001. Shaykh Hamad's son, Crown Prince Shaykh Salman, chaired it. The EDB was initially conceived as a public think tank. Sixteen members comprised the

---

[13] *Times of Oman*, 17 August 2004.

board of directors, including the crown prince, six ministers,[14] the governor of the Central Bank, seven representatives from the private sector, and the chairman of the semi-governmental Bahrain Centre for Studies and Research.

In 2004, the Crown Prince commissioned the American consulting firm McKinsey to draft a comprehensive long-term economic reform program for Bahrain. It proposed a legal and administrative restructuring in three fields:

1. Labor market reform focusing on the competitiveness of Bahraini nationals;
2. Economic reform, including land and juridical reforms and promotion of small-scale private business; and
3. Educational reform.

In May 2005, a royal decree expanded the EDB's authority by moving the "national economy" element of the Ministry of Finance and National Economy to the EDB. The EDB was thus given the overall responsibility for outlining, proposing, and managing economic reforms for Bahrain in a comprehensive manner — including education, labor, tourism, industry, and health care — according to the model of the Singapore Economic Development Board. This extended mission included:

1. Promotion of private sector growth and investment by enhancing incentives for businesses, eliminating investment obstacles, and favoring foreign direct investment;
2. Implementation of a comprehensive labor market reform program to address the structural imbalance in the existing labor market between nationals and expatriates and to reduce levels of unemployment among Bahrainis; and
3. Diversification of the economy away from hydrocarbon revenues.

This Chapter will now concentrate more particularly on labor market reform, which has been organized by regime elites in Bahrain and Oman, and on the capacity of the private sector to influence the path of these reforms.

---

[14]Two ministers are deputy prime ministers, and the others are ministers of the prime minister's court, industry and commerce, finance, and oil and gas.

In Oman, a Ministry of Manpower was created in 2001 by amalgamating the Ministry of Labor with those of Social Affairs and Vocational Training. The sixth Five-Year Plan (2001–2005) estimated that 92 percent of the 110,000 new jobs available between 2001 and 2005 would be in the private sector. The plan provided for total Omanization over five years in 24 low-skill occupations. More technical professions, such as electrician, plumber, goldsmith, tailor, hairdresser, and painter, were to follow suit.

In February 2003, a Five-Year Plan for Omanization (2003–2007) was drawn up that defined ambitious Omanization rates to be achieved by 2007 in key economic sectors.[15] The new labor law, issued by royal decree on 26 April 2003, illustrated these priorities. Under this law, employers had to obtain permits from the Ministry of Manpower to bring in foreign workers only if there were not enough Omanis available for the post and if the company had complied with the prescribed percentage of Omanization in its branch (Article 18). Once the company was granted the permit, a non-Omani, to qualify for a job, could obtain a labor card issued by the ministry (for a duration decided by the ministry) on the condition that the worker had the professional skill or the qualifications required by the position and that the prescribed labor card fees had been paid by the company (Articles 18 and 19).

Moreover, under this law nationals enjoy a set of social measures that expatriates do not, including a minimum wage (OR325 for a full-time unskilled job[16]) and strict protection against dismissal. Indeed, an employer can terminate the contract of an Omani only during the three-month probation period (Article 24) or under two other conditions — if the employee absents himself from work for more than seven consecutive days or more than ten days during one year without justification, or if the employee makes a

---

[15] For instance, the plan called for Omanization rates to increase from 26 percent in 2003 to 77 percent in 2007 in transport, from 25 percent to 55 percent in telecommunications, and from 15 percent to 30 percent in big companies in the contracting sector (*Uman*, 4 February 2003).

[16] In February 2013, the Council of Ministers announced a raising of the minimum gross salary for nationals working in the private sector by 62 percent with effect from July 2013. It consists of OR225 as a basic salary plus OR100 as transport and housing allowance (as of November 2013).

major mistake (Article 40). Thus, the challenge of employing young Omanis, of whom 50,000 every year leave school and university (with or without degrees) and enter the labor market, led to national mobilization driven from above, with the Omanization policy being the main emphasis.

In comparison to similar policies in neighboring countries, the sultanate can be proud of undeniable successes, at least quantitatively. By the end of 2005, the number of active expatriates in the private sector stabilized, while the rate of nationals in the private sector and the overall rate of Omanization (public and private sectors, excluding security and defense forces) increased from 15 percent and 28 percent, respectively, in 2003, to 19 percent and 32 percent two years later. In December 2011, the civil service sector showed an average Omanization rate of 86.3 percent, a figure that had consistently risen during the decade. Moreover, 92.2 percent of employees in the private banking sector were Omani.

Nevertheless, these increases were not enough to hide structural difficulties due to the policy. In 2005, civil servants of the Ministry for Manpower spoke privately of 300,000 job seekers[17] — an unemployment rate of around 25 percent. A former senior state official who joined the private sector summarized the situation: "Never will a government be able to force companies to prefer badly-trained Omanis to experienced Indians, with a salary three to five times lower."[18]

The manager of an oil industry supply company said even more explicitly:

> It is 50 percent more expensive to have an Omani employee than an Indian one, the job and conditions being equal, and even if you take into account the legal penalties linked to the issuing of a labor card for an expatriate ... So I prefer to pay an Omani and ask him to stay at home, and keep the Indian guy working.[19]

Since 2005–2006, the authorities have appeared to realize that Omanization cannot be reduced to a post-for-post substitution of the expatriate

---

[17] Personal interview, Muscat, 30 August 2005.
[18] Personal interview, Muscat, 16 September 2003.
[19] Personal interview, Muscat, 26 January 2003.

workforce with Omanis. As a small business owner, who was also a member of the Majlis al-Shura, noted in 2005:

> Three or four years ago, the government pushed the private sector to hire Omanis. It looked like forcing. With time, the government analyzed that what was done was wrong ... Omanization is not a replacement process. It is necessary to ask instead how to appoint more Omanis! We will always need expatriates.[20]

The fact that most cabinet members are involved directly or indirectly in business explains why the quota-based labor market policy could not be maintained in the long term. These decision-makers had to avoid questions about their supposed promotion of the nation's interests (such as the Omanization policy) versus the particular interests they were defending as businessmen. The major Omani business families who control the Chamber of Commerce and are represented in the cabinet were strategically positioned to express their disagreement with the labor market policy to the ruler and thus to advocate for changes in long-term policy. But even more significantly, they were positioned to prevent the emergence of newcomers in business and alternative voices from the private sector. This is significantly different from the situation in Bahrain, described below.

The Omani authorities have focused on economic liberalization in recent years by giving prominence to national and foreign private capital, even if it means the emergence of lasting inflation and an acceptance of a pause in the Omanization employment policy. For example, the new tax system that came into force in January 2010 cancelled the distinction between local and foreign companies by establishing a fixed tax rate on profits of 12 percent for all companies (both local and foreign) after an initial tax-free exemption of profits of OR30,000 or less. Anwar Ali Sultan, a director of the W.J. Towell Group, explained his satisfaction with this measure:

> The new corporate tax law ... is meant to spur foreign investment into the country. The more foreign investment that comes to the

---

[20] Personal interview, Muscat, 4 September 2005.

Sultanate, the more advantages it will bring for Omanis in terms of jobs and to the country as a whole.[21]

Foreign investments flows doubled between 2005 and 2007, from $0.54 billion in 2003 (2.5 percent of GDP) to $1.5 billion in 2005 (5.9 percent of GDP) to more than $3.1 billion in 2007, amounting to 25 percent of gross fixed capital formation in 2007.[22]

In January 2006 Oman signed a bilateral free trade agreement with the United States, which came into effect in January 2009; many services are excluded from it in order to preserve the local network of small and medium-sized enterprises in the sultanate, and Omanization requirements are still valid, even in the sectors covered by the agreement.

A number of major real estate and tourism projects are being developed, such as the upscale community "The Wave," situated along seven kilometers of seashore behind Seeb Airport near Muscat and worth $4.5 billion. In May 2005 the state, in partnership with the Dubai-based Al-Futtaim Group, launched the first phase of this complex, which houses 4,000 residential properties. It is designed to be completed by 2018, five years later than the original plan. Even more ambitious, on Sawadi beach between Sohar and Muscat, the government approved plans for the Blue City project, worth $15 billion. Covering 35 square kilometers, this new city devoted to tourism will accommodate 200,000 residents in 2020. The government granted investors more control of the project than they would have previously, only retaining the role of facilitator.

As a consequence of this strategic U-turn, the Omanization rate in the private sector decreased from 18.8 percent at the end of 2005 to 12.3 percent in September 2013 — by far the worst rate since 2003. This can be explained by the fact that the number of active expatriates in the private sector (including household workers) has tripled since the end of 2005 (reaching, 1,459,670 in

---

[21] Oxford Business Group, "Oman: Resolving a Taxing Issue," 17 June 2009.
[22] United Nations Conference on Trade and Development, *World Investment Report 2009*, available online at http://www.unctad.org/en/docs/wir2009_en.pdf; United Nations Economic and Social Commission for Western Asia, *Foreign Direct Investment Report 2009*, available online at http://www.escwa.un.org/information/publications/edit/upload/edgd-09-TP2.pdf.

September 2013) — particularly due to the need for foreign workers to labor on construction and infrastructure projects.

From this viewpoint, policies of privatization (which mainly benefited the key players) and the Omanization of private sector jobs (which directly damaged that sector's interests) are reliable indicators of the role business elites have played in the country's balance of powers. The priority granted since 2005 to the private sector and to investment in major projects such as the Sohar port and tourism infrastructure to the detriment of publicly touted objectives such as Omanization and control of immigration of workers has been a clear indicator toward which side the balance has been tilting.

In Bahrain too, labor market reform was planned from above. The country faced endemic unemployment at the end of the 1990s, unofficially estimated to be 30 percent of the national population. In September 2004, the Crown Prince and the EDB held a workshop on the labor market based on the McKinsey study. The key idea was that over the next decade employment must be found for 100,000 new job market entrants, that is, almost 92 percent of the existing local workforce at that time. Until that goal was accomplished, the government's policy was focused, like in Oman, on the nationalization of employment (Bahrainization) through increasing the percentage of nationals to be employed with pre-defined rates to be achieved in each economic sector.

The philosophy of the reform proposed by McKinsey was to deregulate and liberalize the job market and redress the imbalance between the local and cheap expatriate workforce[23] in order to address the structural causes of unemployment of nationals. It included gradually phasing out the Bahrainization quotas, allowing easier termination procedures of Bahraini employees and replacing them with a fee-based system under which employers pay a BD75 monthly fee per expatriate worker and a BD600 visa issuing and renewing fee per worker for each two-year period in order to bring the cost of local and expatriate labor force in line.

---

[23] In 2006, 46 percent of expatriates working in the private sector, but only 1.1 percent of Bahrainis, earned less than BD100 per month (personal calculation based on table 2.1.15.2, available online at http://blmi.lmra.bh/otherdata/surveytables/mi_surveydata.xml; BD1 = $2.65 [as of 11 November 2013]).

In order to implement this reform (which came into effect on 1 July 2008) and regulate the Bahraini labor market, the king issued a law in May 2006 establishing the Labor Market Regulation Authority (LMRA), a government agency with a corporate body under the authority of a board of directors chaired by the Minister of Labor.[24] The other new body, Tamkeen (the Labor Fund), created in 2007 and chaired by the Minister of State for Foreign Affairs, collects the fees paid by the companies employing foreign workers. Twenty percent of the fees go toward the government budget, while 80 percent is invested in training and qualification programs for the national workforce and in consultative and financial services for private companies in order to increase the productivity of Bahrainis. According to an IT businessman:

> By this reform, the crown prince opened a wide battlefront. The prime minister moved quickly. While businessmen usually never talk against the government, the prime minister encouraged the Chamber of Commerce and the leading contractors to speak up to create cracks in the reform.[25]

A number of businessmen did criticize the reform, arguing that preliminary training and education was necessary to adapt the skills of the nationals to the needs of the job market. Adil Fakhro from the Fakhro Group spoke on this issue:

> There isn't Bahraini labor available, the unemployed have no skills, so if you begin to force labor charges and fees on the private sector to make foreign labor more expensive, then the next question is where is the Bahraini? Even jobs like drivers, you can't get them ... Education, training and the labor market reforms must go hand in hand.[26]

---

[24] The board is also composed of the CEO of the EDB, three representatives from the private sector (two of them from the board of the Chamber of Commerce), two members of the Labor Union, the undersecretary of the Ministry of Labor, and the president of the Central Informatics Organization.
[25] Personal interview, Manama, 29 June 2008.
[26] Oxford Business Group, "Bahrain: Labor Dilemmas," 2 October 2004.

The private sector did not spare in its efforts to make its voice heard by the EDB and the LMRA — not only through informal channels and lobbying to the king and the prime minister, but also through repeated public demonstrations outside the LMRA building and the parliament to pressure the authorities and attract the support of the representatives. One of the "privileged" addressees of this lobbying was the prime minister, in whom the private sector knew it had an understanding interlocutor. The business community successfully pushed for cutting the fees so that an agreement was finally reached in 2007: BD10 per month per expatriate plus a BD200 visa renewing fee for each two-year period. Interestingly, the scope of action of the private sector in Bahrain was only indirect, as it responded and adapted to the evolution of the balance of power among the al-Khalifas. The shaping of the labor market reform is a superb illustration of the power struggle within the ruling family, between what many observers label the "old guard," or the prime minister and his supporters among the ministers, and the new generation of technocrats led by the crown prince and the EDB, whose paragon is its CEO since 2005, Shaykh Muhammad bin Isa al-Khalifa. He was educated at the London School of Economics and appointed CEO of the Board following 10 years of working as a close aide of Shaykh Salman.

This difference of perspective within the ruling family surfaced in January 2008 through an open letter the crown prince wrote to the king, complaining about a "persisting disharmony and lack of cooperation between the EDB and certain government bodies [that] are no longer acceptable" and about the "[cabinet's] status quo [that] often thwarted the EDB endeavors."[27] The king arbitrated without ambiguity in favor of consolidating his son's influence by issuing a public statement ordering the cabinet to follow the directives of the EDB, adding that any minister who failed to comply would be dismissed.[28] Also, he introduced a new law that increased the number of

---

[27] Bahrain News Agency, "CP Chairs EDB Meeting," 14 January 2008, available online at http://www.bna.bh/portal/en/news/420622?date=2011-04-20.
[28] Personal interview with a former member of the Council of Representatives, 19 October 2008.

ministers on the board of the EDB from six to 16.[29] As the crown prince explained:

> Our task is to make sure that the government delivers faster by eliminating bureaucratic steps within the Cabinet. Expanding the board makes this easier. We do not need to discuss things twice. We do it just once and pass it along for approval [by the King].[30]

The EDB was granted almost complete independence in decision making, being accountable neither to the cabinet nor to the chambers — a common reason for complaint by the elected Council of Representatives.

From this perspective, the private sector was again forced to adapt to the changing balance of power. In 2006 members of merchant families founded the Bahrain Family Business Association, the first of its kind in the Gulf, to facilitate the resolution of various inherent problems faced by family businesses and to create a unified interlocutor and spokesperson for merchant families. Khalid Kanoo has served as chair since its founding.[31]

In addition, the Chamber of Commerce (BCCI) launched a series of initiatives to increase the role of small and medium companies (SMEs) and to integrate their interests. It created a committee in 2009 to focus on SMEs' particular needs, and it launched two service centers to assist SMEs in promoting their export activities and increasing their international competitiveness.[32] These new initiatives aimed to change the widespread perception of the BCCI as the traditional representative of the leading business groups and to gain

---

[29] These new members of the EDB board are Deputy Prime Minister Jawad al-Urayyid and the ministers of education, labor, social development, cabinet affairs, justice and Islamic affairs, municipalities and agricultural affairs, information, and health and housing.

[30] "The Crown Prince: Why Bahrain Needs Economic Reform," *Middle East Economic Digest*, 16 December 2008, available online at http://www.meed.com/supplements/2008/meed-yearbook-2008/-09/the-crown-prince-why-bahrain-needs-economic-reform/3000205.article.

[31] The association has not proved as active as it could be given that it has duplicated the lobbying work of the Bahrain Chamber of Commerce, which has long been a stronghold of the merchant elite.

[32] "New BCCI Strategies to Help SMEs," *Gulf Daily News*, 2 June 2009, available online at http://www.gulf-daily-news.com/NewsDetails.aspx?storyid=252193.

support from SMEs in order to increase BCCI's capacity to negotiate with and influence the ruling family.

As a further step toward the liberalization of the job market, in May 2009 Bahrain adopted a law (decree 79/2009) that came into effect on 1 August 2009 that reformed the sponsorship system for residency and employment. This new system allowed foreign workers, with the exception of domestic workers, to switch jobs simply by informing their existing employers of their intention to end the contract. Contrary to what was initially proclaimed by the government, the aim of this law was not to abolish the *kafala* (sponsorship) system. The LMRA became the official sponsor of foreign workers, bearing responsibility for issuing two-year work visas once an employment contract had been signed.

Understandably this move raised strong concerns within the private sector, especially the Chamber of Commerce. Along with the General Federation of Trade Unions, the chamber was officially consulted and some of its suggestions accepted, such as a three-month notice by an employee before switching jobs and an option for an employer to terminate a staff member's contract and deport him or her with a month's notice. The BCCI had called for the period before an employee can leave a company to be extended to six months,[33] but this request was rejected. For more than two years after the implementation of the reform on labor fees, the private sector's opposition to the LMRA was vigorous. Public demonstrations of businessmen and trade unions, recurrent appeals to members of parliament and leading figures of the royal family, and tight negotiations on the concrete implementation of the legislation, while possible in Bahrain (until the 2011 unrest) was not conceivable in Oman.

A decisive factor in regard to this difference was the nature of the state-business relationship. In Oman, the al-Said royal family had never occupied any major economic positions and the sultan had never been able to prevent the merchant families from taking political positions and actively participating in (or even determining) economic policymaking. From this point of view,

---

[33] Businessmen, such as BCCI board member Adil al-Maskati, even called for a two-year period. An amendment to the law forcing foreign employees to complete at least one year before being allowed to switch jobs was not adopted by the Consultative Council despite the political weight of the private sector in this chamber. "Bahrain Council Rejects Jobs Switch Bill," *Trade Arabia*, 10 November 2009, available online at http://www.tradearabia.com/news/EDU_170174.html.

rather than encouraging economic mobility that would call into question the established authoritarian order and contribute to a renewal, or at least a revitalization, of the socioeconomic fabric, economic reform in Oman did nothing but confirm the hierarchy of established social and economic positions.

In Bahrain, the elite-driven reform, managed by a technocratic and unaccountable body (EDB), shows that the latitude of action of the prominent business families and their arm (the Chamber of Commerce) was much more restrained. Not only were they not immune to the emergence of competitors, such as the "nouveaux riches" who benefited from diversification policies, but they also had to be careful of not alienating the SMEs. As detailed above, the condition for these families to remain the privileged interlocutor of the political elite and the trusted ally of the SMEs required them to adapt their strategies according to the balance of power among the al-Khalifas.

Since February 2011 and the spread of popular protests in Oman and Bahrain, the vast majority of the business sector in both states has constantly reasserted their closeness to the respective regimes and the necessity to preserve the stability of the country — a thinly veiled allusion to the protesters as troublemakers.[34] Despite the differences between Bahrain and Oman in the business-ruling family relationship, the two countries' business elites have adopted the same attitude in troubled times, aiming to privilege the political status quo over any kind of reform debate. If anything, the 2011 protests are yet again revealing of the extent to which the interest of Bahraini and Omani business elites are intrinsically linked to those of authoritarian rule. This conservative attitude is easily understandable in the context of the Arab awakening, given that the business elites have been accused of corruption, unwarranted privileges, and political and economic opposition to change by youthful protesters in both countries.

---

[34]In a statement on 11 May 2011, the Bahrain Chamber of Commerce explained that "due to the timely measures taken by the leadership and the support of neighboring GCC countries to ensure security and stability in the country, the [national] economy is back on track." Bahrain Chamber of Commerce, "BCCI's Call for Consolidated Efforts to Revive the Economy," 11 May 2011, available online at http://www.noodls.com/viewNoodl/9979018/bcci—bahrain-chamber-of-commerce–industry/bcci8217s-call-for-consolidated-efforts-to-revive-the-eco.

From this perspective, it is not insignificant that early attempts by the Omani ruler to show his supposed benevolence toward the protestors led to an extensive reshuffle of the cabinet in March 2011, with the removal of long-serving ministers widely perceived as embodying corruption and a conflict of interest between business and politics — such as Ahmed Makki, Minister for National Economy, and Maqbul Ali Sultan, Minister for Commerce and Industry.

The fact that demonstrations were particularly active in the town of Sohar, conceived as the international showcase of the economic liberalization of the country, is also highly symbolic. The transition of Sohar within a few years from a sleepy provincial town into the industrial capital of the country led to a disruption of its social structures. This badly-digested economic boom benefited above all a handful of local notables, who have taken advantage of the dramatic rise in land prices, as well as top Omani business groups, such as Umar Zawawi, National Trading Company, Zubair, W.J. Towell, and Bahwan, in partnership with foreign investors, that are already embedded in the heart of the political-economic decision process. Meanwhile, the majority of the local population had no access to the fruits of economic development and experienced a stagnation or a diminution of their living standard due to an increase of costs. The dismantlement of the Ministry of National Economy in March 2011 and the announcement of social and economic measures — such as the creation of public sector jobs for nationals and the sharp increase of public allowances or of salaries in the public and private sectors — that openly contradict the liberalization policies implemented for a decade illustrate the dilemma in which the Omani leadership finds itself. The fundamental question regarding the regime's future relates to the political-economic conflict of interest at the top levels in the country. While this elite has held the levers of power since 1970 and has predominantly benefited from the oil rent, this oligarchic pact has become unacceptable for a new generation who are calling into question the whole economic structure on which authoritarian Oman has relied under Qaboos.

In Bahrain, the massive crackdown that followed the protests in 2011 has once again changed the balance among the ruling family and proven successful in marginalizing the less uncompromising component of the al-Khalifas, that is, the crown prince and the EDB, in favor of the prime minister and his supporters, first among them the Chamber of Commerce and the business elite. In order to reduce the impact of the crisis on the private sector, the Cabinet ordered in April 2011 a six-month freeze on fees on foreign workers levied by the LMRA, then later renewed and extended the suspension until Summer 2013.[35] This measure, which probably marks the death of the EDB-led technocratic plan by robbing the labor market reform of its substance, was strongly praised by the Chamber of Commerce. In March 2012, its chairman wished the prime minister "every success in carrying on the nation-building march" and affirmed that the prime minister's "stances in support of the private sector have always been a source of pride for BCCI and the [...] business community,"[36] an implicit reference to the hated policy pursued by the EDB.

Thus, if the Bahraini merchant elite has turned out to be one of the key beneficiaries of the marginalization of the crown prince since March 2011, there is no doubt that its lobbying for the reversal of EDB policies has only had a limited impact. Both the EDB-led reforms until 2011 and the new balance of power among the al-Khalifas since have confirmed that the royal family is still the decisive economic and political force. Contrary to Oman, where the ruler cannot rely on his small family and has allied with the merchant elite, which has been given political positions to secure public contracts and determine long-term economic policies, the Bahraini business sector has to press for its interests in dealing carefully with the evolving balance of power among the ruling family. It has to make use of the divisions within it in a much more tactical and noisy way than is the case in Oman, where the 2011 protests and the widespread social frustration have not yet put an end to the direct interference of the bourgeoisie in the decision-making process.

---

[35] From September 2013, the BD10 monthly fee per expatriate worker was reintroduced by the Cabinet, but SMEs, that employ less than five workers will only have to pay half this amount. See "Freeze on Expat Levy to be Lifted," *Gulf Daily News*, 28 August 2013, available online at http://www.gulf-daily-news.com/NewsDetails.aspx?storyid=359999.

[36] "HRH Premier Thanked by BCCI Chairman," *LMRA Media Blog*, 26 March 2012, available online at http://blog.lmra.bh/en/archives/1362.

Gulf Governance

Chapter 4

The Rule of Law and Political Liberalization in the Arab Gulf

David M. Mednicoff and Joanna E. Springer

For centuries, until the commercial exploitation of its massive oil and natural gas reserves, Doha, Qatar was a backwater trading city. Many people would still be hard-pressed to find it on a map. Yet, in May 2009 Doha played host to perhaps the most illustrious array of global legal luminaries in modern history. Hundreds of high court judges, respected lawyers, and high-powered legal academics from nearly 60 countries and six continents convened at the first Qatar Law Forum for three days to discuss varied issues underscoring their shared commitment to the rule of law.

One of the United Kingdom's preeminent jurists, former Chief Justice of England and Wales Lord Woolf, helped run the meeting in his capacity as the president of a new tribunal established by Qatar's government to resolve disputes related to the country's widespread financial and construction projects. Professors and administrators from Harvard Law School and several other important American legal academies were among the forum's organizers.

The Qatar Law Forum illustrated an important broader trend. In the past few decades, Arab states generally, and Gulf states especially, have made, or felt pressured to make, the rule of law a central piece of their national politics. This connects to internal citizen demands, as has been shown dramatically since 2011, with calls for the rule of law serving as a major frame for the popular uprising against Hosni Mubarak's regime in Egypt.

This focus on the rule of law also links to a Western foreign policy objective, with the United States at the center, which aims to enhance the rule of law in non-Western countries.[1] This recent vintage of legalist wine fits partly in the old bottles of "law and development" practitioners of the 1960s and 1970s.[2] At the same time, contemporary U.S. rule-of-law reform efforts take place in a setting of globalized inter-connectedness,[3] where international law and the legal norms of one society are easily accessible and often salient elsewhere,[4] and where non-Western domestic and regional legal initiatives are significant, as the Qatar Law Forum exemplified. Thus, multiple and contending discourses and practices around the rule of law suggest a complex political picture.

In fact, such work is complicated further because both internal and external impulses for legalist reform stem from two broad aims. First is an economic stake in facilitating stable market and property transactions for transnational capital. Second is a political concern for improving individual rights and opening up the participatory process.

These two goals may not be mutually reinforcing, and the second can take a back seat to the first. Indeed, efforts to enhance the rule of law to improve

---

[1] The contemporary rule-of-law aid movement generally dates back to the collapse of the former Soviet Union and the rapid political and economic reform needs of Eastern European and Baltic countries. Substantial rule-of-law projects are implemented through the U.S. government's Department of State and Agency for International Development (USAID), as well as semiautonomous organizations like the U.S. Institute of Peace and private contractors. In the case of Middle East work, much of the funding and recent expansion in programs has taken place through the Middle East Partnership Initiative. In the 2007–2012 strategic plan of USAID, rule-of-law reform aid was the top priority within its second broad policy strategy of "governing justly and democratically." USAID, *Strategic Plan: Fiscal Years 2007–2012 — Transformational Diplomacy*, 2007, pp. 18–19.
[2] Thomas Carothers, ed., *Promoting the Rule of Law Abroad: In Search of Knowledge* (Washington, D.C.: Carnegie Endowment for International Peace, 2006), pp. 15–16.
[3] See, e.g., David Held, Anthony McGrew, David Goldblatt, and Jonathan Perraton, *Global Transformations: Politics, Economics and Culture* (Stanford, CA: Stanford University Press, 1999).
[4] See generally Paul Schiff Berman, "Global Legal Pluralism," *Southern California Law Review* 80, 6 (2007): 1155–1238, and Anne-Marie Slaughter, *A New World Order* (Princeton, NJ: Princeton University Press, 2004). On the connection of U.S. judges to foreign legal norms, see Noah Feldman, "When Judges Make Foreign Policy," *New York Times Magazine*, 25 September 2008, p. 50.

the predictability of market transactions and the reliability of contracts can accompany, and possibly enhance, non-democratic regime stability.

Added to this picture is the complex general relationship of the West to the Arab world. At least until 2011, Arab countries were a particularly potent nexus for Western ambivalence about whether to push greater political accountability or maintain support for repressive regimes that accept U.S. security goals, such as the war on terror or the alliance with Israel.

Given the prevalence of non-democratic governments in the Middle East, alongside the significance of political frames around the rule of law for more recent political mobilization, the political and policy sides of the rule of law are worth study. The broad question motivating this work is how the rule of law and its reform can help make Arab political systems more accountable to their citizens. A secondary question is if foreign efforts to amplify the rule of law can be of any use.[5] In this paper, the first of these questions will be addressed with specific regard to the Arab Gulf societies of Qatar and the UAE.

Broad questions about the rule of law share intellectual and practical importance. Theoretically, the imprecise and contested nature of legalist ideals and their confusing relationship with religious norms muddy the waters of how to understand the rule of law in the Arab Islamic world. In practice, despite the influence of courts and lawyers in the West, social scientists and policy practitioners have few clear answers about how promotion of the rule of law can help political liberalization in non-democratic settings.

Yet the monarchical societies of Qatar and the UAE illustrate one possible pathway through which legal growth may connect to political opening. The rapid hyperglobalization that these countries are experiencing has brought to bear pressures to bolster the rule of law both in terms of economic transactions and political rights. If legal reform geared toward improving transnational economic relations need not also advance political rights, the dual factors of hyperglobalization and little indigenous legal infrastructure to administer this

---

[5] Given the unclear relationship between the rule of law as a facilitator of economic transactions and democratization, we bracket out for the purposes of this analysis the economic side of the rule of law in order to focus more clearly on political influences and ideas related to the concept.

hyperglobalization have created environments in increasingly prominent Gulf cities that may suggest linkages between the rule of law and political opening.

The remainder of this Chapter fleshes out this argument and reveals some differences as well as broad similarities with respect to the rule of law and political change in Qatar and the UAE. The contention is that the combination of particular developmental choices and federalism in the UAE have made legal growth, marked though it may be, somewhat less conducive to political change than in Qatar. At the same time, in both cases, hyperglobalization has transformed the legal context of both societies so that a connection to global norms around the rule of law and international rights is highly significant.

Before developing the above argument, it is worth exploring some of the general challenges around the rule of law, as well as in the particular context of the contemporary Arab world.

The Rule of Law: Strong Ideals and Unclear Politics, Particularly in the Arab World

It may be that the rule of law "stands in the peculiar state of being *the* preeminent legitimizing ideal in the world today."[6] Yet the diverse ways in which the term is deployed also has led theorists to dismiss the significance of this "bit of ruling class chatter."[7]

The concept generally refers to two broad political categories. On the one hand, it stands for a single norm or cluster of norms that subordinate aspects of personal political authority to legal equality, fair laws, or perhaps the protection of individual rights.[8] This is at the heart of the pithy if ambiguous formula of a government of laws, not men. On the other hand, the rule of law can describe a particular institution or constellation of functioning legal

---

[6] Brian Z. Tamanaha, *On the Rule of Law: History, Politics, Theory* (Cambridge: Cambridge University Press, 2004), p. 4.
[7] Judith Shklar, "Political Theory and the Rule of Law," in *The Rule of Law: Ideal Or Ideology*, eds. Alan Hutchinson and Patrick Monahan (Toronto: Carswell, 1987), p. 1.
[8] Danilo Zolo, "The Rule of Law: A Critical Reappraisal," in *The Rule of Law: History, Theory and Criticism*, eds. Pietro Costa and Danilo Zolo (New York: Springer, 2007), p. 55.

institutions, certainly including courts but often embracing legislatures and civil society organizations.

When used in the first sense of an ideal, the term "rule of law" is deployed in diverse and imprecise ways.[9] Nevertheless, there is typically an assumption of a separation between a society's politics and law.[10] Specifically, the rule of law is meant to protect people from political anarchy and arbitrariness. It suggests a promise that legal supremacy, stability, and accountability will prevail over the caprice of leaders.[11] Possibly, but not necessarily, related is an emphasis on citizen equality before the law.

It is easy to see the rule of law as a set of measures and institutions united in their tendency to guarantee basic fairness to all people, even *vis-à-vis* the politically powerful. Yet nothing guarantees that the normative pieces of this puzzle fit together. Thus, however it is conceived, the ideal of the rule of law is likely to embed broad goals that potentially cut against each other. Rachel Kleinfeld suggests that the importance of specifying the diverse meanings of the rule of law lies precisely in the near certainty that, in this field, not all good things come together.[12]

A particularly obvious and critical tension is that of the law's importance in providing order and its promise to guarantee the rights of citizens, justice, and equality. Despite the ideal that laws will stand above the self-interested actions of people, the reality is that the drafters, executors, or interpreters of

---

[9] Frank Upham, "Mythmaking in the Rule-of-Law Orthodoxy," in *Promoting the Rule of Law Abroad*, ed. Thomas Carothers (Carnegie Endowment for International Peace, 2006), p. 75, and Richard Fallon, "'The Rule of Law' as a Concept in Constitutional Discourse," *Columbia Law Review* 1 (1997): p. 97.

[10] Gerhard Robbers, "The Rule of Law and Its Ethical Foundations," in *The Rule of Law*, ed. Joseph Thesing (Sankt Augustin, Germany: Konrad-Adanauer-Stiftung, 1997).

[11] For example, "The rule of law ... refers to a principle of governance in which all persons, institutions and entities, public and private, including the State itself, are accountable to laws that are publicly promulgated, equally enforced and independently adjudicated, and which are consistent with international human rights norms and standards." United Nations Security Council, *The Rule of Law and Transitional Justice in Conflict and Post Conflict Societies: Report of the Secretary General*, 2004, p. 4.

[12] Rachel Kleinfeld, "Competing Definitions of the Rule of Law," in *Promoting the Rule of Law Abroad*, ed. Thomas Carothers (Carnegie Endowment for International Peace, 2006), pp. 34–36.

law can flout this ideal unless meaningful accountability, popular awareness, and transparency exist. In other words, the rule of law can bolster democracy or it can slide into rule *by* law and reinforce political repression.[13]

Perhaps because of the tensions among rule-of-law ideals, ideas about implementing the rule of law in non-Western countries often focus on the dimension of institutional reform, especially of courts, with little overt rationalization as to how such reform connects to the ideal. Given the apparent importance of rule of law to democracy in the West, trying to adapt the structures and functions of Western legal institutions to non-Western contexts seems quite reasonable.[14] Indeed, U.S. rule-of-law aid in Arab countries has primarily sought to promote court modernization and judicial training.

The nature of the reform can be highly technical. In Morocco, for example, major U.S.-funded and U.S.-staffed programs have included training judges in alternative dispute resolution, teaching evidence and judicial ethics, and adapting case management computer programs to make it easier for case backlogs to be reduced and for some holdings to be posted on the Internet.

Clearing judicial logjams and increasing the possible transparency of case rulings are clearly reasonable goals, and some of these aid programs are successes in terms of technical judicial efficiency. Nonetheless, it is unclear whether bringing good case management software to an Arab court system helps instill a broader sense of justice, individual rights, or liberalization, since judicial autonomy, the content of the laws, and the laws' sociopolitical context remain analytically underdeveloped.

Understanding how practices of legal institutions link to the ideals of the rule of law is important for appreciating the context and consequences of institutional reform. When reform efforts are confined to legal institutional performance with little reference to the issues of broader justice, a society may be ruled by law without relating to the democratizing goals of the rule of law.[15]

---

[13] Indeed, one vein of scholarship in political science on the rule of law insists that the ideal is unrealizable and that the concept is inseparable from particular political practices. See, e.g., Jose Maria Maravall and Adam Przeworski, eds., *Democracy and the Rule of Law* (Cambridge: Cambridge University Press, 2003), p. 15.
[14] Carothers, ed., *Promoting the Rule of Law Abroad*, p. 21.
[15] Guillermo O'Donnell, "Why the Rule of Law Matters," *Journal of Democracy* 15, 4 (2004): 33–34.

For this reason, promising approaches to conceptualizing the rule of law tie ideals to practices by developing criteria for how political and legal systems approximate rule-of-law values in areas such as legal restraints on government, neutrality, popular respect for law, and observance of human rights.[16] Such criteria can certainly be applied and evaluated in contemporary Arab contexts. There is little empirical research as to how legalist ideals and practices are connected in Arab societies. Existing work tends to focus on judicial opinions and the function of courts, rather than whether or how popular understanding of or respect for law may matter to legal and political systems more generally.[17]

Both the sparseness of this research and the lack of specific arguments as to how legal functionaries contribute to broader rule-of-law ideals or liberalizing political outcomes serve to underscore the problem of knowledge for rule-of-law programs in places like the Middle East.[18] Given that Egypt, now in the process of a revolution, stands as the sole Arab case with a court that has engaged in judicial review for the past several decades, a focus on law beyond a national supreme court would appear to be necessary as a practical matter.

Work relating the rule of law in Arab contexts to the dominant scholarly and policy work coming out of the West, and particularly the United States, faces an added daunting impediment i.e., widespread, Arab skepticism about the United States as the messenger for the rule of law in the Middle East.

Many Arabs believe that American policy makers neither know nor care to know basic aspects of law, politics, and society in Arab countries. And there is an even stronger and equally widespread perception that the United States has not always practiced what it preaches about the rule of law, particularly in the Middle East.

---

[16] See, e.g., Kleinfeld, "Competing Definitions of the Rule of Law."
[17] Erik G. Jensen and Thomas C. Heller, eds., *Beyond Common Knowledge: Empirical Approaches to the Rule of Law* (Stanford, CA: Stanford University Press, 2003), and Eugene Cotran and Mai Yamani, eds., *The Rule of Law in the Middle East and the Islamic World: Human Rights and the Judicial Process* (London: I.B. Taurus, 2000). The former study notes the conflation of the rule of law with institutional programs by reform specialists, as well as the limited impact of such reform programs, pp. 1–3.
[18] See Nathan Brown, *The Rule of Law in the Arab World* (Cambridge: Cambridge University Press, 1997), for work on courts in Arab countries that provides insights regarding embedded Arab authoritarian politics.

Thus, it is not surprising that the rule of law in the Arab world is easily seen as weak, politically unimportant, and perhaps at odds with Western norms and reform efforts. At the same time, many Arab citizens desire more predictable, responsive, and fair laws, particularly as pressure mounts for political change in the region.[19]

The 2004 *Arab Human Development Report* is one prominent statement by a group of Arabs of the central importance of the rule of law to social improvement, as was the Qatar Law Forum itself. Moreover, legalist reform became a subject of much greater attention and funding as a legacy of the George W. Bush administration's broader push for democratic change in the region post-11 September 2001[20] and is likely to be more prominent in the wake of the 2011 popular Arab political movements. If neither the need for legal change nor the problem of legal knowledge is going away, it is important to consider both of these in tandem.

Embedded in this issue are two major questions. How is the rule of law understood generally in the contemporary Arab world? Given diverse political meanings for the rule of law, how might the rule of law be related to political opening in particular Arab societies? How do answers to the above two questions inform the possible role, if any, for outside rule-of-law reformers?[21]

---

[19] Random sample survey research on political topics is increasingly available for at least some Arab societies. For example, the World Values Survey now includes Algeria, Egypt, Iraq, Jordan, Morocco, and Saudi Arabia. See Mark Tessler, "Do Islamic Orientations Influence Attitudes toward Democracy in the Arab World? Evidence from the World Values Survey in Egypt, Jordan, Morocco and Algeria," in *Values and Perceptions of the Islamic and Middle Eastern Publics*, ed. Mansoor Moaddel (New York: Palgrave Macmillan, 2007), pp. 107 and 122, and James Zogby, *What Arabs Think* (Utica, NY and Beirut: Zogby International, 2002).

[20] See the priority attached to rule-of-law reform in the U.S. Department of State's 2007–2012 public strategy document. USAID, *Strategic Plan: Fiscal Years 2007–2012*.

[21] Mednicoff's efforts to address these three broad questions inform an ongoing book project, which will include in different and expanded form the present discussion. The work generally is grounded in diverse methods. Mednicoff and collaborators have conducted interviews with Arab lawyers, legal policy experts, and law students in five country cases of Egypt, Jordan, Morocco, Qatar, Tunisia, and the United Arab Emirates, a group of diverse and important contemporary Arab states. Mednicoff has analyzed data on Arab political performance and popular attitudes that are increasingly available through international projects like the World Values Survey and institutions such as the World Bank. Mednicoff has drawn on the literatures that discuss Arab and comparative law and non-democratic regime resilience, although these are

Out of this broad research comes the present discussion, which focuses on the notion that at least some Arab Gulf states may present a possible pathway for linking rule-of-law development with political opening, in response to the second broad research question.

Identifying such a pathway is important, as there has long been a tension between the egalitarian ideals and legalist nature of Islam and the historical legacy of law in the service of authoritarianism that increasingly subordinated these ideals to centralizing, secular legal praxis in recent decades. In Arab countries in particular, historical experience and comments of interviewees[22] suggest a deep, basic tension in the rule of law as a means of boosting central political enforcement or *state power*, and the rule of law as facilitating individual liberty, or *citizen empowerment*. This basic tension is directly mirrored in actual Western political practice and attitudes toward Arab states, and erupted to strong effect in 2011 in Tunisia, Egypt, and other societies that have repressed legal actors rather than linking them to internal reforms.

The next portion of this analysis looks at these tensions in more detail prior to elaborating on how Qatar and the UAE may represent a pathway connecting change in the rule of law and legal actors with gradual political opening.

The Rule of Law in Contemporary Arab Contexts: How Do Shari'a and History Inform Current Issues?

In one form or another, the rule of law has long been critical as doctrine in the Arab world.[23] Thus, discussion about the rule of law in Arab states cannot proceed without recognizing that the general concept has deep Middle Eastern

---

not usually considered in tandem. Finally, Mednicoff has engaged in participant observation, as well as content analysis and interviews of American rule-of-law aid workers and specialists.

[22] E.g., interviews by Mednicoff with three anonymous Moroccan (May 2008) and two anonymous Qatari (May 2007) law students; interviews by the author with one anonymous senior Moroccan legal official and Moroccan Attorney Amin Hajji (May 2008).

[23] The Middle Eastern origin of two of the most renowned ancient legal codes — the Code of Hammurabi and the Judeo-Christian Bible — should not be forgotten. More to the point, Islamic and Ottoman socio-legal traditions that contribute to contemporary Arab law predate the Anglo-American common law by centuries.

roots. Indeed, Islam's long history of prioritizing law and mechanisms for its evolution means that one indigenous Arab version of rule-of-law ideals remains very popular today.[24]

More specifically, Islam originated as a social system that combined "*al-din wa-l-dawla*" — religion and polity. Naturally, law emerged as the central glue to guide the growth and administration of the millions of people throughout the Middle East, North Africa, and Southern Europe who comprised the early Islamic empire from the seventh through the thirteenth centuries.

While facets of contemporary Western and global articulation of the rule of law cannot simply be retrofitted or read into Islamic political history, the core term for Islamic law, shariʻa, prioritizes legal order and brings together legal doctrine and judicial decisions. In other words, this traditional Arab Islamic term itself is one way of translating, if not necessarily transplanting, some of what is understood as the rule of law; it is likely to be viewed by many Muslim Arabs as the correct Arabic term for the concept. In general, then, the idea of the rule of law was central and well-developed within Islam; political institutional practice was the problem.[25]

The complex political and doctrinal history of shariʻa merits far more detailed treatment than can be undertaken here. Yet several significant points, though they might be partial over-simplifications, facilitate an appreciation of the ongoing influence of Islamic ideals in contemporary Arab politics of the rule of law. First, Islamic law evolved and grew mainly through the role and efforts of scholars and judges but without an ironclad institutional check on the power of rulers. This led the conflict between the empowering and power-enabling tendencies of law to resolve ultimately toward the latter. Second, the ideals of Islamic politics and the rule of law remained a useful political language after the end of Islamic government in many areas of the Middle East and North Africa. Moreover, the scholarly, non-codified history of Islamic law

---

[24] Noah Feldman, *The Fall and Rise of the Islamic State* (Princeton, NJ: Princeton University Press, 2008), pp. 20–21.

[25] For a general account of the tension between the ideal and practice of the rule of law in Islam, see Khaled Abou el Fadl, *Islam and the Challenge of Democracy* (Princeton, NJ: Princeton University Press, 2004), pp. 12–14.

is closer to the Anglo-American common law tradition than subsequent major legal influences in many Middle Eastern countries.

Because Islam emerged rapidly as a system of social governance as well as a creed, it is hardly surprising that a law-forming class of Muslims also developed quickly. Religious scholars were the natural source for legal interpretation, because the Prophet Muhammad's status as God's final prophet meant that either his recorded prophecies in the Qur'an or the sayings (*hadith*) attributed to him, known together with his teachings as the sunna, formed the basis of the most reliable dicta for ordering society. Moreover, the relatively small number of explicitly legal passages in the Qur'an and the governing challenges that grew with the spectacular expansion of Islam in the several centuries after the Prophet's death meant that legal needs and sources were too diverse to allow for simple derivation from the founding documents of the religion. Over time, scholars built an elaborate intellectual interpretative edifice to find ways to codify and extend through reason and analogy (*qiyas*) and interpretation (*ijtihad*) these original authoritative sources of Islam.[26] The result was a diverse, non-monolithic, and long-lasting system of jurisprudence and social growth.

One of the central and enduring doctrines of Islamic jurisprudence was the leader's status as custodian or servant of communal law, rather than its progenitor. As a result, rulers were to be judged by qualified Islamic scholars and Muslims more generally on their record of executing and enforcing Islamic law. This clear theoretical limit to the leader's legislative powers and discretion were subject to the realities of a depoliticized, diffuse, pre-modern imperial citizenry, which could either allow centralized political excess or heighten the importance of the scholars' work. Yet Islamic law's dependency on scholars meant that the ruling political elite "was largely, if not totally, absent from the legal scene."[27] Thus, Islamic scholars exercised a major, often practical role in granting or withholding legitimacy to the leader.

The range and power of the Arab Islamic and subsequent Ottoman Islamic empires decreased over time, while Western economic and military

---

[26] Chibli Mallat, "From Islamic to Middle Eastern Law: A Restatement of the Field (Part II)," *American Journal of Comparative Law* 52 (2004): 285.
[27] Wael Hallaq, *The Origins and Evolution of Islamic Law* (Cambridge: Cambridge University Press, 2004), p. 204.

power posed a doctrinal and practical challenge to Muslim political order in the Middle East and North Africa. In the broad context of Western imperial expansion, the Islamic political order began to take a back seat to the beginnings of local nationalism and efforts at centralization.

Whatever the particular cause,[28] the ideal and reality of Islamic government, including the central place of the rule of law as a check on arbitrary authority, diminished until its death blow after World War I. At that point, the Islamic Ottoman Empire disappeared and the Arab regions were divided into mostly colonial enclaves. More to the point, the system of scholars that upheld the rule of law disappeared, and with it the rule of law itself, other than as a term for colonial government enforcement and bureaucratic centralization.

The fact that Muslim Arab states could not resist modern Western domination doomed Islamic government in most of the Middle East for much of the colonial and early postcolonial periods. However, Islamic political theory remained a significant source of basic ideals, particularly with respect to the rule of law. One relevant normative influence is justice as a value that is centrally and popularly embedded in Islam. Justice as a concept and a discourse is ubiquitous in the Qur'an. Moreover, as is true with American legal ideals, Islam's emphasis on justice in the sunna includes significant attention to social equity and individual rights. Thus, discussions of many of the issues that frame legal discourse are ingrained in the religious identity of a large majority of the people in Arab societies. The importance of justice within Islam also contributed to the fact that Islamic jurisprudence never fully developed a concept of natural law. This has led some to argue that there is no clear theory to ground a completely secular legal order, as natural law helped to do over time in the West.[29]

---

[28] For divergent accounts that nonetheless concur on the importance of legal scholars in developing shari'a and the roots of the collapse of Islamic legal institutions due to modern political developments, see Feldman, *The Fall and Rise of the Islamic State*, pp. 59–75, and Hallaq, *The Origins and Evolution of Islamic Law*, p. 205.

[29] George N. Sfeir, *The Modernization of Arab Law: An Investigation into Current Civil, Criminal and Constitutional Law in the Arab World* (San Francisco, CA: Austin & Winfield, 1998), pp. 11–12.

Islamic political theory can be read as presupposing two more specific tenets that have clear relevance to contemporary Western ideas about the rule of law: 1) Despite the ideal that political authority exists for the benefit of Islam, authority in practice will tend toward absolutism, rather than subordinating itself to communal legitimacy or justice; and 2) resources autonomous from the state are needed to check leaders' actions. This classical Islamic distrust of government and an emphasis on law as a constraint on authority helped ground the influence of Islamic scholars and would sound quite familiar to many Americans.[30]

Such familiarity is not coincidental. As legal anthropologist Lawrence Rosen and others have noted, Islamic law is essentially a common law system, especially in its reliance on local courts and local cultural information as characteristics that distinguish it from the legal centralization of a civil law system.[31] Thus, American and Arab lawyers may share a similar understanding of the importance of locally-based legal processes, among other things. However, Islamic legal development, unlike Anglo-American common law, derived doctrine more from scholarly opinion and consensus than through judicial opinions, which tended to be brief and not necessarily prone to creating binding precedent.[32]

By the twentieth century, Islamic legal rule had been largely banished and tarnished in Arab countries, reduced to the sphere of family law by Western colonial rulers and rejected by many natives who saw Islamic government as outmoded or ineffective in the face of European power. At the same time, late Ottoman centralization and subsequent foreign great power control of law in the Middle East and North Africa fostered three major consequences.

First, it produced a patchwork of legal orders in a given society, rather than the relatively long-standing unitary national legal system that occurred in

---

[30] Ellis Goldberg, "Private Goods, Public Wrongs and Civil Society in Some Medieval Arab Theory and Practice," in *Rules and Rights in the Middle East: Democracy, Law, and Society*, eds. Ellis Goldberg, Resat Kasaba, and Joel S. Migdal, (Seattle, WA: University of Washington Press, 1993), pp. 251, 255, and 263.
[31] Lawrence Rosen, *The Justice of Islam* (Oxford: Oxford University Press, 2000), pp. 48–49.
[32] Chibli Mallat, *Introduction to Middle Eastern Law* (Oxford: Oxford University Press, 2007), p. 61.

the United States. Second, it set up an authoritarian norm that law would in fact be subordinated to imperial political power. Third, it spurred a tendency for constitutions to exist without a significant history of judicial interpretation.

In some states, such as Morocco, this led to frequent postcolonial redrafts of the constitution to reflect changes in the power or preoccupations of political authority, in contrast with the U.S. norm of a single basic constitutional document that can only be modified with difficulty.

The legal system of every contemporary Arab nation is a unique mixture of Islamic, Ottoman, European, and post-independence laws, though this is less true in the Gulf.[33] This mélange of legal sources in most Arab societies did not in itself preclude legal clarity or checks on authority. However, along with the divisive territorial and ethnic logic that European colonial powers frequently evinced in setting borders for many of the contemporary nations of the Middle East, the lack of legal systemic unity in Arab states has two consequences for recent U.S. efforts to enhance the rule of law.[34]

First, it means that the jurisprudential reference points of lawyers in the United States are not likely to be of direct use to most Arab societies. Further, the lack of systemic unity has contributed to political situations in which post-colonial Arab leaders have had many incentives to centralize their authority and no real legal impediments to doing so. This latter point is even more obviously related to the primary legacy of colonialism in the Middle East — an emphasis on control backed by force that was meant to serve the best interests of the colonizer rather than the indigenous citizens. Colonial regimes used invented political forms such as mandates and protectorates to cloak their use of raw power, and Arab nationalist elites were socialized into this system. Legal norms and institutions under colonialism made readily apparent the contradictions between stated and true purposes. These norms and institutions were somewhat successful at centralizing political and economic administration. However

---

[33] For a succinct summary of the combination of sources of law in each Arab area, see Brown, *The Rule of Law in the Arab World*, pp. 3–5. To be sure, a number of territories escaped direct foreign domination, most notably in the Arab Gulf. Yet even in these places, Western legal ideas and practices have supplemented indigenous combinations of Islamic and customary law.

[34] Roger Owen, *State, Power and Politics in the Making of the Modern Middle East* (New York: Routledge, 2000), p. 11.

much Arab nationalists rebelled against colonial rule, they also learned that the lofty promises of colonial political ideas were generally subservient, or even in contrast, to the reality of police control. Facing economic and other challenges, these nationalists unsurprisingly built on, instead of dismantled, the legacies of authoritarian rule that they inherited.

To be sure, the ideal of the rule of law will often be at odds with the centralizing tendency of governments. We have argued that Arab states in the Middle East in general had an especially wide gap between the ideal and the reality because of the combination of a relative lack of an autonomous, precolonial, unified legal order in these states and the particular repressive nature of colonial governments. More subtle is the suggestion that the level of discontinuity between the rational, legalistic values preached by European administrators and their practice of resource extraction and police rule tainted the global, secular ideal of the rule of law in a way that encourages conflict between local and global law.

In short, it is easy for Arabs to view the rule of law in the West in a manner similar to some American legal scholars on the left, as primarily an ideology of political control, not as a possible check on political abuse or guarantee of individual rights. This view is important because it implies that efforts by reformers to strengthen the rule of law, and particularly central legal institutions, need not be associated with political opening within Arab societies. A striking example of how well-formulated ideas of the rule of law can exist alongside repressive political tendencies was the publication by an Iraqi law professor of a thoughtful tract on the rule of law as an ideal in Iraq at the very same time that Saddam Hussein was beginning to consolidate his particular style of brutal, and often legally arbitrary, authoritarian rule.[35]

Despite this authoritarianism, Arab regimes have not lacked clear legal structures. For example, most Arab states have basic laws or constitutions. Thus, Arab constitutions exist and may matter, but they have had much less of

---

[35] Samir Khairi Tawfiq, *Mabda Siyadat Al-Qa'nun* (The Principle of the Rule of Law) (Baghdad: 1978). Considering that it was published a year before Saddam Hussein moved from partial to undisputed political control of Iraq, this thoughtful, philosophical discussion of the rule of law in terms that would sound familiar to Western legal scholars is a particularly interesting treatise on the subject in the Arabic language.

a history of institutionalization and independent judicial interpretation than the U.S. constitution.

This difference is neither surprising nor unknown to American rule-of-law experts. In fact, given Arab political centralization, the very existence of constitutions is at least as interesting a political phenomenon as the dearth of independent judicial interpretative traditions of these documents.[36] For the purpose of this paper, it is worth underscoring the challenge that the juxtaposition of constitutions and political regimes with few genuine legal checks poses for building broad social support, or even judicial competence, for global ideals of the rule of law.

Hence, many Arab citizens have had two broad historical touchstones with respect to the rule of law. One is the twentieth century experience of codified law from many, including Western, sources, most often being used to support centralized, non-democratic rule. A second is the vague collective knowledge and memory of an earlier era, when jurists and judges managed to develop law that could check and delegitimize authority but within the clear norms and bounds of Islamic faith.

Together, these historical experiences mean that the theory and practice of the rule of law in contemporary Arab politics has had a fragmented quality. On the one hand, Islamist political ideology grew throughout the Middle East in the 1980s and 1990s to become the dominant contemporary trope of political discourse and opposition. As a result, Islam and shari'a remain at the rhetorical and actual center of discussions of law in contemporary Arab states. In particular, many Arab constitutions clearly endorse Islamic law as the primary source for legislation.[37] The most frequent rallying cry or demand of

---

[36] For a detailed discussion of the political roles for Arab constitutions, see Nathan Brown, *Constitutions in a Non-Constitutional World* (Albany, NY: State University of New York Press, 2002).

[37] Even a country with as developed secular legal and social traditions as Egypt makes Islam its basic source for legislation in Article 2 of the pre-2011 revolution constitution. For a discussion of this, see Baudouin Dupret, "La Chari'a est la Source de la Législation: Interprétations Jurisprudentielles et Théories Juridiques," in *L'état de Droit Dans le Monde Arabe*, ed. Ahmed Mahiou, (Paris: CNRS, 1997), pp. 125–142.

regime opponents before the 2011 Arab uprisings and a strong slogan since is the amplification or restoration of shariʿa law.[38]

The extent to which Islam and shariʿa should inform the rule of law and what forms this should take is currently a complicated area of great debate and discussion among Arab and non-Arab Muslim scholars. Adding to the complexity of this issue is the theoretical contradiction between the Islamic ideal of *siyasat al-shariʿa* (the government of God's law) and *siyadat al-qaʿnun* (the sovereignty of man-made law). The latter term, the general way in which the Western idea of the rule of law is translated into Arabic, conveys with it a patina of illegitimacy to some, although by no means all, Muslims.[39] Like other broad ideological frames, Islam allows for diverse interpretations about law and politics and is compatible with the actual contemporary Arab practice of mixed legal norms and institutions. For this reason, a broad majority of government and opposition fealty to shariʿa exists alongside more secular courts, bureaucrats, and lawyers' associations in many countries. These are the forces combined for analytical purposes as "the legal complex" in a recent study of law and democratization.[40]

Yet the standing of members of the Arab legal complex is the flip side of the fragmented nature of contemporary rule of law. Lawyers are sometimes part of an active and growing transnational movement of Arabs linked to global rights NGOs and rule-of-law advocates, and are open to more direct import of Western ideas or experiences with legalist reform. Reflected in international fora and documents such as the *Arab Human Development Reports*, this posture does not reject the importance of Islamic identity or law *per se*. Rather, it is a preference, or at least a willingness, to articulate theories of legal and political

---

[38] Feldman, *The Fall and Rise of the Islamic State*, p. 105.
[39] One of the signs of both legal pluralism and the relative novelty of the Western notion of the rule of law in Arab countries is that there is no single phrase that is used in every country to translate the term. For example, in Morocco, the concept is often referred to as *dawlat al-haq wa-l-qaʿnun* (the rule of right and law), instead of *siyadat al-qaʿnun*. This term gained currency through the Moroccan monarchy's efforts to employ it as a slogan for its own purported fealty to the ideal of the rule of law.
[40] Terence C. Halliday, Lucien Karpik, and Malcolm M. Feeley, eds., *Fighting For Political Freedom: Comparative Studies of the Legal Complex and Political Liberalism* (Cambridge: Cambridge University Press, 2007).

reform in terms translated directly from global usage such as *dimuqratiyya* (democracy), *huquq al-insan* (human rights), and *siyadat al-qa'nun* (rule of law). This tendency can be grounded in skepticism about traditional Islamic terms adapting to modern political debates, or a desire to avoid overburdening religious concepts with excess contemporary meaning, or both.

However, this indigenous Arab reformist tendency within sections of the legal complex is not very likely to find broad sociopolitical support, unlike Islamist political expression. In diverse Arab countries such as Egypt, Morocco, and Qatar, lawyers, law students, and lay citizens speak articulately about the rule of law and respect its limited success and broader promise to improve rights, fairness, and political transparency.[41] At the same time, there is tremendous cynicism about American foreign politics and aid generally, and a lack of confidence in domestic legal and political institutions.[42] A century of popular historical associations of Western legal and political ideals with colonial and postcolonial highly centralized governments suggests a broad sense of mistrust with respect to the concrete prospects of rule-of-law reform. Of course, all of this may be changing as the Arab events of 2011, and the demands of many activists around law and justice, reconfigure the nature and politics of law in the Middle East.

Gulf Exceptionalism and the Rule of Law — A Possible Reformist Way Forward?

What is striking about the Arab Gulf is its exceptionalism with respect to much of the above trajectory of Arab legal politics, which may suggest a pathway for legal reform and political liberalization that is not based on the sort of systemic overthrow that has occurred in other Arab societies. This section explores

---

[41] This is on the basis of preliminary qualitative surveys that Mednicoff has administered to lawyers and law students in Morocco and Qatar, as well as several longer interviews. However, Mednicoff is still collecting this data and is careful at this stage to limit general and specific conclusions until data collection has progressed further.

[42] See, for example, the summary information and data files available at the International Foundation for Electoral Systems' project on the rule of law in Arab countries; available online at http://www.ifes.org/features.html?title=Reports%25%20Arabs%20Open%20to%20Democratic%20Reforms%20despite%20Setbacks.

this possible pathway with particular reference to Qatar and the United Arab Emirates.

The recent historical exceptionalism lies in the Arab Gulf states' general lack of intensive colonization, which meant that the triple combination of the growth of strong coercive institutions, the radical diminution of the scope of shariʻa law, and the mosaic hybridity of the legal system was much less potent in those states than elsewhere in the Arab world. This likely created a political background in which state institutions were less centralized and defined. It also created a system in which associations of Western legal ideals and practices with coercion and hypocrisy were less sharply etched.

But what marks the Arab Gulf as most distinct with respect to legal and political reform is its recent pattern of hyperglobalization[43] and the ensuing combination of possibilities for change within the system. The key here is not economic liberalization *per se*, but rather the multiple points of pressure on domestic policy due to economic openness. The sheer quantity of commercial and educational exchanges, high proportion of foreign workers in the labor force, presence of foreign companies and international NGOs, multiplicity of trade agreements, and participation in international organizations and networks combine to globalize most elements of domestic policy. The repercussions of Gulf economic and other open policies entail exposure to foreign expectations and requirements; by participating in transnational business, Qatar and the UAE have implicitly recognized transnational standards for workers' rights, trade regulations, and rule of law more generally. Recognition has opened the door to criticisms of falling short of those standards.

---

[43] By "hyperglobalization," we refer to the accelerated process of globalization that has taken place in societies like Qatar and the UAE. The process is distinguished by both the speed of change and the scope of change, the latter evident from the comparatively limited size and global connectedness of these societies prior to the past several decades of petroleum revenue-funded dynamism. We are not using the term in the more specialized academic sense of the "hyperglobalization thesis," which suggests that recent globalization generally has reduced the scope of action for national leaders. See Evelyn Huber and John D. Stephens, "State Economy and Social Policy in Global Capitalism," in *A Handbook of Political Sociology: States, Civil Societies, and Globalization*, eds. Thomas Janoski, Robert Alford, Alexander M. Hicks, and Mildred Schwartz, (Cambridge: Cambridge University Press, 2005).

International scrutiny comes to bear through the presence of international media, education centers, and human rights organizations. These institutions are those that interrogate whether or not the Qatari and Emirati governments are meeting the standards formally acknowledged or professedly enforced. The crucial question is whether all these international pressure points actually result in *de facto* change, or merely give rise to a plethora of formal laws, reports, agreements, conferences, and events with little substantive repercussions. Countries like Qatar and the UAE face great pressure at the level of workers' rights, but it is precisely at this level that national identity comes into tension with international expectations and creates a dilemma for the government. If improving economic development before political rights has been a model in other parts of Asia, the speed and rapidity of global enmeshment of this broad strategy in Gulf Arab countries creates the possiblity of a novel legal framework.

Given the Arab Gulf's extraordinary amount of capital and imported labor, hyperglobalization exposes in particularly acute ways tensions between national development/control and universalizing international legal norms. One manner in which this plays out with respect to the status of non-native workers is a general tendency for Western-based lawyers to assume the need and possibility for bringing global human rights law to Qatar and the UAE based on the relative under-development of formal legal institutions in these countries. On the local side, this can lead both to sensitivity around perceived Western condescension and neo-imperialism, or, more likely, official governmental efforts to highlight the compliance, and even leadership, of the Gulf in fealty to international law. This helps make sense, for example, of Qatar's role in hosting global legal luminaries at the Qatar Law Forum in May 2009. The event was meant to signal that Qatar was a global player in the arena of law — hardly the backwater center of weak legal institutions and protections for non-natives that Western rights lawyers and legal consultants might assume it to be.

Gulf hyperglobalization means an intensification of points of contact between diverse perspectives and actors relevant to the rule of law. The multiplicity of these actors, because of the influx of workers and institutions from all over the world and the heightened international scrutiny that this entails, creates variation and hybridity around the rule of law that is unusual, particularly given the Arab Gulf societies' relative dearth of legal and other sociopolitical infrastructure prior to the oil boom.

The most significant of these hyperglobalized legal points of contact are:

- Law enforcement
- Legal education
- Activism around human rights
- Media expansion and openness

The above areas each entail diverse ideas about the meaning of the rule of law and justice that allow for varied outcomes and do not generally reduce to simple conflicts between the religious and the secular, Western and Arab.[44]

Both conflictive and consensual elements of rule-of-law ideals and institutions are highly visible in the Arab Gulf. A state like Qatar, which has shown a fairly strong ability to moderate conflicts between and among domestic and global rule-of-law issues, illustrates a possible pathway for political liberalization without system overthrow. The UAE, which has been somewhat less successful at mitigating these conflicts, presents a more problematic picture with respect to specifically political liberalization.[45]

Law enforcement is central to the contestation of legal norms and its relation to more open politics. With respect to non-citizen visitors and workers, this tension is front and center. On the one hand, the essence of these countries' hyperglobalized growth strategies requires relatively open borders and legal reforms that address the worst abuses of labor exploitation. Indeed, both Qatar and the UAE have legislated specific improvements for non-citizen workers in recent years. On the other hand, concern around the control of large majorities of non-native populations, along with general global patterns of migration

---

[44] Indeed, the majority of South Asians among the resident population of both Doha and the two major cities of the UAE suggests the importance of moving beyond simple dichotomies between the West and the Arab world more generally.

[45] We do not wish to overstate the possible differences in the liberalizing trajectory of the rule of law between these two Gulf societies, especially with the likely pressures around political opening that regimes are experiencing after the popular overthrow of the Tunisian and Egyptian governments.

securitization in general, have led these same countries to apply state-of-the-art biometric and other arguably intrusive measures of enforcing visa holders' subjection to host state control.

Legal enforcement with respect to non-citizens can also be used to appeal to elements of national culture. This, too, has been more evident in Dubai than in Doha. Prosecutions and harsh judicial punishment by Dubai courts of instances of public lewdness, sexual behavior, or drinking, despite the city's cosmopolitanism, are clear cases of legal enforcement triggered by strong symbolic native concerns about threats to traditional culture represented by contemporary hyperglobalized development. Such legal enforcement confirms the delicacy of the tightrope with respect to foreign workers and citizens that Arab Gulf officials walk.

The extraordinary, perhaps unprecedented, trajectory of rapid development of Gulf cities like Doha and Dubai from backwater trading posts to cities of global influence has required an enormous influx of professional experts in law itself. Because these cities lacked indigenous tradition around the teaching, practice, and regulation of law, they have had to build legal infrastructure in a very short time. This has entailed a very fluid environment for both conflict and consensus around global and local legal training, ideas, and practices.

Qatar and the UAE presented close to a tabula rasa in many areas of contemporary national bureaucratic development, particularly education. They have attracted and continue to attract world class universities, opening themselves to the influence of preeminent global academic establishments and the world-class professors associated with them. These foreign academics have their own ideas about liberal arts and education, which are highly globalized notions that cluster around free enquiry. Lacking generations of an education system and established administrative subcultures, Qatari and Emirati students are therefore exposed to diverse global ideas in an environment of rapid restructuring.

Both Qatar and the UAE have shown signs that their diverse populations of global and native residents and broader international connections have fostered legal reforms that might be associated with more open politics. In Qatar, in recent years, these include:

- The College of Law at Qatar University splitting from the College of shariʻa, with accompanying curricula reform and global legal influence.
- A new dedicated tribunal for international commercial and civil disputes.
- The formation of and efforts to establish standards for the Qatar Bar Association.

In the UAE, examples are:

- More pervasive legal enforcement in non-rights arenas such as vehicular traffic laws.
- Increasing the use of courts, including against prominent citizens, such as the Shaykh Issa trial (despite Issa's ultimate acquittal).[46]
- Increased rights for non-citizen workers, based on substantial labor law overhaul.[47]

The above reforms only indirectly relate to the oil wealth of Arab Gulf countries. The rapid developmental imperatives that hydrocarbon revenues have made possible created the dynamic patterns of global and native interactions around law both within the resident populations and across borders. It is these interactions that create possibilities for legal change that are politically opening. At the same time, distinctions in development strategy, as can be teased out between comparative discussion of Qatar and the UAE, also suggest possible differences in legal reforms and their political consequences.

---

[46] Shaykh Issa is a brother of the ruler of the UAE who was acquitted on charges of torture, despite the existence of a video of him beating an Afghan merchant in 2004. For a summary of the Shaykh Issa case, see Marten Youssef, "Sheikh Issa Acquittal: Government 'Does Not Interfere' in Court Matters," *The National*, 13 January 2010, available online at http://www.thenational.ae/apps/pbcs.dll/article?AID=/20100113/NATIONAL/701129852/1010; Human Rights Watch, *UAE: Sheikh's Trial Insufficient to Stop Torture*, 10 January 2010, available online at http:// www.hrw.org/en/news/2010/01/10/uae-sheikh-s-trial-insufficient-stop-torture. For a general analysis that confirms and suggests many of our points here, see Christopher Davidson's 10 January 2011 blog discussion, "Rule of Law in the United Arab Emirates: 2010 Review," available online at http://www.currentintelligence.net/gulfstream.

[47] For more on these increased rights, see Mednicoff's work on this issue sponsored by the Center for International and Regional Studies at the Georgetown School of Foreign Service in Qatar, currently under review. An overview of this work is available online at http://cirs.georgetown.edu/publications/summaryreports/.

Qatar, which has prioritized educational reform through Education City and other developments, and regional media openness through Al Jazeera, has generally been building legal educational and associational infrastructure. More open discourse among lawyers and the public, which highlights the politically liberalizing potential of law, would seem to be the result. Since the first Qatar Law Forum in 2009, the country has continued to seek to establish itself as an internationally recognized regional and even global leader in rule-of-law development. The second forum, which took place in May 2012, covered topics ranging from courts and constitutions to Islamic finance dispute resolution, global legal questions, and freedom of expression. Later the same year, the forum held a symposium on anti-corruption and the rule of law in London; partnership between the United Kingdom and Qatar on improving the rule of law was emphasized at a gathering of prominent legal professionals and academics from several countries.[48]

Qatar has also utilized the UN as a forum and partner in building international prominence on rule of law and anti-corruption. In 2009, Qatar hosted a UN session on anti-corruption; two years later, in December 2011, the Rule of Law and Anti-Corruption Center opened in Doha as an independent institution functioning in partnership with the UN.[49] The following April, Qatar committed $4 million to the United Nations Development Programme's Anti-Corruption and Integrity in the Arab Countries initiative. Qatar has been actively involved in the implementation of the project, and stands out in the region by virtue of this (financial) commitment to anti-corruption.[50]

By its own account, Qatar has demonstrated commitment to rule of law through participation in UN meetings, as well as through efforts to participate

---

[48] "Qatari Attorney General Talks Anti-Corruption and Rule of Law in London," Qatar Law Forum, 17 December 2012, available online at http://www.qatarlawforum.com/wp-content/uploads/2012/01/QLF_17_December_2012_news_release.pdf.

[49] Francesca Astorri, "Qatar Opens Anti Corruption Center," *The Peninsula*, 12 December 2011, available online at http://www.thepeninsulaqatar.com/qatar/175469-qatar-opens-anti-corruption-centre.html.

[50] United Nations Development Programme (UNDP), "Qatar and UNDP Finalize Agreement to Set Up Arab Region Anti-Corruption Initiative in Doha," 25 April 2012, available online at http://www.undp.org/content/undp/en/home/presscenter/articles/2012/04/25/qatar-and-undp-finalize-agreement-to-set-up-arab-region-anti-corruption-initiative-in-doha/.

in international conventions on rule of law and human rights. Qatar asserts successes at the national level by making rule of law an organizing principle for public life and by promoting transparency in political administration.[51] These efforts have been driven by the desire to attract foreign investment, as demonstrable commitment to anti-corruption and rule of law signals an attractively reliable and familiar environment for investment capital from abroad. Qatar has succeeded in gaining a number one rating among Middle Eastern countries for low levels of corruption, according to the 2011 public perceptions index published by Transparency International.[52]

Qatar has also shown commitment to developing a national judicial apparatus whose standards, frames of reference, and procedures are familiar and acceptable to foreign investors and businessmen. The Qatar International Court and Dispute Resolution Center (QICDRC) was founded in 2009 with the mandate to adjudicate transnational disputes involving Qatar or relating to entities based there. The court is empowered to make judgments on the basis of international common law and itself is independent from all other Qatari legal institutions, although it is supported by the Qatari government.

In February 2013, the QICDRC issued a publication laying out a plan for improving judicial and legal education in Qatar. Central to the plan is the creation of an International Judicial and Legal Education Institute, building on the success of Qatar's Centre for Legal and Judicial Studies. Again, the goal is to rise to a place of international prominence, this time in the field of educating members of the legal profession itself. The legal referents would be international, rather than indigenous to Qatar or the region more broadly. The content and purpose of the curriculum will be provided by the Institute, thereby establishing a flagship role for Qatar in international legal development.

Qatar has demonstrated much less willingness to respond to international pressure to address the treatment of foreign workers, despite intense pressure and international publicity surrounding construction for the 2022 World Cup.

---

[51] "Qatar Stresses Importance of Rule of Law," *The Peninsula*, 12 October 2012, available online at http://thepeninsulaqatar.com/latest-news/210579-qatar-stresses-importance-of-rule-of-law.html.

[52] See http://www.transparency.org/cpi2011/results.

Human Rights Watch in particular has relentlessly pressured the country to address the working conditions of its largely migrant construction labor force. In May 2012, Qatar vaguely promised to consider ending its highly criticized sponsorship (*kafala*) system and replace it with a contract system for foreign workers. In response to pressure from the International Trade Organization, Qatar also agreed to organize a labor committee as a substitute for a labor union. However, non-citizens would not be eligible to participate.[53] As of March of 2013, Qatar has announced that it is working on a new law to protect worker health and safety. Thus, Qatar's focus remains on legislation rather than enforcement. Though Qatari courts have been cracking down on local commercial fraud under the auspices of the Consumer Protection Department, this is yet another example of Qatar's preference for promoting smooth and efficient business transactions while making little headway in terms of substantive rights of foreign workers.

The UAE has done far less than Qatar to encourage more politically open or globalized education, at least now that the excitement of having satellite campuses of New York University and the Sorbonne has ebbed. And while legal education and process are growing in the UAE, the country's developmental strategy prioritizes rapid economic and tourist growth, which favors legal regulation that maximizes financial transactional stability and order.

On the other hand, the UAE has felt compelled to respond more directly to pressure in relation to its labor law, leading to extensive new legislation. A new federal labor court system was set up to provide a fast track for labor dispute resolutions. These courts were first in place in Dubai and Abu Dhabi and are being implemented across the country.

In 2011, a major labor law reform addressed complaints against the *kafala* system of sponsorship for foreign workers by granting workers the right to move between employers. Provisions regarding minimum wages, vacation time, and

---

[53] "Good News For Migrant Workers — Qatar to Drop Sponsorship and Adopt Recruitment on Contract System," *Asian Tribune*, 6 May 2012, available online at http://asiantribune.com/news/2012/05/06/good-news-migrant-workers-%E2%80%93-qatar-drop-sponsorship-and-adopt-recruitment-contract-sy.

safety and health protection for construction workers have also been put in place. The Ministry of Interior made it illegal for a company to withhold any workers' passports, although there has been difficulty in enforcing this provision. The Ministry of Labor also cancelled new licenses for foreign recruiters who are not in compliance with the laws. The UAE also signed bilateral agreements with labor source countries upholding particular workers' rights insisted on by their governments. Finally, the UAE has been the first in the region to put in place legislation regulating the relationships between domestic help and employers; the law upholds the Convention on the Elimination of All Forms of Discrimination against Women.

The UAE has claimed that its enforcement of these reforms is robust. Among other things, the government employs hundreds of inspectors, fines companies that fail to pay employees adequately or in a timely fashion, and has established a 24-hour hotline for workers' complaints. In August 2012, 20 new sanctions for breaches of labor law were put in place.

Yet there is considerable inconsistency about enforcing labor rules and policies. One reason is the diversity of actors in the UAE's relatively young federal system, in which courts have only recently gained experience and legitimacy as actors. Grievances are supposed to be resolved through the Ministry of Labor prior to entering the court system. Also, because countries like the UAE frame the presence of non-native workers partially as a security issue, it is not easy enforcing non-citizen rights, at least when they are perceived as a possible threat to natives. A final and important issue is the lack of transparency of the policy process in the UAE. For example, in 2006 a senior official pledged to allow labor unions in the construction sector; however, a strike in 2007 along with citizens' general insecurities regarding foreign workers led to this promise going unmet. Labor unions remain illegal.

As this unfulfilled pledge suggests, statements around enforcement mechanisms for non-citizen workers' rights have a strong symbolic rather than practical content, especially given the difficulty for external data collection regarding their enforcement. The Shaykh Issa case mentioned above is a prominent example of officials' ability to claim that a fair enforcement process favoring foreign workers' rights took place. Yet despite the case going to court, officials protected the evidence presented in the case, which resulted in an acquittal that did not favor the victim, a foreign worker. Thus, announcing or setting up mechanisms to enforce foreign workers' rights appeals to officials, but only if those same mechanisms do not later put them in a position in which their political standing is under threat. This calculus may help make sense of why Qatar, in contrast to the UAE, has announced fewer specific enforcement mechanisms for workers' rights, instead asserting leadership through global conferences on the rule of law.

Further highlighting the complex relation between legal reform and democratic opening, increased Emirati use of the courts and even clarified rights for workers may serve the interests of procedural smoothness more than political opening. Indeed, the use of the judicial system to threaten politically outspoken Emiratis in the spring of 2011 is a sign of the potential for increased legalism to be a tool of repression rather than reform.[54]

We are not suggesting, therefore, that young Arab Gulf countries fit into a simple pattern of legal growth based on Western-propelled or inevitably politically liberalizing responses to their relative legal underdevelopment. Rather, the wealth and global ambitions of Gulf countries, together with their prior insulation from widespread global legal penetration, create diverse opportunities and intense encounters around different notions of locally appropriate best legal practices. The result of this rapidly-growing and rapidly-shifting terrain for legal reconfiguration is a variety of areas and possibilities for either expansion or retrenchment, which are based on different Arab Gulf societies' particular national or sectoral developmental priorities.

Conclusion

One can find examples of, as well as points of divergence in, the way that Arab Gulf societies have avoided the pitfalls of connecting global ideals and historical practice around the rule of law to reformist politics. The unique combination present in Doha, Dubai, and Abu Dhabi of limited conflictive historical encounters between Western legal domination and shari'a, the dearth

---

[54] See Human Rights Watch, "UAE: Activists Arrested for 'Opposing Government'," 25 April 2011, available online at http://www.hrw.org/en/news/2011/04/25/uae-activists-arrested-opposing-government.

of strong legal establishment development, and the logic of hyperglobalization, have united to make Qatar and the UAE possible laboratories for contemporary globalist legal hybridization. Such hybridization contains the potential for particular legal norms and structures that are congruent with both international law and local historical practice. When this happens, the politically liberalizing potential of law can be realized.

Yet the global and regional environments in which Gulf societies find themselves are far from easy. The inequalities left in hyperglobalization's wake are alarming, while the pressures for rapid political reform unleashed throughout the Arab world are mounting. There is some evidence that Gulf rulers after 2011 may be pulling back on reforms that increase the linkage of legal ideals and institutions to political accountability.[55] One might hope, nonetheless, that these rulers might draw the opposite conclusion from regional events about the need for both law and open politics.

---

[55] See Christopher M. Davidson, "Why the Sheikhs Will Fall," *Foreign Policy*, 26 April 2013, available online at http://www.foreignpolicy.com/articles/2013/04/26/why_the_sheikhs_will_fall.

Chapter 5

The Dynamics of Distribution in the Gulf: Selective Allocations, Agency, and Bureaucratic Accessibility in Kuwait

James C. A. Redman

For more than three decades the rentier framework has provided researchers and scholars alike with a model for discerning the nature of interactions between states and their citizens throughout the Gulf. However, only within the past few years have specialists begun to question its overly deterministic, almost predictive, shortcomings, and its failure to address the multiplex roles that individual and collective agency clearly account for in this political environment.

More specifically, the classical rentier paradigm inadequately assumes that rent distribution by the government is either completely equitable or that rent-seeking on the part of the populace is uniform. Fortunately, this top-down emphasis is now being reevaluated, and this Chapter will further contribute to this process by examining these issues as they pertain to Kuwait by considering the following interrelated factors: Partiality in the distribution of rent income, the ascendancy of bureaucratic brokerage, and the institutionalization of interpersonal modes of access via the men's guestroom (*diwaniyya*).

Rentier Dynamics: The Limitations of a Framework Without Agency

The rentier state concept garnered much of its current recognition from Hossein Mahdavy's analysis of the Iranian political economy and what he termed the "fortuitous *étatisme*"[1] that accompanied the nationalization of the country's hydrocarbon industry. Although he focused on Iran, Mahdavy proposed that his analytical approach was applicable to any number of states both within and outside of the Middle East as long as their revenue sources are external, accrued directly by the government, and are substantial enough to dwarf any local productive capacities. Mahdavy also contended that intensive oil exportation engenders governmental spending and investment within its own sectors without the hindrances of public accountability, since the citizenry is effectively excluded from the generation of state wealth.[2]

Following Mahdavy's lead, many scholars subsequently were quick to adopt the rentier model and, unfortunately, pervert it through gross generalizations, assumptions, and inappropriate applications. These fallacious notions ranged from basic economic determinism without any sociopolitical context[3] to broad classifications of universal rentier ethics[4] that brazenly dismissed the realities of local, historically specific circumstances. The most conspicuous of these oversights is the simple fact that not all rentier states have been created equal and there are considerable disparities between them. Aside from the innumerable contextual variations, demographic factors arise as the most noticeable variable.[5]

---

[1] Hossein Mahdavy, "Patterns and Problems of Economic Development in Rentier States: The Case of Iran," in *Studies in the Economic History of the Middle East: From the Rise of Islam to the Present Day*, ed. M. A. Cook (Oxford: Oxford University Press, 1970), p. 432.
[2] Mahdavy, "Patterns and Problems," pp. 428–429, 432.
[3] Gwen Okruhlik, "Rentier Wealth, Unruly Law, and the Rise of the Opposition: The Political Economy of Oil States," *Comparative Politics* 31 (1999): 296.
[4] Hazem Beblawi, "The Rentier State in the Arab World," in *The Arab State*, ed. Giacomo Luciani (London: Routledge, 1990), p. 98.
[5] Michael Herb makes a convincing case that population size is one of the most underappreciated factors of rentierism. Herb demonstrates that whereas most means of analysis focus heavily on the degree to which oil exports account for a nation's GDP, this approach fails to account for

States with small populations like Kuwait have been categorized as ideal types of rentierism[6] due to the excessive impact of external rents on the national economy, coupled with the negligible existence of any secondary wealth generating activities.[7] Politically, this small-state dynamic in the Gulf has served to amplify the effectiveness of governmental distributive efforts.[8] It is also notable that ideological dispositions rooted in a range of sociopolitical and historical experiences have prompted rent recipients to invest their revenues differently in accordance with their domestic agendas.

More pertinent for this Chapter is the misperception that for oil states the concentration of so much wealth derived from external sources places incontestable powers and resources at the disposal of their ruling establishments.[9] In comparison to extractive administrations in productive economies[10] that rely upon the economic activities of their populations to generate state revenues,[11] it has been argued that a rentier regime fosters a "ruling bargain"[12] between itself and its citizenry whereby the state, in its role as the primary link connecting the

---

the effect of such revenues by overlooking its impact per capita. This oversight negates the economic realities that separate rentier states by haphazardly labeling them all the same. By Herb's measurements, based on per capita indicators, the discrepancies between the oil producing nations become more apparent. Hence, there are rich rentiers and poor rentiers, with countries like Kuwait and the UAE falling into the first category while Angola and Nigeria occupy the latter. Michael Herb, "A Nation of Bureaucrats: Political Participation and Economic Diversification in Kuwait and the United Arab Emirates," *International Journal of Middle East Studies* 41 (2009): pp. 376–377.

[6] Hootan Shambayati, "The Rentier State, Interest Groups, and the Paradox of Autonomy: State and Business in Turkey and Iran," *Comparative Politics* 26 (1994): 310.

[7] Mahdavy, "Patterns and Problems," p. 431.

[8] F. Gregory Gause, *Oil Monarchies: Domestic and Security Challenges in the Arab Gulf States* (New York: Council on Foreign Relations Press, 1994), p. 42.

[9] Gause, *Oil Monarchies*, p. 42.

[10] Alexander A. Cooley, "Booms and Busts: Theorizing Institutional Formation and Change in Oil States," *Review of Institutional Political Economy* 8 (2001): 166.

[11] Dirk J. Vandewalle, *Libya Since Independence: Oil and State-Building* (London: I. B. Tauris, 1998), p. 18.

[12] Wanda Krause, "Gender and Participation in the Gulf," Kuwait Programme on Development, Governance and Globalisation in the Gulf States, No. 4, London School of Economics and Political Science, 2009, p. 20.

local economy to external rents,[13] allocates its income to support the well-being of its nationals.

Of course, these allotments are far from indicative of a charitable ruling establishment. The most credible inference is that these distributive domestic policies by oil-receiving regimes discourage political discourse and invite compliance to spread among their people.[14] Through the mechanisms of allocation, the rentier government aspires to depoliticize the public and alleviate discord[15] while legitimizing itself as the preeminent central actor in state affairs.[16]

By using astute spending tactics like the allowance or withholding of official funds, "The intention is to provide benefits with the aim of gaining political loyalty or being able to deny such benefits … to those who oppose the government."[17] It is assumed that what this amounts to for all practical intents and purposes is an attempt by the state to purchase popular consent[18] by virtue of the overwhelming resource imbalance between it and the rest of society.[19]

The official instruments of this political co-optation commonly take multiple forms through the conspicuous privileges of citizenship[20] signified by subsidized goods, municipal services,[21] and socialized benefits such as standardized medical care and universal education.[22] Moreover, government employment and periodic gifts in the guise of loans[23] and debt forgiveness[24] epitomize a sense of national entitlement.

---

[13] Shambayati, "The Rentier State," p. 309.
[14] Okruhlik, "Rentier Wealth," p. 308.
[15] Kiren Aziz Chaudhry, "Economic Liberalization and the Lineages of the Rentier State," *Comparative Politics* 27 (1994): 18–19.
[16] Cooley, "Booms and Busts," p. 166.
[17] Gause, *Oil Monarchies*, p. 43.
[18] Wanda Krause, *Women in Civil Society: The State, Islamism, and Networks in The UAE* (New York: St. Martin's Press, 2008), p. 21.
[19] Steffen Hertog, "The Sociology of the Gulf Rentier Systems: Societies of Intermediaries," *Comparative Studies in Society and History* 52 (2010): 285.
[20] Cooley, "Booms and Busts," p. 166.
[21] Chaudhry, "Economic Liberalization," p. 18.
[22] Sulayman S. al-Qudsi, "Pre and Post-Fiscal Distributional Patterns in Kuwait," *Middle Eastern Studies* 17 (1981): 401.
[23] Chaudhry, "Economic Liberalization," p. 18.
[24] Gause, *Oil Monarchies*, p. 61.

Yet, what this reductionist approach creates is an acute overemphasis on a "top down dynamic"[25] that leads to assumptions about rentierism's effects on individuals without actually exploring the options available for individual agency. Although the rentier state is not internally extractive it nonetheless must be well entrenched in local affairs and not be set apart from society;[26] otherwise, it would be unable to dole out its surpluses with any degree of efficiency.

But in small states like Kuwait with expansive bureaucracies that employ all but a fraction of the nationalized populations,[27] nearly everyone enjoys some sort of privileged access to the state and its resources.[28] From ubiquitous civil servants and "paper pushers"[29] to midlevel technocrats and administrative fiefdoms[30] there are seemingly endless ranks of intermediaries standing between citizens and services.[31]

With so many opportunities for brokerage and influence peddling, a condition intensified by such bureaucratic vastness that proper channels and efficiency are either not forthcoming or altogether absent without personal intervention,[32] individual rent-seeking becomes a standardized, day-to-day modus operandi for those who require basic public amenities as well as even more discretionary dispensations.[33]

Therefore, the rentier image of social dormancy that is presumed to result from the state's distributive munificence is shortsighted and neglects the fact that these civic properties are oftentimes unevenly dispatched and guarded

---

[25] Pete W. Moore and Bassel F. Salloukh, "Struggles under Authoritarianism: Regimes, States, and Professional Associations in the Arab World," *International Journal of Middle East Studies* 39 (2007): 59.
[26] Okruhlik, "Rentier Wealth," pp. 308–309.
[27] Hertog, "The Sociology of the Gulf," p. 286.
[28] Steffen Hertog, "Segmented Clientelism: The Political Economy of Saudi Economic Reform Efforts," in *Saudi Arabia in the Balance: Political Economy, Society, Foreign Affairs*, eds. Paul Aarts and Gerd Nonneman (New York: New York University Press, 2005), pp. 130–131.
[29] Hertog, "The Sociology of the Gulf," p. 292.
[30] Hertog, "Segmented Clientelism," p. 131.
[31] Gause, *Oil Monarchies*, p. 60.
[32] Hertog, "The Sociology of the Gulf," pp. 291, 306.
[33] Vandewalle, *Libya Since Independence*, p. 24.

within closed, personalized networks[34] that easily transpose any distinctions between the private and the public.[35]

Rentier Distribution: Selective and Unequal Allocations in Kuwait

While it is true that in Kuwait there are wide-ranging perks that affect the citizenry, such as guaranteed civil service employment,[36] particular support is directed toward specific groups such as the old merchant families[37] and the tribes in the hopes of securing their political cooperation.[38]

On the one hand, this scenario is the basis for conventional rentier analysis: The local distribution of externally derived rents in exchange for popular obedience toward the state.[39] Yet this analysis also pinpoints exactly why the rentier approach demands further examination. The unequal disbursement of payments and privileges,[40] rather than breeding passivity and contentment, actually cultivates resentment and discord. It was along these same lines that Gwenn Okruhlik attested that

> [The] long-stated corollary of the observation that distribution replaces extraction as the primary function of the state is that oil wealth can be distributed and used to placate potential dissent. Thus, the government can effectively buy off opposition. Yet in Saudi Arabia, Kuwait, and Bahrain opposition has arisen and

---

[34] Alena V. Ledeneva, *Russia's Economy of Favours: Blat, Networking and Informal Exchange* (Cambridge: Cambridge University Press, 1998), pp. 100–101.
[35] Vadim Volkov, "Patrimonialism versus Rational Bureaucracy: On the Historical Relativity of Corruption," in *Bribery and Blat in Russia: Negotiating Reciprocity from the Middle Ages to the 1990s*, eds. Stephen Lovell, Andrei Rogachevski, and Alena Ledeneva (New York: St. Martin's Press, 2000), p. 38.
[36] Mary Ann Tetreault, *Stories of Democracy: Politics and Society in Contemporary Kuwait* (New York: Columbia University Press, 2000), p. 156.
[37] Gause, *Oil Monarchies*, pp. 54–57.
[38] Nicolas Gavrielides, "Tribal Democracy: The Anatomy of Parliamentary Elections in Kuwait," in *Elections in the Middle East: Implications of Recent Trends*, ed. Linda L. Layne (Boulder, CO: Westview Press, 1987), p. 160.
[39] Okruhlik, "Rentier Wealth," pp. 295–297.
[40] Cooley, "Booms and Busts," p. 166.

with it a discrepancy between the expectations derived from the rentier framework and empirical reality. Not simply the receipt of oil revenue, but the choices made on how to spend it shape development...The rentier framework has proven inadequate in elucidating the rise of dissent because it reifies the state and overemphasizes state resources and autonomy from the social consequences of expenditures.[41]

Thus, instead of merely buying the citizenry's affections, the rentier state's position as the overwhelming source of national wealth places it at the forefront of debates when questions arise over its spending habits.[42] Hence, while the rentier framework is suggestive of the state's immunity from its citizenry's appeals,[43] it cannot assume or guarantee the public's quiescence when the official distributive mechanisms are skewed in the favor of so few.[44] Even in Kuwait, where the ruling family has been keen to dispense state monies in accordance with its political agendas, these programs have not passed unnoticed.

Perhaps the first high profile case that exposed the ruling al-Sabah family to accusations of malfeasance with the public treasury was the Land Purchase Program of the late 1950s and early 1960s, a thinly veiled reallocation of state funds to private accounts under the pretext of urban development.[45] John Daniels neatly described this ploy as one in which "the government purchased the land on which construction or development was to take place at a very inflated price, and a minority of nationals exploited the advantage of buying and reselling land at a very handsome profit. Some officials, with inside knowledge of future developments, were reputed to have staked their claims on sites which they knew construction was to take place."[46]

---

[41] Okruhlik, "Rentier Wealth," pp. 296–297.
[42] Vandewalle, *Libya Since Independence*, p. 27.
[43] Krause, "Gender and Participation," p. 20.
[44] Okruhlik, "Rentier Wealth," pp. 296–297.
[45] Ragaei El Mallakh, "Planning in a Capital Surplus Economy: Kuwait," *Land Economics* 42 (1966): 427.
[46] al-Qudsi, "Pre and Post-Fiscal," p. 403.

A reward to the wealthy meant to secure their loyalty and gratitude toward the regime,[47] the Land Purchase Program reinforced the pre-oil dominance of the mercantile elites and their tribal counterparts in local dealings.[48] But to appreciate the sheer magnitude of these initial transfers of capital and the costs associated with privatizing public assets, the following report by the International Bank for Reconstruction and Development is instructive.

> In 1959 the amount spent on land was roughly double the increment to public foreign investments.... During the six and a quarter years ending March 31, 1963, over KD295 million was spent by the Government to acquire land, or more than a third of total government income. Over the same period, the increase in public foreign investments was about KD140 million, or 16 percent of government revenue.
>
> From a financial standpoint, in addition to the fact that over 50 percent more has been spent on land in the last six years than on capital projects, a striking fact is the relatively small amount which the Government has obtained from the resale of land or from rentals on government-owned property. Despite the fact that the housing program would seem to provide for the turnover of a good deal of this land, only KD15.4 million or about 5 percent of the cost of land acquired by the Government has been recovered by sale in the last six years.[49]

Clearly, though, the government had no intention of recovering its investments in any way that would have been measurable by monetary standards. Rather, its aim was to placate the old merchant families and those close enough to the al-Sabah family to be privy to its designs.[50]

---

[47] Tetreault, *Stories of Democracy*, p. 156.
[48] Gause, *Oil Monarchies*, p. 54.
[49] International Bank for Reconstruction and Development (IRBD), *The Economic Development of Kuwait* (Baltimore: The Johns Hopkins University Press, 1965), pp. 88–89.
[50] Jill Crystal, *Oil and Politics in the Gulf: Rulers and Merchants in Kuwait and Qatar* (Cambridge: Cambridge University Press, 1995), pp. 76–77. El Mallakh remarked that several years after the original land purchases were made from the wealthy landholders the state began to direct its acquisitions in such a way that included low and middle income property owners. Nevertheless, the budgetary allocations for these later purchases were comparatively reduced

In less than two decades after the commencement of the Land Purchase Program, the government was again afforded several opportunities to funnel its state monies into specifically targeted private pockets. In 1977, the prices of shares on the Kuwait Stock Exchange (KSE) collapsed due to pervasive speculation and a preponderance of postdated checks. The government swiftly stepped in and compensated traders for their losses with a bailout of over KD150 million.[51]

However, at this time the country's market operated on single transactions of large quantities of stocks — minimally one thousand shares per exchange that, in practice, barred the involvement of small investors. As a result, once the bottom fell out and the treasury propped it back up, hundreds of merchants were saved from bankruptcy[52] while ordinary Kuwaitis watched.

But only a few years later, the average citizen would have a chance to venture into the market, hopeful in the knowledge that the government had already shown that it would not allow for a financial catastrophe, self-induced or not, to cripple its populace.[53] Thus, with oil prices soaring, public spending multiplying, and few outlets available for domestic investment[54] since the KSE remained limited to the old families,[55] a parallel market arose in the al-Manakh building that catered to newcomers.[56]

(See El Mallakh, "Planning in a Capital Surplus," p. 431), and it can be assumed that the financial impact for individual families was only slight given that the highly lucrative downtown properties were already in the hands of the connected classes. See Crystal, *Oil and Politics*, pp. 76–77.
[51] Abdelghani A. Elimam, Maurice Girgis, and Samir Katob, "A Solution to Post Crash Debt Entanglements in Kuwait's al-Manakh Stock Market," *Interfaces* 27 (1997): 90.
[52] Crystal, *Oil and Politics*, 97.
[53] Mohammad A. al-Yahya, *Kuwait: Fall and Rebirth* (London: Kegan Paul International, 1993), p. 76.
[54] Elimam *et al.*, "A Solution," p. 90.
[55] Crystal, *Oil and Politics*, p. 98. As almost a matter of propriety, these established families guarded the market and traded privately amongst themselves. In this closed market, the "system of dealing …[worked] well as a mechanism for moving large sums of money among a small number of investors." See Ayman Shafiq Fayyad Abdul-Hadi, *Stock Markets of the Arab World: Trends, Problems and Prospects for Integration* (London: Routledge, 1988), p. 44.
[56] Fida Darwiche, *The Gulf Stock Exchange Crash: The Rise and Fall of the Souq Al-Manakh* (London: Croom Helm, 1986), p. 95.

Absent of any regulatory oversight, Suq al-Manakh, as it came to be known, avoided the state's safeguards that limited the participation of companies,[57] brokers,[58] and investors[59] in the KSE.[60] In this anarchic trading environment, fictitious Gulf companies that existed only on paper[61] were bought and sold with either postdated checks[62] without a deferment period or traded for real assets. When an investor tried to cash a check for KD55 million from one of al-Manakh's largest traders before it was due, the account was found to be insolvent and the market crashed[63] under the weight of a $94 billion debt that was over four times the amount of the country's GDP.[64]

In spite of this crisis, the government did not respond with the same sense of urgency as it did during the 1977 meltdown that paralyzed the merchants' banking activities. The leadership, though, was rightfully cautious given the enormity of the sums involved,[65] the lack of any standard accounting methods,[66] and the illegality of the whole 1982 predicament.[67] Besides, the

---

[57] In 1977 the government banned the creation of new public companies to boost the market for existing firms. Also, Gulf companies that were not incorporated in Kuwait were prohibited from being traded on the KSE. See Darwiche, *The Gulf Stock Exchange*, pp. 54–57.

[58] Most of the brokers in Suq al-Manakh "were ignorant about the nature of the work of a stock exchange. Land and property brokers by origin, when share trading was introduced, they automatically changed to the new business. Moreover, they were mostly interested parties, since they took stakes in the companies they traded. Stripped of the impartiality of disinterested advisers, they promoted those companies in which they were personally interested." See Darwiche, *The Gulf Stock Exchange*, p. 60.

[59] In addition to those citizens excluded from the legal market by the old merchant families (See Abdul-Hadi, *Stock Markets*, 44), al-Manakh was also available to non-Kuwaitis who were prevented from directly accessing the official market. See al-Yahya, *Kuwait*, p. 32.

[60] Abdul-Hadi, *Stock Markets*, pp. 21–26.

[61] Abdelghani A. Elimam, Maurice Girgis, and Samir Kotob, "The Use of Linear Programming in Disentangling the Bankruptcies of Al-Manakh Stock Market Crash," *Operations Research* 44 (1996): 666.

[62] A postdated check premium of 60 to 300 percent was added to spot prices to compensate sellers for their delayed payment. See Elimam *et al.*, "A Solution," p. 91. Some of these checks bore future dates that ranged from months to years. See Darwiche, *The Gulf Stock Exchange*, p. 60.

[63] Darwiche, *The Gulf Stock Exchange*, pp. 60–61, 88.

[64] Elimam *et al.*, "A Solution," p. 92.

[65] Darwiche, *The Gulf Stock Exchange*, p. 101.

[66] Abdelghani A. Elimam, Maurice Girgis, and Samir Kotob, "The Use of Linear Programming," p. 666.

[67] al-Yahya, *Kuwait*, p. 33.

government realized that it was ill-equipped to tackle a problem on this scale by itself, so it called upon the services of the one concern that still remained unscathed: The elite dominated Kuwait Chamber of Commerce and Industry (KCCI),[68] whose representatives enjoyed access to the official market[69] and did not have to resort to al-Manakh.

The inclusion of these traditional power brokers allowed the KCCI merchants to regain some of their hold over the country's policies that they had lost in the post-oil years after the state replaced them as the nation's employer and welfare provider.[70] For instance, to manage the fallout from al-Manakh, the Supreme Planning Council was formed with seven of its ten independent members drawn from the KCCI. Next, in 1986, "direct pleas by KCCI president al-Sagr resulted in the creation of the Economic Reactivation Committee, a high-level advisory board of KCCI board members and state technocrats. The state also reversed its controversial personnel decisions of the 1970s by appointing KCCI loyalists and eventually the director-general of the KCCI to head key economic ministries."[71]

As expected, the old guard seized this turn of events as a chance to reassert its control over the private economy while penalizing the upstarts who had facilitated the al-Manakh debacle — a class of investors who were depicted as "new speculators with little to lose, people of modest origins or former civil servants, who seized an unrepeatable opportunity to improve their financial status. The majority of those involved in al-Manakh belonged to the families of the nouveaux riches rather than to the traditionally wealthy families prominent in the economy and in major businesses."[72]

Despite any evident conflict of interests, the principals of the KCCI also oversaw the Kuwait Clearing and Financial Settlements Company and

---

[68] Pete W. Moore, "What Makes Successful Business Lobbies? Business Associations and the Rentier State in Jordan and Kuwait," *Comparative Politics* 33 (2001): pp. 137–138.
[69] Crystal, *Oil and Politics*, p. 100.
[70] Jill Crystal, "Coalitions in Oil Monarchies: Kuwait and Qatar," *Comparative Politics* 21 (1989): 434.
[71] Moore, "What Makes Successful Business Lobbies," p. 137.
[72] Darwiche, *The Gulf Stock Exchange*, p. 95.

acted as legal agents for 85 percent of the debtors, a process that strengthened the KCCI's position as an intermediary between the government and its citizens.[73]

More profitably, though, the merchants' involvement yielded significant incentives. In 1983, over the course of only two months, the state injected a sum of KD250 million into the commercial establishment's preferred official stock market.[74] In addition, the succession of bankruptcies that followed in the wake of al-Manakh[75] transferred extensive newly moneyed properties back to the business aristocracy at liquidation prices, and the declining economy even convinced the government to reintroduce its Land Purchase Program.[76]

The cordial working relationship with the state throughout the entire al-Manakh episode also led the merchants to marginalize their counterparts[77] and pursue more restrictive policy measures to protect their own trade interests.[78] As just one example of this, the 1983 Decree on the Regulation of the Kuwait Stock Exchange instituted the Market Management Committee

---

[73] Moore, "What Makes Successful Business Lobbies," pp. 138–139. Illustrating the suspect motives of the KCCI in its role as mediator and whether it represented its clients' best interests is a meeting that was held between its finance committee and the cabinet economic committee. In this session, the KCCI representatives sought to cease further bankruptcies and lower the debts of existent bankrupts. Not only was this proposal unlawful but "creditors of bankrupts would have suffered an injustice, in that they would have incurred a part of their debtors' insolvency. The injustice would have been flagrant, because dozens of other creditors had received what they were owed in full through the [Security] Fund. A double standard would have been created between those who had recovered their monies in full and those asked to make sacrifices." See Darwiche, *The Gulf Stock Exchange*, p. 120. Nevertheless, the passage of Law 100/1983 was indicative of the KCCI agenda (See Moore, "What Makes Successful Business Lobbies," p. 139): a ceiling of 25 percent on postdated check premiums. Debtors who settled before this law lost money by paying a higher premium as well as losing the premiums they had expected to collect as creditors (See al-Yahya, *Kuwait*, pp. 41, 76). Thus, for the dealers caught in the middle, having paid their debts in full but now legally bound to collect only one quarter of their outstanding dues, bankruptcies "followed one another ... in a chain reaction." See Darwiche, *The Gulf Stock Exchange*, p. 127.

[74] al-Yahya, *Kuwait*, p. 38.

[75] Elimam *et al.*, "The Use of Linear Programming," 666; Darwiche, *The Gulf Stock Exchange*, p. 127.

[76] Crystal, *Oil and Politics*, p. 100.

[77] Pete W. Moore, *Doing Business in the Middle East: Politics and Economic Crisis in Jordan and Kuwait* (Cambridge: Cambridge University Press, 2004), pp. 134–135.

[78] Crystal, *Oil and Politics*, p. 100.

and mandated that four of its 12 members be taken from the ranks of the KCCI.[79] Entrusted with overseeing the market and approving brokers' applications as well as setting the fees for new brokerage companies,[80] the committee gave its KCCI majority recognizable leverage in the post-parallel market. This correlates well with Crystal's conclusion that once al-Manakh was contained, ultimately it was the "older merchants [who] had thus benefited from the crisis."[81]

The last serious disruption to this implicit "business as usual" domestic rule commenced in the early hours of 2 August 1990, as Iraqi units poured across the border into Kuwait. Coming after many seasons of internal turmoil — the al-Manakh collapse, the unresolved suspension of the National Assembly in 1986, and the continued calls by pro-democracy activists for reforms — the regime could not have been in a weaker position as it fled the country.

Once in Saudi Arabia, however, the exiled government quickly moved to prepare the groundwork for its return. Politically, it appeased the opposition by pledging to restore the constitution[82] and reinstate the National Assembly upon liberation.[83] On the other hand, more pressing was the issue of how to reestablish the relations that had endorsed the status quo for so long. To this end, the regime symbolically reached out to the old merchants and selected KCCI Chairman Abd al-Aziz al-Sager to speak on behalf of the people at the October 1990 Jeddah Conference, an event staged to show the world that the legitimacy of the ruling al-Sabah family was backed by popular solidarity.[84]

But to regain its grasp on local affairs the government had to do more than publicly reconcile with its critics; it had to reaffirm its own pre-war function

---

[79] Darwiche, *The Gulf Stock Exchange*, p. 128.
[80] Abdul-Hadi, *Stock Markets*, pp. 27–28.
[81] Crystal, *Oil and Politics*, p. 100.
[82] Tetreault, *Stories of Democracy*, pp. 78–79, pp. 81–85.
[83] Rosemarie Said Zahlan, *The Making of the Modern Gulf States: Kuwait, Bahrain, Qatar, the United Arab Emirates, and Oman* (Reading: Garnet Publishing, 1998), p. 54.
[84] Ghanim Alnajjar, "The Challenges Facing Kuwaiti Democracy," *Middle East Journal* 54 (2000): 253–254.

as the nation's unrivaled distributor[85] despite the fact that the invasion had erased its capital surplus and driven the regime to seek loans.[86] Accordingly,

> The amir worked hard to adopt the prewar strategy of placating the population economically. Despite severe economic constraints, the government announced it would pay all existing consumer loans, car loans, and mortgage loans to Kuwaitis, pay back salaries to government employees for the occupation period, exempt Kuwaitis from utility and other public service charges and rents incurred during the occupation, and increase government entitlements in a variety of categories (marriage grants, child allowances, aid to orphans, widows and the poor). In March 1992 the government granted a 25 percent salary increase to all Kuwaitis in the public sector. It also bailed out the ailing banking sector.[87]

Supplementing this general welfare package for the populace were several initiatives intended to rescue and mollify the nation's commercial establishment.

Included in the post-invasion bank bailout was a provision for the government to purchase the debts of investment houses. All told, this would have cost the treasury an estimated $20 billion[88] and, as was to be expected, the KCCI was very supportive of this plan. Later, the National Assembly amended the original proposal[89] although it accepted a revised version from the KCCI in 1995.[90]

In the rush to rebuild the country, the government also oversaw several modifications to its existing trade policies that appealed directly to the interests of the old families. Former housing minister Ibrahim Shahin was entrusted with approving all reconstruction contracts, a task for which he was woefully inept,

---

[85] Crystal, *Oil and Politics*, p. 178.
[86] Jacqueline S. Ismael, *Kuwait: Dependency and Class in a Rentier State* (Gainesville, FL: University Press of Florida, 1993), p. 175.
[87] Crystal, *Oil and Politics*, p. 178.
[88] Ismael, *Kuwait*, p. 175.
[89] Gause, *Oil Monarchies*, p. 56.
[90] Moore, "What Makes Successful Business Lobbies," p. 139.

and many believed that his appointment was orchestrated by the country's merchants to ease their access to lucrative state contracts.[91]

Whether this was actually the case or not, the annulment of the Public Tenders Law No. 37 lowered many of the barriers between contractors and public monies, particularly the prohibition on direct negotiation for tendering that bypassed the Central Tenders Committee's powers of review[92] that were in place to control the use of government money.[93] With a price tag of up to $30 billion[94] there were ample enticements for businessmen to take part in the rebuilding efforts[95] now that they could operate unimpeded by procedural supervision.

The preceding examples are illustrative of selective allocation on the part of the Kuwaiti government — a discretionary dispensation of its revenues[96] according to its prevailing inclinations and needs.[97] Moreover, as the aforementioned cases illustrate, these inclinations are hardly equitable despite any ideals to the contrary.

In 1996, parliamentarian Ahmad al-Sadun spoke out against the Kuwait Investment Authority, accusing the state of "simply selling its assets to a select number of Kuwait's elite."[98] Just a few years earlier, the Kuwait Investment Office, chaired by Shaykh Fahad Muhammad al-Sabah, could not account for several billion dollars ventured in Spain.[99] In the ensuing outcry, National Assembly member Abdallah al-Nobari said disparagingly that "it seems that some members of the Kuwaiti royal family just helped themselves to a financial grab equivalent to Saddam Hussein's invasion."[100]

---

[91] Tetreault, *Stories of Democracy*, pp. 85–86.
[92] John O. Gerald, "Legal Aspects of Doing Business in Kuwait," *Arab Law Quarterly* 6 (1991): 328.
[93] Arab Law Quarterly, "Kuwait: Government Tendering Procedures," *Arab Law Quarterly* 4 (1985): 460.
[94] Huda H. al-Bahar, "Kuwait's Post-War Reconstruction," *Mimar* 40 (1991): 15.
[95] Tetreault, *Stories of Democracy*, p. 86.
[96] Vandewalle, *Libya Since Independence*, p. 27.
[97] Gause, *Oil Monarchies*, p. 43.
[98] Tetreault, *Stories of Democracy*, p. 189.
[99] Crystal, *Oil and Politics*, p. 177.
[100] Roger Cohen, "Missing Millions — Kuwait's Bad Bet — A Special Report: Big Wallets and Little Supervision," *The New York Times*, 28 September 1993, C1.

Not surprisingly, "while the development of oil contributed to a tremendous growth and proliferation of the economy, it has simultaneously generated all kinds of inequalities."[101] These disparities become even more amplified against the arbitrary nature of state allocations, as the examples cited above[102] have shown, a characteristic of rent distribution in the Gulf states that is aided by opaque bureaucratic channels and restricted magisterial access.[103]

Rentier Channels of Accessibility: The Case for Agency in Kuwait's Distributive Apparatus

In Kuwait, the confluence of colossal national wealth, limited non-state productive capacities, and the near total reliance by local populations on public services in the forms of jobs and subsidies[104] have made the state a near constant focal point for its citizenry.

Indeed, it is certainly plausible that this civic scrutiny is heightened given that the state is the sole recipient of all oil-generated rents[105] and the selective dispenser of these revenues[106] via unequal and, at times, obscure avenues. Such traits, Alena Ledeneva argues, lead to "closed distribution systems" that "are closed particularly in terms of information. Whereas privileges are common knowledge, there is no open information about the criteria for entitlement, services, and rations."[107] Combined with the absence of administrative impartiality at any level of government, from the routine daily offices for licenses and permits to the more specialized requests that require higher-ranking intervention,[108] it becomes a regular expectation that informal

---

[101] Fuad I. Khuri, *Tribe and State in Bahrain: The Transformation of Social and Political Authority in an Arab State* (Chicago: The University of Chicago Press, 1990), p. 152.
[102] Vandewalle, *Libya Since Independence*, p. 27.
[103] Hertog, "The Sociology of the Gulf," p. 292.
[104] *Ibid.*, pp. 285–286.
[105] Khuri, *Tribe and State*, p. 153.
[106] Vandewalle, *Libya Since Independence*, p. 27.
[107] Ledeneva, *Russia's Economy of Favours*, p. 100.
[108] Ralph E. Crow, "Confessionalism, Public Administration, and Efficiency in Lebanon," *Politics in Lebanon*, ed. Leonard Binder (New York: John Wiley & Sons, 1966), pp. 174–175.

and personalized connections must constantly be sought to mediate transactions between the citizen and the state.[109]

This process of deploying one's contacts in order to make some desired result come to fruition requires the discriminative use of *wasta*, a colloquial usage of the formal Arabic *waseet*,[110] the root of which means "middle,"[111] although in actual practice it functionally denotes "either mediation or intercession …[both] the person who mediates/intercedes as well as the act of mediation/intercession."[112]

Not infrequently, *wasta* has taken on a less constructive tone to indicate the promotion of individual, private interests that circumvent formal procedures and potentially deprive others of their rights.[113] *Wasta* in this sense entails the deployment of influential liaisons on one's behalf to secure some benefits that, without *wasta*, might not have been reasonably attainable.[114]

While this may, at first glance, appear to insinuate that petitioners are always trying to stake their claims to entitlements that are rightfully owed to others — although this does happen more often than not[115] — it is also true that supplicants must regularly seek agents simply to find any satisfaction in their legitimate dealings with government offices.[116]

For Kuwait, whenever there are the inevitable meetings that bring the nation's inhabitants into contact with the state's hierarchical agencies, it is expected that some intermediary *wasta* will have to be sought. In the brief narratives below, the need for *wasta* and the admittances it can provide permeates every level of Kuwaiti society regardless of citizenship. In the first instance, the experience of Faisal, a very well-connected retiree, highlights some of these

---

[109] Hertog, "The Sociology of the Gulf," p. 284.
[110] Jihad Makhoul and Lindsey Harrison, "Intercessory *Wasta* and Village Development in Lebanon," *Arab Studies Quarterly* 26 (2004): 25.
[111] Hertog, "The Sociology of the Gulf," p. 289.
[112] Robert B. Cunningham and Yasin K. Sarayrah, "Taming Wasta to Achieve Development," *Arab Studies Quarterly* 16 (1994): 29.
[113] Saeda Kilani and Basem Sakijha, *Wasta: The Declared Secret* (Amman: Jordan Press Foundation Printing Press, 2002), pp. 18–20.
[114] Makhoul and Harrison, "Intercessory *Wasta*," pp. 25–27.
[115] Carrie Rosefsky Wickham, *Mobilizing Islam: Religion, Activism, and Political Change in Egypt* (New York: Columbia University Press, 2002), p. 55.
[116] Kilani and Sakijha, *Wasta*, p. 32.

arrangements as they are used to expedite the government's public coverage of its populous.

Faisal once held a low-level governmental post. When he was active in this position, he developed an impressive number of contacts within the different ministries. Today, people visit Faisal precisely for his access to this broad range of decision-makers. Faisal finds himself regularly out during the day calling on people all at the request of others.

One of Faisal's acquaintances, Abu Bakr, provides a good example of Faisal's networking capabilities. Faisal and Abu Baker first met one afternoon when they both happened to be visiting the Ministry of Health. In the hallway outside of the personnel offices, Abu Bakr lamented to Faisal that for the past three months he had been trying to get his paperwork signed but, regrettably, he did not know any of the managers or directors. Faisal, from his previous work, was on personal terms with the director that Abu Bakr needed. He took Abu Bakr's papers and returned them to him, signed, within an hour.[117]

Given these complications that the citizenry faces in its dealings with the bureaucracy, it is not unexpected that for expatriates there are also considerable barriers that hinder those trying to find their way through the state's immense networks of regulatory offices and redundant paperwork. Like the urban laborers and working classes that Suad Joseph depicts in Lebanon, Kuwait's foreign workforce also must confront an obstructive bureaucracy as they are burdened by the weight of their substantial "handicaps: lack of time, money and resources, the likelihood of illegal statuses, and negative past encounters with public officials."[118]

These obstacles, and the means by which to resolve them, are all present in the commentary of Tamer M., a young Pakistani man from Lahore employed in Kuwait's private sector as an office assistant, who expressed his aggravations with trying to get a driver's permit.

> If I get my [driver's] license I will buy a car to get around; it will make going to work and coming home easier because right now I

---

[117] Interview recorded in Kuwait City, Kuwait, 3 March 2007.
[118] Suad Joseph, "Working the Law: A Lebanese Working-Class Case," in *Law and Islam in the Middle East*, ed. Daisy Hilse Dwyer (New York: Bergin and Garvey, 1990), p. 145.

have to ride with friends. I have stayed on [at] my new job for nine months and I have my [civil identification] card, but even with the card it is hard to get a driving license. I have tried many times [to get one] but they want more papers... signed from many ministries and offices. My friend at work is Kuwaiti and he knows someone he can give my papers to. I think this will take care of it.[119]

Comments like these by Faisal and Tamer M. make it unmistakable that *wasta*, whether manifest as trustworthy connections[120] or outright favoritism,[121] defines those junctures where the interests of the state, the polity, and the body politic all intersect. It is, in Frederick Charles Huxley's estimation, the linkage that "operates on and between [the] micro and macro levels"[122] of society.

But what becomes increasingly apparent in these accounts of *wasta* is that it is infused with the qualitative attributes of interpersonal aid. Although it distinctly exudes the veneer of what some have called dependency[123] and others have criticized as the trappings of nepotism[124] or corruption,[125] such labels ignore the fundamental centrality that relationships occupy in a country like Kuwait.

From the self-framed image at the state level, where leadership and governance are personified[126] rather than cast in abstract institutions,[127] to

---

[119] Interview recorded in Kuwait City, Kuwait, 17 November 2007.
[120] Kilani and Sakijha, *Wasta*, p. 20.
[121] Sylvia Haladjian-Henriksen, "Social Stratification Obstacles to Reducing Inequality and Alleviating Poverty: The Case of Lebanon," in *Poverty and Social Deprivation in the Mediterranean: Trends, Policies, and Welfare Prospects in the New Millennium*, eds. Maria Petmesidou and Christos Papatheodorou (London: Zed Books, 2006), p. 315.
[122] Frederick Charles Huxley, "Wasita in a Lebanese Context: Social Exchange among Villagers and Outsiders," *Anthropological Papers* 64 (University of Michigan, 1978): 12.
[123] Volker Perthes, *The Political Economy of Syria under Asad* (New York: St. Martin's Press, 1997), p. 181.
[124] Haladjian-Henriksen, "Social Stratification Obstacles," p. 315.
[125] Kilani and Sakijha, *Wasta*, p. 17.
[126] Zahlan, *The Making of the Modern*, p. 79.
[127] Mohammad Ali Al Oudat and Ayman Alshboul, "'Jordan First': Tribalism, Nationalism and Legitimacy of Power in Jordan," *Intellectual Discourse* 18 (2010): 71.

the complications of "meritocratic individualism"[128] in a social climate in which "mutual favor-doing"[129] is simultaneously a marker of success[130] and a community expectation,[131] any boundaries that would delineate individual concerns and the dynamics of kinship from the business of statecraft and industry[132] are either unclear[133] or completely negotiable.[134]

Further distorting any structural lines that would demarcate where the "webs of informality"[135] end and the offices of state begin is Nazih Ayubi's view that throughout the Gulf, "just as the *état providence* is also an *état famille*, the *raison d'état* is not easily distinguishable from the *raison de famille*."[136] What must be added to Ayubi's reasoning is that the synthesis of the *raison d'état* and the *raison de famille* becomes possible only once the former has been loaded with the same "moral and emotional content"[137] as the latter.

---

[128] Andrew Shryock and Sally Howell, "'Ever a Guest in Our House': The Emir Abdullah, Shaykh Majid al-Adwan, and the Practice of Jordanian House Politics, as Remembered by Umm Sultan, the Widow of Majid," *International Journal of Middle East Studies* 33 (2001): 266.

[129] James A. Bill, "The Plasticity of Informal Politics: The Case of Iran," *Middle East Journal* 27 (1973): 138.

[130] A. Nazir Hamzeh, "Clientalism, Lebanon: Roots and Trends," *Middle Eastern Studies* 37 (2001): 176.

[131] Kilani and Sakijha, *Wasta*, p. 33.

[132] Hisham Sharabi, *Neopatriarchy; A Theory of Distorted Change in Arab Society* (New York: Oxford University Press, 1988), p. 131.

[133] Shryock and Howell, "'Ever a Guest'", p. 249. In this respect it is worthwhile to quote Hisham Sharabi's thoughts on personalized institutions, or what he concluded to be neopatriarchal institutions, in the Middle East: "For the typical bureaucrat, for instance, the workplace (one's office) is no more than an extension of the place of sociability and relaxation. There is little qualitative difference between what goes on in the office or what goes on in the salon, living room, or *diwan* ... .This is not just a pattern of local behavior, but an institutionally embodied and socially prevalent practice. Thus bureaucracy — in government, the military, education, business — projects a modernized exterior, but internally its structure is essentially patriarchal, animated by an elaborate system of personal relations, kinship, and patronage." See Sharabi, *Neopatriarchy*, p. 131.

[134] Paul Kingston, "Patrons, Clients and Civil Society: A Case Study of Environmental Politics in Postwar Lebanon," *Arab Studies Quarterly* 23 (2001): pp. 56–57.

[135] Bill, "The Plasticity," p. 134.

[136] Nazih N. Ayubi, *Over-stating the Arab State: Politics and Society in the Middle East* (London: I. B. Tauris, 2006), p. 229.

[137] Joseph, "Working the Law," p. 144.

Whether or not this is signified through the lexicon of kinship[138] or some alternative device intended to prompt requital, such as gift-giving[139] or visiting,[140] it is the design and management of relational indexes[141] like these that collapse the dichotomies of executive duties and customary commitments.[142] Khaled A. R. qualified this judgment after he took a moment to collect his thoughts on how indispensible connections are for attaining anything in Kuwait. In his opinion,

> Our government is strong in the sense that no one can overthrow it ... [But] it is weak in [its] power .... The government and its laws, the legal system, [are] not respected or feared. [It is] respected by those without *wasta* or relations [because] *wasta* or relations let people get away with things. [Why?] [This is a] small country, everything is built on relationships.[143]

Yet, in a state system like Kuwait in which the government and all of its appendages are at the epicenter of nearly every distributional allowance, from support services to economic provisions,[144] *wasta* can scarcely be expected to exist either entirely independently or far beyond administrative inducements. This is especially true when the pathways through the bureaucracy are littered

---

[138] Suad Joseph, "Connectivity and Patriarchy among Working-Class Arab Families in Lebanon," *Ethos* 21 (1993): 454.
[139] Pierre Bourdieu, "The Sentiment of Honour in Kabyle Society," translated by Philip Sherrard, *Honour and Shame: The Values of Mediterranean Society*, ed. J. G. Peristiany (Chicago: University of Chicago Press, 1966), pp. 204, 206.
[140] Andrea B. Rugh, *Within the Circle; Parents and Children in an Arab Village* (New York: Columbia University Press, 1997), pp. 218–219.
[141] John F. Padgett and Christopher K. Ansell, "Robust Action and the Rise of the Medici, 1400–1432," *American Journal of Sociology* 98 (1993): 1310.
[142] Lawrence Rosen, "Law and Culture in the Popular Legal Culture of North Africa," *Islamic Law and Society* 2 (1995): 201.
[143] Interview recorded in Kuwait City, Kuwait, 22 March 2009.
[144] Jill Crystal, "Civil Society in the Arabian Gulf," in *Civil Society in the Middle East, Volume Two*, ed. Augustus Richard Norton (Leiden: E.J. Brill, 1995), pp. 260, 272.

with "secondary and tertiary"[145] intermediaries who are strategically situated in positions to negotiate the terms of governmental favors.[146]

By recognizing the centrality of the welfare state's place in everyday life, these networks, in one way or another, eventually lead back to a state sponsored patron even though the participating actors might actually regard themselves as being equivalent in status. But this lack of interpersonal differentiation does not mask the unavoidable fact that in the oil-rich Gulf monarchies, "the broader structure[s] in which such relationships are embedded tend to be hierarchical, and by and large societal partners function as clients of the bigger institution involved."[147]

In fact, a redistributive welfare economy like Kuwait's bears a striking likeness to the allocative monopolies that typify command markets.[148] Most illustrative of this similarity is the lopsided public employment sector in Kuwait that provides jobs for 90 percent of the country's citizenry[149] in line with the government being in a position to inundate its nationals with services, subsidies,[150] and favorable business opportunities.[151] Furthermore, attempts toward increased privatization have been staunchly opposed on the grounds that it would seriously undercut the massive dispensational benefits that so many Kuwaitis have grown accustomed to receiving[152] and, it can be supposed,

---

[145] Amaney A. Jamal, *Barriers to Democracy; The Other Side of Social Capital in Palestine and the Arab World* (Princeton, NJ: Princeton University Press, 2007), p. 15.

[146] Samih K. Farsoun, "Family Structure and Society in Modern Lebanon," in *Peoples and Cultures of the Middle East, Volume II: Life in the Cities, Towns, and Countryside*, ed. Louise E. Sweet (Garden City, NY: The Natural History Press, 1970), pp. 275–276.

[147] Hertog, "Segmented Clientelism," 130.

[148] Sheila Fitzpatrick, "Blat in Stalin's Time," in *Bribery and Blat in Russia: Negotiating Reciprocity from the Middle Ages to the 1990s*, ed. Stephen Lovell, Andrei Rogachevski, and Alena Ledeneva (New York: St. Martin's Press, 2000), p. 167.

[149] Shafeeq Ghabra, "Kuwait and the Dynamics of Socio-Economic Change," *Middle East Journal* 51 (1997): 361.

[150] Hertog, "The Sociology of the Gulf," p. 285.

[151] Herb, "A Nation of Bureaucrats," pp. 384–386.

[152] Michael Herb indicates that this great imbalance between the public sector and private enterprises is fermenting "a distinctive form of class conflict in the Gulf in which salaried citizen employees of the state have a jaundiced attitude toward the private sector while the private sector views most citizens as parasites on the state and avoids hiring them." See Herb, "A Nation of Bureaucrats," p. 383.

the intercessional capacities of the well-placed intermediaries who provide these allowances.[153]

This is the point that is the key to understanding the existence of brokerage between state and society in Kuwait: Its top-heavy, unnavigable bureaucracy lends itself to an abundance of go-betweens who possess insider knowledge of how to satisfy most demands.[154]

However, the state's absolute control over the local economy must be included in any formulations of the parameters of Kuwait's *wasta*-type intermediation. What this means is that instead of subjecting one's own assets to petitioners, it is actually the government's resources, already destined for eventual redistribution, that are being sought through the mobilization of these informal relationships; the only personal outlay is accessibility.[155] In addition, these state properties are widely looked upon as belonging to the citizenry[156] despite the difficulties that come with trying to retrieve these resources through formal measures without the right personal backing.[157]

Institutionalizing Credentials in the Rentier Milieu: The Kuwaiti Guestroom

Situated between the individual and the state are the country's ubiquitous guestrooms, or the Kuwaiti *diwaniyya* (pl. *dawawin*), that fill the social spaces

---

[153] Steffen Hertog, "Defying the Resource Curse: Explaining Successful State-Owned Enterprises in Rentier States," *World Politics* 62 (2010): 287–288. One of the most notorious liaisons acting between the state and its nationals is a politician who is diminutively regarded locally as "al-Hout," or "The Whale," due to his ability to funnel large sums of government *wasta* into his own personal networks.

[154] Hertog, "The Sociology of the Gulf," pp. 291–292.

[155] Alena V. Ledeneva, "Continuity and Change of Blat Practices in Soviet and Post-Soviet Russia," in *Bribery and Blat in Russia; Negotiating Reciprocity from the Middle Ages to the 1990s*, ed. Stephen Lovell *et al.* (New York: St. Martin's Press, 2000), pp. 185, 188. This description of how *wasta* operates in Kuwait is closely linked to Alena Ledeneva's remarks on Soviet era *blat*: "By helping out, people gave out not goods of their own, but benefits of which the other was deprived." See Ledeneva, "Continuity and Change," p. 190.

[156] Ledeneva, *Russia's Economy of Favours*, p. 101.

[157] Hertog, "The Sociology of the Gulf," p. 303.

that have been called the "raw material of politics"[158] to denote the utility of ostensibly non-political institutions in shaping political capital. These forums cannot be overlooked as indispensible resources for providing attendees with avenues to access and trade and to apply influence in its various manifestations.

Valerie Marcel succinctly summarized these tendencies and their effects for the Kuwait Petroleum Company:

> Diwaniyyas are the channel through which *wasta* is exercised and special favors are granted. *Wasta* can help KPC by enabling its professionals to appeal to MPs in these informal networks and counter pressure from other, interfering MPs. The diwaniyya practice has strong potential applications to the extent that it allows informal relationships across the formal hierarchy. It is also a place in which to raise awareness of problems, to debate issues, and to promote a better understanding of the needs of the oil industry. On the other hand, some favors are detrimental to the NOC [National Offset Company] because they are won through the diwaniyya-*wasta* channel and bypass regular management processes. For example, favors sometimes involve granting a job to someone who is not qualified. Thus it is important for KPC to insulate its management decisions from the social pressure of these networks.[159]

Certainly, these *dawawin* are the country's veritable marketplaces through which brokers with resources negotiate their petitioners' requests. They do not deal at the level of solitary individuals, but through an institution in which membership or attendance can confer the valued credentials[160] needed to tap into the repertoire of privileges that the rentier state can provide.

In the spheres of Kuwaiti politics, the intervention of group solidarities within the *dawawin* to restrict the pool of candidates contending for the

---

[158] J. A. Barnes, "Networks and Political Process," in *Local-Level Politics: Social and Cultural Perspectives*, ed. Marc J. Swartz (London: University of London Press, 1969), p. 107.

[159] Valerie Marcel, *Oil Titans: National Oil Companies in the Middle East* (Washington, D.C.: Brookings Institution Press, 2006), p. 61.

[160] Alejandro Portes, "Social Capital: Its Origins and Applications in Modern Sociology," *Annual Review of Sociology* 24 (1998): 4.

National Assembly is a well tested, though formally outlawed, device in Kuwait. While the tribal primaries, a process through which members of tribes meet to preselect their candidates in order to eliminate the weakest and improve the tribe's chances at the polls,[161] easily attract the most attention,[162] comparable non-tribal mechanisms[163] amongst the nation's *hadhar*[164] constituencies are no less prevalent. Mary Ann Tetreault, in her description of *diwaniyya* voting, underscores this trend for those without tribal affiliations:

> *Diwaniyya* voting is not unusual in Kuwait. It is a strategy that works like a tribal primary or a family council where participants agree ahead of time on one or two candidates as a way to concentrate their votes and improve the likelihood that their choices will win.[165]

The gains that are expected from this type of voting strategy are multidimensional for hosts and guests alike. For the proprietors, there is the prospect that gains can be accrued by parlaying one's status as a *diwaniyya* host into that of an "election key" (*al-mufta al-intikhabi*) for parliamentary candidates in order to open "the gates for them to reach certain families, tribes, and other social groups."[166] This support comes with the expectation that a successful candidate will channel the rewards of his office — his government sanctioned *wasta* — back to those who endorsed him during the elections; i.e., the *diwaniyya* hosts who mobilized their guests into voting blocs. The analysis below reflects this phenomenon as it took place before the 2006 redistricting:

> Kuwait's small, two-member districts offer closely knit *diwaniyya* communities the opportunity to affect elections directly. Members pledge support to a favorite candidate and sometimes, to increase his chances of winning, agree to cast "one-eyed" ballots.

---

[161] Alnajjar, "The Challenges," pp. 245–246.
[162] Gavrielides, "Tribal Democracy," pp. 166–170.
[163] Yagoub Yousef al-Kandari Ibrahim Naji al-Hadben, "Tribalism, Sectarianism, and Democracy in Kuwaiti Culture," *Digest of Middle East Studies* 19 (2010): 278.
[164] Historically, the urbanized town dwellers of Kuwait.
[165] Tetreault, *Stories of Democracy*, p. 118.
[166] Gavrielides, "Tribal Democracy," p. 178.

> By selecting only one candidate instead of two, these *diwaniyya* members increase the concentration of the vote for their favorite and thereby the chance that he will win — and be grateful for their support. *Diwaniyya* members are sure to be the first to inform him of that, too.[167]

Consequently, the availability of MP *wasta* can, as the visitor to one *diwaniyya* put it, elevate hosts into men who "can make things happen ... they have power in the country."[168] Of course, there are also those MPs who host their own *dawawin*, some of which are disparagingly called "service" *dawawin*, or simply "services" (*khadamat*), for the reason that they are the sites where bureaucratic privileges are most easily dispensed to supplicants from the very politicians who have the accessibility that is required. This type of politician has been described as trading in favors.

> Favors for favors, measured in votes as well as in direct campaign contributions, are the province of the "service candidate" who acts both as ombudsman and benefactor to individual constituents in his district ... constituents who approach service candidates find it easier to obtain scarce and selective benefits ... than if they were to apply through regular bureaucratic channels.[169]

What can be added to this synopsis is that so many solicitors find that their quest for favors leads them directly to the nighttime facility where their claims will be given more careful consideration: a service *diwaniyya*.

Frequently, though, most *dawawin* exist outside of any functional capacity that would allow them to leave their mark on Kuwait's national elections. In spite of this, these *dawawin* still crystallize networks of informal relations beyond the boundaries of official institutional settings[170] to produce,

---

[167] Mary Ann Tetreault, "Advice and Dissent in Kuwait," *Middle East Report* 226 (2003): 38.
[168] Ali A. K. Interview recorded in Kuwait City, Kuwait, 16 March 2008.
[169] Tetreault, *Stories of Democracy*, p. 115.
[170] S. N. Eisenstadt and Louis Roniger, *Patrons, Clients and Friends: Interpersonal Relations and the Structure of Society* (Cambridge: Cambridge University Press, 1984), pp. 283, 297.

reproduce, and maintain the social inroads of connectivity needed in Kuwait to insure that the benefits of the rentier state do not remain too far out of reach.

Within these settings, intercessory patronage is approached to "weave in and out of the bureaucracy, the offices of politicians … workplaces … [and] schools … in order to fulfill individual and collective needs."[171] The encounters that Fahad, a professional in his mid-20s, has gone through illustrate this trend quite well:

> I do not enjoy my father's *diwaniyya* because little important information is exchanged, just the normal, "How are you?" and "Oh, fine." But I do attend the *diwaniyya* held by the men on my mother's side of the family. [Why?] *Wasta*. If I need anything I go there and ask. If I have a problem with a ministry, I go there. They [the guests] say, "Oh, what do you need? We will talk to them." And everything will be taken care of and there is no problem. So, I go there instead of to my father's [*diwaniyya*].[172]

As this case indicates, Fahad, like so many others, finds that the connections engendered by a *diwaniyya* serve as an outlet to a broader spectrum of contacts that can assist one's search for redress. Rather than acting alone, the *dawawin* offer a familiar, reassuring location that alleviates any misgivings or anxieties that attendees may have been harboring, thereby affording all of the participants with some feeling of security since these engagements transpire in a predictable setting[173] with commonplace conventions.[174]

Although the present day extent of Kuwait's *dawawin* would be seriously curtailed without the proceeds from the state's "luxury employment"[175] and the

---

[171] Diane Singerman, "Restoring the Family to Civil Society: Lessons from Egypt," *Journal of Middle East Women's Studies* 2 (2006): 17.
[172] Interview recorded in Kuwait City, Kuwait, 11 November 2007.
[173] Erving Goffman, *The Presentation of the Self in Everyday Life* (New York: Anchor Books, 1959), pp. 92, 95.
[174] Douglass C. North, *Institutions, Institutional Change and Economic Performance* (New York: Cambridge University Press, 2004), pp. 25, 34–36.
[175] Nasra M. Shah, "Workers in Kuwait: Implications for the Kuwaiti Labor Force," *International Migration Review; Special Issue: Temporary Worker Programs: Mechanisms, Conditions, Consequences* 20 (1986): 826.

discretionary income that affords such prolific hosting and visiting throughout the country,[176] not all of Kuwait's residents are directly served by the *dawawin*. With some notable exceptions, these are exclusively Kuwaiti male institutions and, as such, they restrict women's and expatriates' opportunities for brokerage. In an environment rife with connections this is a considerable hindrance for any woman or foreign laborer seeking advancement, promotion, or support within their profession.

The resulting effect is that Kuwaiti women and non-Kuwait workers can find themselves more or less cut off from the closed circles of information that circulate within the *dawawin*. Without the proper proxies, this can be a serious deficit. Conversely, for a Kuwaiti woman at least, absence from the *diwaniyya* scene can actually play to her advantage at the professional level because her performance and decision-making will not be criticized as arising from *diwaniyya* favoritism or *diwaniyya* pressures,[177] a perception that readily serves to underline the institutional value of the *dawawin* in Kuwait for providing facilitatory favors.

Conclusion

Kuwait, without a doubt, is a prime example of a country with a specific mode of governance that is neither extractive nor coercive. Instead it relies upon the circulation of entitlements and privileges to assuage discontent, yet it still cannot stifle the expression of agency within its own borders. Furthermore, the colossal sums of cash generated by oil exports has hardly led to popular passivity or increased equity for the citizenry. To the contrary, as the preceding cases have shown, it requires a far more nuanced rentierism to fully explain the interpersonal and intergroup disparities that have actually been amplified by the arbitrary nature of state allocations, a characteristic that is even more

---

[176] Yagoub Yousef al-Kandari, *Al diwaniyya al kuwaitiyah* (Kuwait City: University of Kuwait, 2002), pp. 68–69.

[177] Hani Alsarraf, "Policy Administration and Political Rights: The Experiences of High–Level Women in the Kuwaiti Government," PhD. dissertation, Cleveland State University, 2008, pp. 101–103.

heightened by obscured bureaucratic channels and restricted magisterial access. When this is merged with the conspicuous lack of bureaucratic evenhandedness that is a hallmark of administrative offices, the pursuit of personalized connections and *diwaniyya* contacts to successfully navigate the labyrinthine agencies of the rentier state becomes an invaluable resource.

The Gulf and Beyond: Relations and Tensions

Chapter 6

Rethinking Regional Organization in the Gulf and the Greater Middle East

Malik R. Dahlan

Introduction

Over the past few years, Arab citizens, intellectuals, and outside observers have expressed strong concern about the current state and future course of development in the Gulf and the Greater Middle East. In light of the still ongoing turmoil across the region, this global attention has generated intense debates on the choices confronting the region's governments and citizens.

While many countries in the Middle East are eager to tap into the global economy through various channels, including bilateral accords or multilateral institutions such as the World Trade Organization (WTO), instability and turmoil fueled by armed conflicts and violence tend to eclipse such aspirations and efforts. Particularly in the aftermath of September 11, which saw increased instability due to the U.S. war on Iraq and Afghanistan, an acute case is to be made for progressive steps toward economic integration and stability.

Challenges in the region include young and expanding populations, long-standing issues of ethnic and social diversity, conflict, poverty, unemployment, and energy security. In addition, the region's links with the rest of the world are increasing and becoming more complex through the process of globalization. As a result, the Gulf and the Greater Middle East are more vulnerable to regional and global crises, as strikingly seen in Dubai in 2008 due to the economic crisis as well as today due to the current and widespread social unrest.

In order to achieve global economic integration in the Middle East, domestic reform and trade liberalization are necessary. At a fundamental level, there are three possible approaches: unilateral action taken within each state; multilateral and regional cooperation and integration; and global processes through such institutions as the WTO. It is particularly the second approach, regional integration or regionalism, that I take up in this Chapter, including its intersection with the structures of global level processes and trade governance.

Regional cooperation poses an unprecedented opportunity for regional organizations such as the Gulf Cooperation Council (GCC) to rethink and restructure their policy planning, mission, and objectives so that they can play a greater role in addressing regional integration and the needs of the global political economy.

From the perspective of disciplines, this study draws upon both international law and the political economy of international trade. Regionalism will be analyzed in two ways: Firstly, as a set of alternative schemes that serve as solutions to the shortfalls of the WTO; and secondly, as a connection to the intellectual community of Middle Eastern law and policy studies.

The overall thrust of this study flows from the acknowledgment of grave problems in the Gulf region and the Greater Middle East. These problems represent a collective failure on the part of these countries and their regional organizations to deal with global and economic realities, as well as the need for a regional agenda that leads to economic and social development with greater individual freedoms and prosperity.[1] The central argument is that policy options for the Gulf and the Greater Middle East must include a stronger emphasis on the contribution of economic-legal frameworks to ensure regional stability, growth, and peace. This Chapter will also look into the greater role that regional organizations such as the GCC can potentially play, and ultimately posits that the GCC could draw lessons from the Asia-Pacific Economic Cooperation (APEC) model to promote regional integration and economic development.

---

[1] The 2002 UNDP Arab Human Development Report (and the 2003 restatement) dealt with many such problems.

The Failure to Address Economic and Political Challenges

Despite ample opportunities in the Gulf and the Greater Middle East, regional organizations have failed to play a leading role on issues of economic stagnation and political and social unrest. In addition, despite their wealth, or perhaps because of it, as their economies are driven by oil reserves, these countries are lagging behind others in economic development and integration. As a result, the region has not been able to transform its economic and political structures to compete globally, improve its communities, and prevent internal conflicts.

Economists generally agree that to break this cycle of stagnation, the Middle East must sustain rapid and high levels of economic growth on a par with India, China, and the Asian Tigers, about 8 to 10 percent GDP growth per annum. Below that rate, economic activity will not create enough capacity to absorb the region's growing populations and alleviate the citizenry's "misery and hopelessness," as concluded by the Council on Foreign Relations, "that characterize much of this part of the world [and] lie at the heart of international terrorism."[2]

According to the traditional gauge of economic openness, the Middle East is comparable to lower and upper middle income countries.[3] Yet the region's total GDP is only half that of the United Kingdom or France. With a population almost the size of the European Union, the Middle East is potentially a large market. However, this market remains small and politically fragmented. Also, in contrast to other regions in the developing world, the GCC and the Greater Middle East have not significantly expanded or integrated trade relationships. This lack of economic integration has suppressed growth opportunities, frozen trade structures, hindered economic diversification, and has led to an overall rigidity in the economy that constrains the increase of modern manufacturing industries, research and development, and service sectors. Essentially, achieving the aforementioned high-level economic growth necessitates the political leadership of the main states and regional organizations

---

[2] Bernard Hoekman and Patrick Messerlin, *Harnessing Trade for Development and Growth in the Middle East,* Report by the Council on Foreign Relations Study Group on Middle East Trade Options (New York: Council on Foreign Relations, 2002), Foreword, p. vii.
[3] *Ibid.*, pp. 2 and 8.

to work toward the rule of law, economic and political regional integration, and an active participation in the global political economy.

Regional political ties have become more strained due to the widespread social unrest across the region. The speed with which the economically stagnant and politically moribund orders of the countries in the GCC and the broader Middle East are crumbling under the weight of their often unemployed and technologically connected youth is remarkable. With the benefit of hindsight, it is easy to see why the region's demographic bulge — 75 percent of the population is under the age of 25 — would ultimately challenge and defeat Hosni Mubarak, Zine el-Abidine ben Ali, and other anachronistic Arab regimes.

Yet few, if any, foresaw the shared social and economic consciousness among the youth that is rooted in language, history, and policies and was spread by new media that served to mobilize them quickly and decisively. With the help of Al Jazeera, Facebook, and Twitter, the region's constituencies, including those in Algeria, Bahrain, Egypt, Libya, Syria, Tunisia, and Yemen, realized their shared problems and took collective action. Although the turmoil is ongoing and the end is not yet within sight, there is little doubt that new and hopefully more democratic governments will emerge in some Arab capitals, and that other regimes will introduce varying levels of political and economic reform to meet the demands of their restive populations.

But even if we assume that the current unrest leads to positive political transformations in certain GCC and other Middle Eastern states, the chronic economic stagnation and degeneration that afflict these societies will continue under the weight of global economic processes, unstable trade balances, and violent regional political issues such as the Israel-Palestine conflict. Indeed, legitimate democracy in the region may in the short term lead to a continuation of, and in some cases, increased, state regulation of industry. While it will be necessary to create a competitive private presence where absent and to improve regulatory capacity where necessary, creating a competitive investment climate takes time. It requires the development of human capital and technology, as well as reforms to enable the development of strong backbone services. The state and its continued regulatory function will be important in any development toward increased liberalization.

Domestic and regional forces are not the only pressures on the economic and political status quo. Outside demands, mainly stemming from globalization efforts, are pressurizing these countries as well. To a certain degree, Middle Eastern governments have recognized the benefits of international trade and the compelling logic of participation in international economic institutions, such as the WTO. However, the unbalanced and fragmented nature of the regional economy hinders the process of integration with the global economy.

Moreover, the governments face the challenge of needing to align domestic legal, political, and economic structures to conform to regulatory standards and processes set by these global institutions. These adjustments challenge pre-existing alliances and interests within each country's political economy. Different domestic actors seek to understand the benefits and the costs of greater economic openness and expanded trade and investment relationships.

Regional organizations such as the GCC have missed a critical opportunity to play a leading role in this process of increasing economic openness. The GCC's inadequacy is even more apparent when compared to the success of other regional organizations such as APEC, the European Union, and even the Shanghai Cooperation Organization, all of which are effectively expanding.

The grave economic and political challenges in the region are tied directly to the absence of strong regional organizations. Traditional organizations in the region have very limited impact across the area and have largely failed to unite, integrate, and harmonize the regional political economy. For instance, the GCC is essentially a private club of "conservative, oil-drenched monarchies along the Persian Gulf"[4] that has focused on economic development among its own. It has simply provided a dialogue regime for its members in order to coordinate economic and political positions.

The economic and geographical constraints of GCC membership severely undermine the potential role that it could play if it presented a united wider Arab world. Consequently, many of the GCC's previous efforts to integrate the region both economically and politically were watered down. For instance, Jordan unsuccessfully applied to join the GCC in the mid-1980s

---

[4]Tobias Buck and Eileen Byrne, "Gulf States' Overtures Delight Jordan," *Financial Times*, 12 May 2011.

and again after King Abdullah II ascended to the throne. It was not until May 2011 that Jordan's request to join the GCC was accepted and Morocco was also invited to join the union. In September 2011, a five-year economic plan for both countries was put forward after a meeting between their foreign ministers and those of the GCC States — the first GCC meeting since May that included the Jordanian and Moroccan ministers. Though a plan for accession was being looked into, no timetable had been set as of this writing in early 2013.

Progress has been slow even within the GCC. For instance, the planned establishment of a GCC single currency in 2010 was postponed pending further studies and harmonization measures. This delay followed the decision of two members (Oman and the UAE) to opt out, and, more recently, other members have voiced concerns about readiness in the wake of the financial crisis in Europe and mounting pressures on the euro. The four remaining member countries have nevertheless established a GCC Monetary Council in Riyadh to continue the technical steps toward establishing a monetary union.

In addition, the similar economic and production structure within the GCC restricted economic incentives for improving intra-Middle East development. As such, the GCC lacks the capacity to represent the wider Middle Eastern region, including North Africa.

A Regional Approach to Address Problems

Globalization challenges both the legal and the political economic status quo of countries in the GCC and the Greater Middle East. Despite the need for a concerted regional action on issues such as water security, economic development, and the permanent threats of conflict and political violence, there is still no regional body designed to bring together all the states of the region. It is not only reticence and distrust that prevents such a body but also the very real and often violent realities of politics in the region. In a part of the world where the potential for war is ever-present, acceding to binding obligations with bitter enemies is a major challenge.

The first step in framing a regional approach is to determine how the GCC and the Greater Middle Eastern countries could fit into a regional framework and the benefits and drawbacks that could result from it. Certain countries may play more of an important role. Due to the size of their economies and political standings in the region, Saudi Arabia, Egypt, Turkey, Iran, and Israel must take on leading roles in the effort to develop a regional arrangement in order to regulate the oil trade, a common market, a common currency, and general trade with Israel.

Among the compelling arguments for greater economic integration, regionalism offers Middle Eastern states a less threatening approach to transnational cooperation and integration than one that is premised on a more custom-tailored path to joining the international community as a productive economic actor subject to the rule of law.[5] A regional approach takes into full account the cultural, geopolitical, and religious dynamics of the countries in question. Religions, cultures, and the "clash of civilizations" are not sufficient to explain the dynamics in the Middle East.[6] The key challenge will be the reconciliation of the traditional ways of life, such as shari'a and welfare, with the intensifying mainstream of the global economic order.

At this point, it may be unrealistic to expect individual Middle Eastern countries to aspire to an advanced, highly integrated trade regime such as the North Atlantic Free Trade Agreement (NAFTA) or the European Union (EU). As the scholar William Alford points out, "Many nations — including virtually all of the world's poorest countries — are not now nor are soon likely to be full members of any such economically significant trading blocs."[7]

Consequently, the real and immediate challenge lies in how to maintain the necessary flexibility and socioreligious sophistication of the GCC and the Greater Middle East while at the same time allowing these countries to benefit from the stabilizing effects of regional trade and improving their participation in the global order.

---

[5] Robert Z. Lawrence, *Regionalism, Multilateralism and Deeper Integration* (Washington, D.C.: Brookings Institution Press, 1996), pp. 21–42.
[6] Michael N. Barnett, "Sovereignty, Nationalism, and Regional Order in the Arab States System," *International Organizations* 49, 3 (1995) 479–510.
[7] William P. Alford, "Introduction: The North American Free Trade Agreement and the Need for Candor," *Harvard International Law Journal* 34 (1993): 293.

To join the WTO, Middle Eastern countries are required to comply with WTO rules. Many countries have aligned their national reform goals to comply with these requirements, particularly regarding investment policies. Nevertheless, challenges remain. A central issue for these countries is the need for a deeper transformation of governing structures, particularly regulatory bodies, as well as an increased transparency of processes and a uniform application of laws. These more substantial changes require revamping the government and the private sector, leaving foreign investors and nongovernmental organizations uncertain about the efficiency and stability of the new structure.

To be clear, Middle Eastern countries have already made concessions and compromises to the traditional ways in which they have operated to become a part of the international order. In particular, changes to Arab business and cultural practices have been required in some instances to bring Arab countries more in line with international standards. These changes can be very difficult to implement in practice, particularly where there are internal socioreligious divisions that may be opposed to adherence to new standards. The issues of political economy add another layer of complexity, as certain institutions refuse to be regulated. Considering these factors, it makes more sense for these countries to integrate regionally and work toward similar political economies before they can integrate into the global system fully.

The regionalism approach questions whether the established international institutions represent the only or most direct path to prosperity for Middle Eastern countries. Countries could stay outside of the WTO while prospering from a more customized multilateral or regional trading or economic bloc that requires fewer legal and political transformations. Devising institutional methods for regional integration among the developing countries of the Middle East could spur growth and development for other Middle East countries that are not currently members of the GCC, enhancing their leverage and bargaining power with developed countries. Moreover, regionalism in the Middle East should be open and outward-looking enough to accept the form of modernization capable of affecting these countries positively while at the same time maintaining the national and sociopolitical integrity unique to each of them.

The Checkered History of Regional Efforts

According to Roger Owen, in the nineteenth century the Middle East remarkably contained few economic resources beyond agriculture. Even though most of the region was administratively and politically united under the Ottoman Empire, no regional market existed.[8] Since the Second World War, the Middle East has witnessed several attempts at regionalism through economic integration and development.

Amongst them, the 1953 treaty to organize transit trade among the states of the Arab League was perhaps the most memorable attempt. Following this treaty, in the wake of the formation of the European Economic Community (EEC), was a short-lived first attempt to create a better integrated form of an Arab common market in 1957, followed by the 1964 agreement that established an Arab common market among Egypt, Iraq, Jordan, and Syria. None of these initiatives were successful. The most important reason behind their failure was that the final agreements were only a compromise between the Egyptian proposal, which called for full economic union with common directions and policies, and the desire of other states to go no further than the creation of a regional market for certain goods by means of the reduction or elimination of certain barriers.

Kuwait, for its part, devised an interesting model for economic integration through the creation of the Kuwait Fund for Arab Economic Development in 1961. This scheme called for integration by means of spreading oil wealth. It possessed many advantages, yet it never fully developed, as the country's oil-driven economic plans did not prevail until the early 1970s. As intriguing as the idea is, oil distribution has never assumed a significant role in international trade theory.

The Middle East also witnessed a wave of sub-regional integration attempts, starting with the Maghreb Arab Union (MAU), which Algeria, Libya, Mauritania, Morocco, and Tunisia established in 1964. As in broader cases, individual states were more dedicated to their own industrial development

---

[8] Roger Owen, "Arab Integration in Historical Perspective: Are There Any Lessons?," *Arab Affairs* 6 (1988).

programs as well as to structural problems more generally in the Middle East, a preoccupation that resulted from the monopolies of government organizations on imports. As such, the most important factor contributing to the failure of these sub-regional economic structures was the fact that individual members negotiated agreements separately, hoping to obtain better results.

The second sub-regional economic organization created was the GCC, established in 1981 by Bahrain, Kuwait, Oman, Qatar, Saudi Arabia, and the United Arab Emirates. Seen as an ambitious attempt to create a dynamic form of union, ultimately the GCC has failed to integrate its countries' economies, largely due to the minimal amount of trade that exists among them. Trade integration has limited possibilities in the group since the Gulf economies are all oil-driven and nearly identical.

Another example of a sub-regional organization was the short-lived Arab Cooperation Council, formed in 1981 by Egypt, Iraq, Jordan, and Yemen. It was formed under the Agreement for Facilitation and Promotion of Intra-Arab Trade and was signed by 18 member states of the Arab League. The Arab League itself is considered the dominant intra-Middle East forum for regional cooperation on economic matters through its arrangements of the Greater Arab Free Trade Agreement (GAFTA). The member states of the Arab League currently aim to revive the 1981 Agreement for Facilitation and Promotion of Intra-Arab Trade. The main shortcoming of the agreement was its nature as a declaration of intent on the part of the country signatories. It had no binding terms and everything was open to negotiation. Moreover, the liberalization scheme adopted by this agreement was a product-by-product approach. Negotiating countries were allowed to pick and choose some manufactured products but not others for tariff exemptions. In addition, the agreement did not lay out a time schedule for the elimination of tariffs and trade barriers. Political barriers also worked against efficiency and mutual confidence. In contrast, the recent GAFTA Executive Program to revive the 1981 agreement came up with specific commitments with regard to tariffs and tariff-like charges, non-tariff barriers, and rules of origin.

GAFTA, which was launched on 1 January 1998, is structured as a traditional preferential trade agreement, and it embodies specific commitments and the elimination of tariffs, import duties, and other barriers to outside trade. These goals were to be achieved in ten years, by 2008. However, GAFTA is limited to goods and does not include services; thus it is a traditional preferential trade agreement.

Finally, two external regional initiatives — one American and one European — were attempted. The U.S. government's "Greater Middle East" initiative, proposed at the G8 Summit in June 2004 under the administration of then president George W. Bush, identified democracy as the all-encompassing cure for the region's afflictions. By 2006, it was clear that the Bush plan, at least when judged by its own objectives, had failed. The plan jeopardized any serious collective internal effort in the Middle East for fostering credible democratic efforts and raised an outcry among Arab leaders that America was attempting to impose external political models on the region.

The European effort, in the form of the Union for the Mediterranean, was established in 2008 at the instigation of then French president Nicolas Sarkozy. The organization is comprised of all 27 EU member states, eight Arab states of the Mediterranean, Turkey, and four non-EU European states of the Mediterranean. Sarkozy's original conception, in which the organization would have a structure based on that of the EU, with common institutions, was far more ambitious and was opposed by many of France's EU partners, particularly Germany. Perhaps as a partial consequence, the establishment of the Union has had no substantive impact in the Mediterranean or the Middle East.

In addition, Turkey spearheaded an initiative to bring together Syria, Turkey, Lebanon, and Jordan to sign a quadripartite free trade agreement in August 2010. The four nations agreed to follow up on creating a free trade zone to boost trade exchanges, particularly to support small and medium-sized businesses (SMEs) in these countries by eliminating trade barriers. This was a groundbreaking agreement in many respects, particularly because it transcended deeply held grievances on the part of Lebanon and Syria toward Turkey, their former imperial ruler. Furthermore, it demonstrated the potential for interstate economic priorities to rise above issues of territorial contest, such as the pestiferous dispute between Syria and Turkey over the Iskenderun (or Hatay) region that was a part of Syria until 1938 and has a significant Syrian population.

Most recently, President Obama's Fourth Policy Principles were released on 19 May 2011, in which he stated:

> It is important to focus on trade, not just aid; on investment, not just assistance. The goal must be a model in which protectionism gives way to openness, the reigns of commerce pass from the few to the many, and the economy generates jobs for the young. America's support for democracy will therefore be based on ensuring financial stability, promoting reform, and integrating competitive markets with each other and the global economy.[9]

President Obama also announced his intention to launch the Trade and Investment Partnership Initiative in the Middle East and North Africa (TIPI-MENA). The initiative was intended to establish a Marshall Plan-like external agenda led by the United States, EU, and G8. In essence, TIPI-MENA was formulated to serve as a comprehensive regional economic assistance program following the turmoil surrounding the so-called Arab Spring. However, despite the Obama administration's ambitions, the initiative has yet to move forward in a coherent and financially viable approach.[10]

The challenges that have riddled the program include internal politics, financial constraints, as well as diplomatic sensitivities within the Middle East principally the situation in Syria and the Iran-5+1 agreement. Having said that, it is worth noting that TIPI-MENA entailed: (1) Working with the EU to facilitate more trade within the region; (2) building on existing agreements to promote integration with American and European markets; (3) opening the door for those countries that adopt high standards of reform and trade liberalisation to construct a regional trade arrangement; and (4) creating a powerful force for reform in the Middle East and North Africa following the

---

[9] Barack Obama, Second Middle East Speech, Benjamin Franklin Room, U.S. State Department, 19 May 2011.

[10] The initiative has been pushed to the Office of the United States Trade Representative and has only focused on Small-Medium Enterprise (SME) development in Egypt, Morocco, and Jordan. See CRS Report for Congress: "U.S. Trade and Investment in the Middle East and North Africa: Overview and Issues for Congress" March 2013. Available online at http://www.fas.org/sgp/crs/misc/R42153.pdf.

success in the European Union. The long-term effect of TIPI-MENA has yet to be tested.

Rethinking the Role of Regional Organizations

Regrettably, most of the aforementioned initiatives and actions had little practical impact. They represented a collective failure by regional governments and organizations to deal with global and economic realities and to support a regional agenda that leads to economic and social development with greater individual freedoms and prosperity. Yet the GCC's recent initiatives have shown that it is capable of repositioning and expanding itself. Its active involvement in the social unrest in Bahrain and Yemen and the invitation to Jordan and Morocco to join the GCC are but a few examples. It is still too early to identify the precise consequences of these developments, but the GCC's intention to expand beyond the traditional boundaries of regional economic issues is clear. These inclinations could lead to an opportunity for the GCC to ultimately harmonize regional politics and economies and expand development throughout the region. In light of this leadership opportunity, the GCC still needs to clarify its developing model and strategy.

Policy decisions by regional entities such as the GCC must extend integration to Middle Eastern countries beyond the Gulf and to issues beyond the economy if leaders hope to contribute to regional stability, growth, and peace. The process will not be easy and may take several major steps. Due to the size of their economies and political status in the region, the GCC countries could take on a leadership role in the effort to develop a regional trade arrangement to regulate the oil trade, common market, common currency, and trade with Israel.

What the GCC's Recent Actions Mean to the Region

The GCC's recent initiatives are significant to the region and to the organization's fundamental transformation. The entry of GCC troops into Bahrain was critical in attempting to regain order and prevent further violence. While there is still some way to go to improve stability in Bahrain, the assistance provided by the GCC troops and the message this sent arguably limited the progression of violence in other Middle Eastern states. The GCC has also been actively involved with the mediation and peaceful transfer of power in Yemen, which is labeled as the "last hope" action by the United States and Europe.[11] Although the process is difficult, such a step is important to the GCC in several regards.

Firstly, the GCC is closely related to Yemen geographically, culturally, and historically. For many years, Yemen and the GCC countries have been negotiating its accession. As a result, a certain level of cooperation has been established. This cooperation with Yemen illustrates the GCC's willingness to open the door to less developed and non-oil dominated countries in the region. The success of this step is key to the GCC's efforts to integrate the region both economically and politically. Second, as in Bahrain, the social unrest in Yemen could potentially trigger divisions throughout the GCC countries. Third, Yemen sits on the GCC's oil lifeline to Asia via the Arabian Sea and the Indian Ocean. Finally, stability in Yemen would provide GCC countries with inexpensive human resources that are vital to the potentially fast growing GCC economy.

The GCC's invitation to Jordan and Morocco to join the organization was a move that surprised some observers and analysts. Regardless, a general consensus concurred that the closer association would provide economic benefits to all the countries. This expansion clearly indicates that the GCC aims for enlargement, but not strictly through closely related economic or geographical means. Neither Jordan nor Morocco are oil-rich countries and, more importantly, they are not located in the Gulf.

This move can be explained by geopolitical factors. Jordan is a buffer between the GCC countries and Israel and Iraq, while Morocco controls the oil route to North America through the Mediterranean Sea. Another explanation for this move is that it provides the GCC with the foundation to further expand across the Arabian Peninsula and into the wider Middle East and North Africa.

---

[11] "Qatar Pulls Out of Yemen Crisis Mediation," *Financial Times*, 13 May 2011, available online at http://www.ft.com/cms/s/0/1ebe7316-7d76-11e0-b418-00144feabdc0.html#axzz1MhIMTBJw.

The GCC and the region would benefit greatly from an integrated regional market and harmonized cooperation on economic matters, including the free movement of workers, goods, and capital. The integration could also give the GCC and Middle Eastern countries political leverage throughout the Arabian Peninsula and the Mediterranean Sea. In sum, these recent steps by the GCC reveal that it is capable of transforming itself into a powerful regional force not confined to economic issues or geographic boundaries.

APEC as a Model

Notwithstanding the positive indications revealed in the GCC's recent actions, there is still a long way to go before the GCC can complete its transformation. Rather than crafting a novel system or having one imposed by external powers, the GCC and the Middle East can benefit from examining the experiences of other regions and then adapting those frameworks to suit their specific needs. While the European Union offers inspiration, the model of the 21-member Asia-Pacific Economic Cooperation (APEC) forum is more readily applicable to the realities of the Middle East. As an organization with Asian, Oceanian, North American, and South American member economies, APEC's primary goal is to engender and facilitate greater cooperation in regional trade and investment liberalization in the Asia-Pacific region, thereby bolstering economic growth and prosperity. Such a framework is well suited to the Middle East. Priorities of national governments will differ but economic prosperity is a common goal. Economic prosperity requires institutional unity, with a focus on soft laws and institutions.

The key virtues of the APEC Model Include:

Open Regionalism: Perhaps the most important characteristic of APEC is its tendency to be more compatible with the WTO regime than other regional structures. Its adaptation of "open regionalism," which eliminates problems stemming from preferentiality and exclusivity that are usually found in regional trade agreements, attests to that end. APEC's non-exclusive membership policy allows for deeper integration with other trading regimes in the world, which effectively extends the scope of liberalization agendas of the various members and promotes cross-cultural dialogue.

Soft Institutionalization: APEC's organizational cooperative scheme provides for informality, or "soft institutionalization," "soft laws," and a "non-binding" character. These attributes make it an inherently more efficient system for regional integration and avoid the shortcomings of the more formalized and rigid EU system. Collectively, these aspects allow for flexibility, making the organization an ideal vessel for developing legal norms that ensure economic integration suitable for both domestic and international agendas.

Instrumentalism: APEC's approach to policy integration is one that sets the principles and guidelines of the region and fosters dialogue that ultimately allows member countries to accept the terms on their own timeframe. Such flexibility makes it easier for developing countries to assess their commitments when it comes to the pressure of deregulation and liberalization. In introducing new trade policies, APEC members can factor in domestic issues and smoothly incorporate cushioning measures. Indeed, APEC's "Individual Action Plans" and "Early Voluntary Sectoral Liberalization" helps implement trade policies and encourages members to assume bolder steps to adapt "best practices" from other developed states and ultimately join a formal forum such as GAFTA or the WTO,[12] but on their own time.

In addition to these features, APEC promotes transgovernmental networking, which promotes political and regulatory cooperation. Furthermore, private involvement in APEC, which seems almost a legacy in the Asia Pacific region, allows the business sectors to play a critical and constructive role in operating institutions. This buy-in by the private sector has been critical to APEC's success, and it has enabled efficient diversification of economies.

An APEC-Structured GCC

By using the APEC model as a framework, wider intra-Middle East integration can foster regional cooperation in the regulatory arena. The form of this

---

[12] Sungjoon Cho, "Breaking the Barrier Between Regionalism and Multilateralism: A New Perspective on Trade Regionalism, *"Harvard International Law Journal* 42, 2 (2001): 419.

regional structure is critical. There is not just one prototype or archetype of regionalism such as regional trading agreements. The GCC approach should not necessarily mean forming any tangible "bloc" among neighboring countries. A loose alliance like APEC may be better suited to the Middle East, as it could be open to non-regional members such as China and the United States or even Israel. This scheme, known as "open regionalism,"[13] as described above, would also be compatible with and complementary to the international trading system.

While APEC's purview is limited to economic matters, the reorganization of the GCC in the Middle East necessitates a broader mandate that encompasses other factors of crucial importance to the region. Three categories of explicit goals would be keys to address.

The primary goal of the GCC should be to enhance economic co-operation among the member states. This goal could be achieved through an APEC-like "Three Pillar" strategy: (1) A region-wide liberalization of laws by reducing trade barriers and even creating a region-wide free trade zone; (2) the facilitation of interstate trade and investment by allowing individuals and companies from member states to do business in other member states; and (3) regional collaboration that enhances the economic capacity and capabilities of member states.

In addition to fostering the development of stable, sustainable, and mutually gainful economic relations, this body should create even greater incentives for resolving more complex issues of dispute. As such, the secondary goal would be to address non-economic issues among Middle Eastern countries that have a detrimental impact on economic relations. These issues include domestic conflicts and transnational disputes, weapons of mass destruction, energy and water resources, and other environmental issues.

Framing the discussion of these issues in an economic context would counter much of the entrenched political positioning and permit an alternative to what might be seen as conventional wisdom. For example, disputes over water resources could be addressed from the perspective of economic benefits and detriments rather than from foreign policy perspectives, stripping

---

[13] *Ibid.*

away questions of nationalism and ideology. Such an approach may appear superficial, but at least the GCC could have the modest and attainable goal of containing such crises, increasing the opportunities for arbitration and lessening the occurrence of heated debates. As a tertiary goal, the GCC should attempt to provide a forum for institutional issues that require sustained, long-term efforts. These issues include low-to-mid level transnational disputes and domestic governance issues such as political and administrative transparency and access to the judicial redress of grievances.

Even a modest form of enhanced regional cooperation centered on these three goals has the potential to affect the underlying cause of Middle Eastern instability in a significant way. Though the problems of the Middle East are multitudinous, one issue more than any other lies as the fountainhead of the region's ills — the Palestinian–Israeli conflict. This conflict has lasted for 60 years and has infected almost every facet of the geopolitical context. In 2002, all 22 member states of the Arab League offered Israel a comprehensive solution by which they would agree to complete peace and normalization of relations with Israel in exchange for the absolute end to the Israeli occupation of all Palestinian, Syrian, and Lebanese territories and a just settlement to the Palestinian refugee crisis. This offer was reaffirmed by the League in 2007. While Israel has thus far refused to accept the Arab Peace Initiative, it has not rejected it outright, and therefore there is still hope for settlement of the problem with help from regional efforts. More importantly, the mere fact that the entire Arab League has found the consensus necessary to make such a bold offer is remarkable, and proves in some small measure that the region has matured and its leaders capable of coming together for the common good.

Conclusion

The enormous social and economic changes sweeping across the region present a new era of danger and opportunity. A meaningful and politically feasible regional approach is urgently needed to fulfill the promise of the rule of law, economic opportunity, and social justice that the Arab citizenry demands. In this process, regional organizations such as the GCC could play a significant role in paving the way for a better tomorrow for the people. Without such a framework, the forces of reregulation and global liberalization may render this momentous political period a means of consigning the region's populations, be it Arab, Israeli, or Iranian, to continuous protracted violence and instability.

The GCC's recent movements toward expansion could be a plausible step toward robust regional integration. This process is far from completion, but the long-established and successful APEC model could provide the GCC with a roadmap for the future.

Chapter 7

Sources of Continuity in Iran's Foreign Policy

Mahmood Sariolghalam

The key elements of Iran's foreign policy since 1979 have shown remarkable stability and continuity.[1] The basic approach in Iranian policies regarding the United States, Russia, Europe, and major Arab countries and the Palestinian issue has fundamentally remained unchanged. Much of this consistency and continuity stems from Iran's regime type, which is one that does not quite fit the conventional understanding of the nation state, with its interests and policies defined and charted on the basis of political and geographic realities.[2] Instead, it is based on universalism, or a global order with an Islamic worldview that is found within the geographic boundaries of Muslim societies. Such universalism also includes the "have-nots" of the world.

---

[1] The original idea for this article first appeared in an article in Persian: "The Foreign Policy of the Islamic Republic of Iran: Possibilities for Change," *Foreign Relations* 1, 1 (Spring 2009). Later, the idea was further developed in a comparative context and appeared in another article in Persian: "The Concept of Power and Foreign Policy Performance: Comparing China and Iran," *Foreign Relations* 2, 9 (Spring 2011). The current Chapter is a further elaboration of the two aforementioned articles. This contribution may be related to a more substantiated theoretical framework that draws on the relevance of social constructivism to the study of Iran's foreign policy.

[2] On this issue, see Daniel Brumberg, *Reinventing Khomeini* (Chicago: The University of Chicago Press, 2001); Hamid Dabashi, *Theology of Discontent: The Ideological Foundation of the Islamic Revolution in Iran* (New York: New York University Press, 1993); and Said Arjomand, *The Turban for the Crown: The Islamic Revolution of Iran* (Oxford: Oxford University Press, 1988).

Since the Islamic Revolution, Iran's policies toward major issues and countries have been predicated on the unchanging nature of the "national interests of Iran." These national interests are driven by the desire for regime security, which in turn has underpinned the country's foreign policy. As a result, Iranian foreign policy has reinforced the legitimacy, sovereignty, and security of the state. Economic needs have been positioned at a distant second.

It can be argued that ideological states are not at liberty to be flexible in their definition of events or political entities, and therefore are compelled to justify their approach on the basis of philosophical or structural roots. In the Iranian case, the so-called "national interests" of the state extend beyond the territorial boundaries of Iran. As an "Islamic state," Iran has been obliged to reach beyond itself to serve the interests of "deprived Muslims" of all sects. This belief emerged from a school of thought in Shi'i political theology that matured during the nineteenth and twentieth centuries in which Iranian religious and nationalist activists fought side by side for the country's independence from Western intrusions.[3] The differences between these activists did not surface until the overthrow of the Pahlavi regime in 1979.

In fact, the first clash of ideology over the national or Islamic interests of the state occurred after the Revolution, with the Islamists prevailing. Mehdi Bazargan, the first prime minister after the Revolution, was not alone in losing the ideological battle to the Islamists. The moderates of the Rafsanjani period (1989–1997) and the reformists of the Khatami era (1997–2005) did as well.[4]

State administrations since 1979 have not been able to mobilize political and social forces to define national interests. The Islamists argued vigorously that the tenets of the Revolution were Islamic and that Islam did not follow the Westphalian logic of the nation state. As such, political Islam and liberalism could not be merged.[5] Yet policies that would serve Iran and the Iranian people

---

[3] In my search for a relatively objective and comparative analysis of "modern" versus Shi'i interpretations of politics, I have found Mashallah Ajoudani's work original, fair, and enlightening. Mashallah Ajoudani, *The Iranian Constitutionalism* (in Persian) (Tehran: Nashr-i Akhtaran, 2003), in particular pp. 73–188.

[4] Eric Hooglund, *Twenty Years of the Islamic Revolution: Political and Social Transformation in Iran since 1979* (Syracuse, NY: Syracuse University Press, 2002).

[5] Mahmood Sariolghalam, "Understanding Iran: Getting Past Stereotypes and Mythology," *The Washington Quarterly* 26, 4 (Autumn 2003): 77.

exclusively, such as an Islamic order extending from Morocco to Indonesia that would administer Islamic laws and create an economic setting distinct from the global capitalist system, have not been constructed.

Still, Iran's Islamists have benefited from the advantage of being empowered by the state to politically and logistically direct its major institutions to uphold Islamist foreign policy of engagement in the Middle East, in particular supporting the Palestinian cause, countering Western interests, and sidelining economic interests in favor of geopolitical and military interests. As a result, a duality in belief and policy, which manifested itself as an "us" versus "them" stance, has become entrenched. A plethora of textual evidence supports this view from an Islamic perspective.[6]

In addition, politics in Iran have followed the logic of a zero-sum game. With room for only one perspective, those who had other views were either forced underground or fled the country. In 1971, even the Shah advised his opponents to take their passports and leave the country.[7] The Iranian Islamist social and political psyche has not embraced coalition building, compromising, concessions, or conciliation. The consequence of this stance has limited discourse; policies are not reevaluated, trends are not studied, and the art and process of consensus building within an inclusive institutional setting is almost nonexistent.[8]

Therefore, Iranian foreign policy in the post-revolutionary period has been effective at marginalizing the "national interest" paradigm and universalizing the "Islamist" paradigm, which has espoused regional involvement and the defense of Muslim interests in the face of Western intervention. However, the Iranian perspective has little relevance to most other Muslim countries. An overwhelming number of these countries embrace Western and American partnership.

If Iran's foreign policy can be said to have remained the same in its ideology, it has somewhat varied in its function. In the first decade after the

---

[6] Ervand Abrahamian, *Khomeinism: Essays on the Islamic Republic* (Berkeley, CA: University of California Press, 1993); Dabashi, *Theology of Discontent;* Arjomand, *The Turban for the Crown.*
[7] Irfan Qani'ifard, *In the Net of Events: An Interview with Parviz Sabeti* (Los Angeles: Ketab Corporation, 2012), p. 235.
[8] Sariolghalam, "Understanding Iran," p. 77.

revolution (1979–1989) Iran's foreign policy outreach more purely served the ideological function of "us" against the "West" more broadly. In the years after 1989, Iran's regional outreach has been more suited to a more particular endeavor: the containment of the United States. Iran's conflict with Israel and its denial of the Holocaust perhaps represents the most noteworthy single feature of its conflict with the United States and, consequently, with the Western world. This issue in itself explains how the Islamist paradigm has dominated the discourse of Iran's foreign policy institutions and has set the stage for the nation's international conduct.

In the 1990s, both the United States and Iran developed elaborate and operational containment strategies toward one another. On this basis, Iran's Islamist foreign policy has survived for some three decades. Though different state administrations in the 1989–2011 period may have followed diverse approaches, styles of diplomacy, and vocabulary, the overall direction of foreign policy toward the United States and other major Western countries and issues have fundamentally remained consistent.[9] These policies include:[10]

a. Preference for causes and movements over governments in foreign policy relations.
b. Institutionalized confrontation with Israel and the United States.
c. Fostering strategic enclaves in the Middle East to contain potential U.S. confrontation.
d. Separating foreign economic relations from foreign policy pursuits.
e. Supremacy of ideological interests over economic interests for the purpose of maintaining domestic security.

Analysis

Four areas of reasoning develop the claim that the Islamic Republic has maintained a rather static foreign policy founded on the stances listed above.

---

[9] Sariolghalam, "Understanding Iran," pp. 58–62.
[10] Mahmood Sariolghalam, "The Foreign Policy of of the Islamic Republic of Iran: A Theoretical Renewal and a Paradigm for Coalition," (Tehran: Center of Strategic Research, 2000), p. 27.

The Islamic regime separates economic policy from foreign policy

From the outset, the officials of the Islamic Republic did not shy away from declaring that the purpose of the Revolution was not solely the economic development of the country. In speech after speech, revolutionary leaders elevated justice above development — and justice that emanated from spirituality and egalitarianism rather than economic distribution. Much of this outlook is derived from Islamic interpretations of man, society, and politics.[11] The idea was not just to change governments, but to change the structure of the government.

Thus, since the Iranian Revolution, it can persuasively be argued that political issues have always overshadowed economic concerns. Income from oil has provided enough political stability and security and has met the everyday needs of the public. Over the years, somewhere between 80 and 90 percent of the Islamic Republic's national budget has come from oil revenues. National resources have been devoted to enriching moral values and freeing Muslim territory from alien control. Iranian military and non-military resources have gone toward supporting such groups as Hizbullah in Lebanon and Islamic Jihad in Palestine to promote Islamist and anti-Western causes.

Post-revolution Iran focused on national planning and Third Worldism and self-reliance. These post-colonial axioms of the non-aligned movement were adopted as the pillars of a national strategy for development. Sanctions and delinking the economy from the West were welcomed. Essentially, the grand strategy aimed to create an alternate civilization to the "materialistic" Western world. While Brazil, Turkey, South Korea, Malaysia, and Singapore provide models of economic growth, such growth required cooperative relations with the centers of economic, trade, and technological power, especially the United States.

Due to its vast internal market and technological superiority, the United States has been an indispensable pillar for any country that aims for economic

---

[11] Ayatollah Khomeini, *Kashf al-Asrar* (Tehran: Nashr-i Safar, 1979) and *Sahifa-yi Nur*, Vols. 2 and 3 (Tehran: Sazman-i Madarik-i Farhangi-yi Inqilab-i Islami).

growth. By distancing itself from the United States, the revolutionaries of Iran lost opportunities for technology transfer. Subsequent American unilateral sanctions have also deprived Iran of opportunities to acquire new technologies from other countries in order to upgrade its oil and gas industry. Iran also cannot develop a strategy to penetrate Arab markets and benefit from the expanding economies of the Arabian Peninsula. Security, religious, and ideological differences and frictions have served as major obstacles for cooperation with neighboring countries, particularly in the Persian Gulf. Under such conditions, regional economic integration has been inconceivable.

Yet, as long as oil income pours in, Iran does not need to worry about maintaining its subsistence economy. Developing high tech industries, expanding the petrochemical infrastructure, and nurturing the ability to export durable and non-durable commodities to the major markets have not been (and cannot be) in the national political agenda. Indeed, had Iran defined its national interest as the promotion of its economic capacity, it would have pursued a different course in its foreign policy. It would have, for example, encouraged technology transfer and direct foreign investment, especially in its deteriorating oil and gas industry. China did not begin to develop economically until it normalized relations with Washington.

In short, Iran's economy is not interdependent with the rest of the world. It is essentially a barter economy in which oil is traded for goods and services.[12] By reducing its foreign economic relations to mere barter trading, Iran has largely emerged as a state outside of the global collective decision-making processes, somewhat resembling North Korea.[13] The politics of Iran's foreign policy is therefore not intertwined with economic relations. It is Iran's desire to maintain strategic distance from medium, large, and great powers. Its self-imposed isolation provides decision makers space and room to maneuver. In this respect, it is pertinent to note that the internationalization of an economy not only mobilizes the domestic productive capacity of a country, but over

---

[12] On the motives of localization of the economy, see Kaveh Ehsani, "Survival through Dispossession: Privatization of Public Goods in the Islamic Republic," *Middle East Report* 250 (2009), available online at http://www.merip.org/mer/mer250/ehsani.html.

[13] On the state of the Iranian economy see Jahangir Amuzegar, "Iran: The Rial Saga," *Middle East Economic Survey*, 6 August 2012.

time it also incrementally elbows the system to conform to the norms of the global power structure.

From the Iranian state perspective, interdependence is incompatible with political independence and causes gradual foreign meddling, a trend the Islamic Revolution battled against passionately. If Iran were to seek to emerge as another Turkey or Malaysia, its internal power structure and the ideals that legitimize the system would have to be altered. Like parallel railroad tracks, Iran's foreign policy and its foreign economic relations are destined never to meet.

The ideological nature of power in the Islamic Republic is reflected in its foreign policy

The nature of power in both industrialized and developing countries is founded on promotion of the private sector, the accumulation of wealth, the empowerment of the middle classes, and the expansion of the national GDP. One indicator of the economic health and political stability of a country is its domestic economic, social, and administrative capacity to attract foreign direct investment. Foreign policy in such states serves these policies and is an instrument for national power. If one regards the expansion of economic wealth as an ideology, it is an ideology that serves the average person. It is evident that the average citizen in Asia today lives far better than a generation ago and, unlike in Western Europe, the middle classes in Asia are increasing in vast numbers.[14] In 12 years, from 2000 to 2012, China's foreign reserves grew from $165 billion to $3.2 trillion.[15]

The Iranian political establishment cannot detach itself from history, particularly from the wrongdoings and interventions of external powers in the nineteenth and twentieth centuries. Ideology is a policy to combat great powers, to compensate for damages incurred in the past. In the Iranian version of Islamic ideology, maintaining distance from great powers is thus a virtue. It allows space and provides potential for developing a customized model of

---

[14] See the statistics provided by the World Business Council for Sustainable Development, available online at http://www.wbcsd.org/web/vision2050.htm.
[15] See http://www.chinability.com/Reserves.htm.

development and system sustainability. When a country such as Iran defines and declares itself unique and uninterested in engaging others, it loses the opportunity to enter coalitions and identify common objectives with politically and economically relevant countries both at the regional and global level. Ideology in its strict and revolutionary sense divides the country from others.

Non-cooperation with foreign powers is a closely guarded principle in the Islamic Republic. Potential negative economic consequences for the average person or for the state are immaterial. If the Islamic Republic engages in global politics and economics, it will no longer be the Islamic Republic, but would simply be another developing country absorbed into the global neo-realist system.[16] Because the Iranian leadership craves to remain exceptional, it must champion its ideological authenticity at all costs.

It is hard to dismiss the religious component of this attitude. The religious circles of Iran have produced considerable literature throughout the twentieth and twenty-first centuries calling for distance and particularism.[17] From these antecedents, political Islam evolved as a doctrine both to oppose the Westernized Shah's regime and to combat Communism.

A distinct repercussion of Iran's ideological foreign policy has been security conflicts with most of its neighbors. For instance, because of the tenets of political Islam, which strive for the interests of a collectivity rather than a nation state, Iran has engaged in a standoff with Israel for more than three decades. Many pundits are puzzled by Iran's attitude toward Israel, but there is a straightforward explanation. If Iran stood by its Westphalian national interests, it would choose only to sympathize with the Palestinian people. But, as a bastion of political Islam, Iran cannot rightly overlook the plight of the Palestinian liberation movement.

As outlined in the previous section, political Islam places politics and culture above economic interests, and therefore it could not position itself alongside the great powers. In theory, it rejects capitalism and does not value the expansion of national commercial and financial power. Within this framework,

---

[16] Sariolghalam, "The Foreign Policy of the Islamic Republic of Iran."
[17] Mahmood Sariolghalam, *Iranian Authoritarianism during the Qajar Period* (3rd edition) (Tehran: Farzan Rooz, 2012), pp. 139–153.

the concept of power is equal to ideological power. Though political Islam has diverse philosophical underpinnings, its internal processes and foreign policy outcomes resemble those of the Eastern bloc of the 1950s and the 1960s. As efficiency, productivity, and good governance have become universal values for a large majority of states, mechanisms for ideological sustainability have instead been the logic of political Islam.[18]

History tells us that revolutions cannot triumph and experience continuity without an ideological force. The Iranian revolution was no exception. However, whereas in the 1980s, foreign policy and its "export of the revolution" basis supplied more ideological vigor, in today's Iran ideology is needed at home. Foreign policy is only domestic policy's natural extension.

The sovereignty and the legitimacy of the Islamic Republic depend on the ideological nature of its foreign policy

The Islamic Republic unmistakably distanced itself from nationalism, secularism, and capitalism. It was also instituted on the principle of "no normalization" with the United States and the illegitimacy of Israel. As such, its state configuration became exclusive and has prolonged its legitimacy and sovereignty via the ideology of political Islam. If Iran were to change its policies and respond positively to American overtures, it would increasingly face contradictions in its definition of national sovereignty and its legitimacy. Moreover, if Iran were to make concessions to Israel as did Jordan or Egypt, its revolutionary credentials would be questioned by the vast security apparatus indoctrinated on ideological foundations.

Yet over the past three decades many changes have occurred in Iranian society that may challenge this ideology and hence legitimacy. A myriad of thoughts and political attitudes have surfaced during this period, particularly recently. Given the state's rejection of capitalism, ironically a good majority of Iranians are now worldly, materialistic in the Western sense, and are interested in the goods and services of rich and modern countries. For example, in late

---

[18] Ali Mirsepassi, *Political Islam, Iran and the Enlightenment: Philosophies of Hope and Despair* (Cambridge: Cambridge University Press, 2010).

March 2011, at the time of the Iranian New Year, millions of Iranians spend billions of dollars vacationing in Turkey, the UAE, Armenia, and Malaysia by going to concerts, sunbathing, shopping, and dining. This has been a New Year practice for years, but 2011 was noteworthy because of the number of Iranian involved and the amount of money spent. If the Iranian polity continues to indulge in such tastes, the state's logic of sovereignty and legitimacy will have to at least be somewhat modified. Normalization with the United States could present itself as indispensible, and the battle with Israel would become a non-issue.

To make any changes, ideology must be sidelined, or at least the Chinese model be applied, that is, change of policies and not change of structure. The political structure in China over the last three decades has not altered in any visible way; instead, policies in almost every single economic, political, and social area have been redefined and adjusted to new realities. China's embrace of capitalist practices, its growing trade with the West, and its new role in regional and global conflict resolution are all in contrast to the confrontational and politically isolated Mao period. In economic and foreign policies, the Chinese government has incorporated business interests in its calculations.

The redirecting of Iran's foreign policy would dictate a new consensus that would reach out to a diverse composition of elites comprised of professionals, business people, and the youth who have been exposed to international norms. The ramifications of this potential new consensus arguably extend beyond that of an ideological consensus. If carried out, the configuration of power would then have to be demarcated anew.

However, such internal conceptual conflicts have not served to bring about change; they have only spurred the Iranian elite to use ideology as an even more vigorous device to sustain itself. As was the case in Egyptian and Russian history, during which the art of consensus building and its processes were deficient, ideological centralism has become the only means of maintaining national sovereignty and state legitimacy. Such focused ideological interpretations of reality tend to limit possible modifications and adjustments.

Over time, these fixed ideologies become even more calcified and are eventually regarded as untouchable and sacred. Ideology calls for permanence, which is in contradiction to the constant variations of human life. Hence,

Iranian political culture has regrettably only experienced centralization.[19] Iran's foreign policy is the reflection of a social order that lacks trust among its members. The liberty to organize at the social level appears to be a prerequisite to organizing at the elite level and allowing debates to take place. But it is not only the ban on organizing that has caused rigidity in ideology at the top levels. Disorganization in Iranian society has also facilitated ideological centralism at the elite level.[20] Indeed, in Iranians' century-old struggle for statehood and progress, consensus building on major national issues has proven to be a weakness. The social contract among Iranians is still in the making.

The national security of the Islamic Republic is intertwined with its current foreign policy

All countries require a central organizational concept for their national security doctrine. Terrorism is such a concept for most Western countries. Though there are numerous issues that threaten Iran's national security, such as drug trafficking, brain drain, desertification, and the youth bulge, none can equal the salience of external adversaries such as the United States and Israel. Indeed, the priority of guarding against these opponents[21] defines the parameters of social order in Iran. It constitutes a highly efficient instrument to construct the *raison d'être* of a system and whatever may potentially agitate its existence. It should also be noted that Iran's rhetoric and behavior also serve as a convenient excuse for Middle Eastern countries and extra-regional actors to pursue military buildup, regional reach, political alliances, and security consolidation.

The behavior of the Islamic Republic increasingly demonstrates that it cannot "mix" with the great powers. This behavior is often explained in terms of political Islam, in that it cannot coexist with capitalism and liberalism. Philosophically, political Islam also cannot accept "the rule and the primacy

---

[19] This idea and other ideas relating to political culture are based on the author's field research. See Mahmood Sariolghalam, *Iran's Political Culture* (3rd edition) (Tehran: Farzan Rooz, 2010).
[20] David Patrick Houghton, "Reinvigorating the Study of Foreign Policy Decision Making: Toward a Constructivist Approach," *Foreign Policy Analysis* 3 (2007): 24–45.
[21] For illuminating research on the "enemy image," see Richard K. Herrmann and Michael P. Fischerkeller, "Beyond the Enemy Image and Spiral Model: Cognitive-Strategic Research after the Cold War," *International Organization* 49, 3 (1995): 415–450.

of others." Logically, political Islam is more a reaction than a construct, and "Islamic democracy" is a theoretically trumped up euphemism for built-in contradictions. Confrontation and denunciation therefore has become a way of life. For argument's sake, if Iran were drafted as a member of the G20 because of its geoeconomic and geopolitical significance, it would have to redefine its identity, its internal legitimation processes, and its national security priorities. The consequence of such refurbishing would be a new consensus at home with new faces and new ideas. Normalization with the United States would especially disturb the parameters of the internal power configuration in Iran.

Such a new arrangement would entail a new worldview. For an ideological order, engagement initially necessitates a deconstruction of the old order. China is a classic illustration. As long as Mao's interpretation of the world set the pattern in security and economic debates, the country could not engage with the outside world. A genuine deconstruction of Mao's thinking was a strategic precondition to embark on a new path.[22] Maoist thinking that aimed to keep China distinct and politically distanced from the rest of the world vividly inhibited that country's economic integration with other countries and regions. Ideological states usually fear mixing with other societies in order not to disturb their tightly controlled domestic orders.

The situation in contemporary Iran can be compared to that of Maoist China, except that the contemporary ideological, and hence political and social, divisions in Iran in terms of tradition and modernity cannot enable and qualify such a transformation. Unlike in China, Iranian groups that are striving and competing for power are too polarized to reach a consensus.

Many of Iran's discourses are almost a half-century old. For example, conceptions of the state, the West, management, deterrence, and power are based in the preachings of the nonaligned movement of the 1950s. A good number of engineers and physicians turned politicians, in addition to locally trained and below average social scientists, indulge in articulating these obsolete and old-fashioned misconstructions.[23]

---

[22]Wang Hui, *The End of the Revolution: China and the Limits of Modernity* (London: Verso, 2009), pp. 3–18.
[23]Mahmood Sariolghalam, "Iran in Search of Itself," *Current History* (December 2008): 427–428.

National security, then, is the extension of preserving the ideological order. As mentioned earlier, support for non-state actors and liberation movements has been valuable in strengthening bargaining power for the ultimate safeguarding of an ideological disposition. In other words, sustaining the ideological construct and all of its derivations is the most significant pillar of Iranian national security. In the end, however, it is an ideology that is under threat. Issues such as the slow rate of economic growth, the depletion of natural resources, environmental decay, limited technological know-how, and poor educational quality receive only temporary attention when accidents take place or crises erupt. As a result, the power and relevance of the Islamic Republic arises almost solely from its ideological uniqueness. Whether or not this can be sustained in the face of rising on-the-ground troubles is the larger question.

A Fractured National Identity

Despite attempts from the 1950s through the 1970s, Iran could not construct the foundations of a modern society based on a sizeable middle class. In recent decades, Iranians have proved unable to build a unified national identity and have thus failed to position their country as a *nation state*. A standoff between the joint forces of religion and political Islam, on the one hand, and those of modernity on the other, continues to this day.

There is a peculiar dichotomy between pre-revolutionary state-society relations and the popular roots of the Islamic Republic of Iran. The former was exclusively an edifice of individuals and an elite structure, while the Islamic state, through the logic of the revolutionary process, produced a social base for its domestic and foreign policy pursuits. The Islamic Republic found legitimacy particularly in the rural areas and among the urban poor. Some may dub the new polity as populist, but it goes beyond populist ideology.

The latest modus operandi among Iranians has fulfilled some tangible needs and furnished plenty of psychological blandishments for the masses. For the anti-globalization generation now living under the Islamic Republic, there is constant psychological gratification because there are no foreigners telling it what to do. This generation who fought against *l'ancien régime* is impervious and inattentive to technological joint ventures, the IT revolution, the nine percent economic growth rate in China, e-government, and impressive infrastructure investments around the world. After all, there is enough petroleum income to let time pass by untrammeled. It is argued that though knowledge, organization, and networking are required to produce wealth, one may lose political independence as a result of acquiring these attributes. Purity is ensured through isolation.

According to the statistics compiled from many sources,[24] Iran's income from petroleum since its discovery around 1908 is about $1 trillion. In comparison, Japan's average GDP over the last decade has consistently been around $4.7 trillion annually. Both countries embarked on a course of transformation in the latter part of the nineteenth century, in Japan through the Meiji Dynasty and in Iran through the constitutionalist movement. This simple comparison may guide one to the salience of economic growth as a major prerequisite to accomplish social coherence, political stability, and an improvement in human development indexes.[25]

Indeed, a pivotal deficiency has caused distress in Iran's new social and political arrangements: The ideological system defers modification, adjustment, and adaptation to new global realities. Conceivably, the revolutionary polity cannot reorder or redefine itself since such an undertaking would inadvertently bring about revisions in the power configuration of the country.

The points outlined above regarding Iran's economic policy, foreign policy, sovereignty, legitimacy, and security underpin the consistency of post revolutionary Iran's foreign policy behavior. While in the early days of the revolution, uniqueness meant commitment to political Islam, increasingly in the 1990s and the 2000s uniqueness became a means of affording legitimacy and security.

Conclusion

The ideology of the Islamic Revolution is fundamentally a response to a historical legacy — the legacy of extensive foreign intervention in the social and

---

[24] Iran's Central Bank, Iran Centre for Statistics, BP and OPEC.
[25] Fareed Zakaria, *The Future of Freedom* (New York: W. W. Norton & Company, 2003).

political life of Iran. The long period of foreign intervention resulted in Iran's constitutionalist, and ultimately revolutionary, activities that disentangled the country from its humiliating experience and aimed to raise up the decaying empire. Similar to other revolutionary experiments, it created domestic structures that were consonant with foreign policy bearings.

The essential approach in Iran's foreign policy behavior has remained intact over the course of three decades. It is worth noting that despite its rigid fixations, Iran has occasionally exhibited flexibility in the service of its ideological construct. For example, despite their apparent mutual animosity, Iran and the United States pursued a win-win game plan in Iraq and Afghanistan in the 2001–2007 period.[26] Normalization was seemingly not necessary for such a high level of harmony between purpose and process, as this unexpected and narrow engagement was designed for short-term gains.

To avoid isolation in the past, Iran even reached out to Mubarak's Egypt, numerous Saudi officials, Jordan, and Morocco to expand relations. Iran's dealings with Turkey have been the most stable in its entire post-revolutionary foreign policy, though as a result of the Syrian crisis since 2011, in which Iran has sided with the Bashar al-Asad regime and Turkey against it, relations have become strained. Iran's interactions with Russia and China have been businesslike. It should be noted that none of these bilateral relations have borne any threatening impact on the ideological character of the state and its internal structures. Most countries neither have the interest nor the capability to want to change the systemic features of the Islamic Republic.

Iran's confrontation with the United States has provided a prevailing stimulus for the continuity of the Islamic Republic and its foreign policy over a span of three decades. At the core of this confrontation is the meaning that Iran attaches to the concept of Israel: A state with no legitimacy. Iran's characterization of Israel and its narrative of the Israeli–Palestinian conflict excite Iranian–American encounters. This depiction of reality assists Iran in bequeathing itself with legitimacy, sovereignty, security, and stability.

---

[26] Kenneth Katzman, *U.S.-Iranian Relations: An Analytic Compendium of U.S. Policies, Laws and Regulations* (Washington D.C.: Atlantic Council, 2010).

For states that aspire to project uniqueness, conflicts and crises may be strategically valuable and psychologically comforting. In the absence of interstate wars in the Middle East, the concept of the Islamic Republic may also be beneficial to many regional and extra-regional players. Given the competition between China and the United States over raw materials and energy resources, the idea of the Islamic Republic may also serve numerous interests for both global powers in the Arab world and in the wider Middle East.

Though the Chinese do not want Middle Eastern issues and conflicts to become stumbling blocks in their relations with Washington, they utilize such cases in their broad geopolitical and economic calculus to soften or harden certain policies. Particularly in the last decade, in which Iran's nuclear policy and widespread sanctions have shaped American policy toward Tehran, China has emerged as an economic beneficiary both by defusing pressure on Iran and drawing political advantages in its interactions with the United States.

One pertinent query looms on the horizon: Will the Iranian–American rivalry that serves many interests endure in the medium to long term? That may depend on a number of dynamics, namely, Iran's succession issue; the aptitude and the political skills of social forces in the country to redefine national priorities; and the price of oil. But it also may more fundamentally depend on whether Iran's elite is able to continue its ideological centralization. If real change comes to Iran, its rivalry with the United States may become moot.

The United States stands out as the only country that has the geopolitical and strategic interests to bring Iran into its orbit. American unilateral sanctions coupled with European Union and United Nations multilateral sanctions have had crippling consequences for Iran's economy, bringing daily and chaotic policy changes as well as social unrest and dissatisfaction. Iran's economy cannot possibly improve unless fundamental shifts take place in its foreign policy orientation and particularly in its denial of the regional political order. Based on the preceding four-part analysis, the key question is: Can Iran emulate the Chinese example and generate changes in its foreign policy and economy without jeopardizing its political order? The only plausible proposition in this regard is a policy of political inclusiveness by the current military-industrial complex. Survival, territorial integrity, and political cohesiveness of the state rather than ideology and Islamist orientation may coerce current elites to transform.

Settlement of disputes with the United States is at the center of Iran's national challenges and survival of the political order. As chronicled above, the most noteworthy clash with the United States is Iran's characterization of the state of Israel, which has unleashed tremendous energy to oppose Iran over the last three decades. As such, the future of the Islamic Republic rests on its willingness to revise its depiction of Israel.

The United States and the Gulf

Chapter 8

American Policy in the Persian Gulf: From Balance of Power to Failed Hegemony

F. Gregory Gause, III

American policy in the Persian Gulf region has gone through three phases since the 1940s. The first, which lasted until about 1970, was driven by a mix of commercial energy interests and strategic Cold War interests, but exhibited only minimal American military commitment. The second, from about 1970 through the end of the century, was driven by strategic considerations and saw a steady buildup of American military forces in the region. During this period Washington in effect abandoned the commercial interests of American oil companies and defined its interests completely in terms of strategic Cold War and regional power considerations. Those considerations revolved around access to oil, no doubt, but not around the competition between American oil companies and other foreign oil companies or the local national oil companies. Strategic "stability" was the byword for American policy during this period, despite the important changes that were occurring in the region itself. The third period, from 2001 to the present, saw the United States abandon its interest in regional "stability" and focus on changing the status quo. This period of failed hegemony has its origins in the attacks of 11 September 2001 and crashed on the rocks of the occupation of Iraq. The Obama Administration came to power intending to return to the policy that characterized the second period, one based on American military power preserving, not challenging, the regional status quo. However, the Arab upheavals of 2011 might call into question that return to a "realist" approach to the Persian Gulf in American policy.

Periodization rests on identifying turning points. I see the important turning points in American Gulf policy as the oil revolution of the early 1970s and the 9/11 attacks. Within the second period, I see the Iranian revolution as an important change in the strategic map, one that led to the buildup of American military force in the region. However, the revolution did not significantly change the overall definition of American regional interests, merely how Washington set out to safeguard them. I do not see the end of the Cold War as a major turning point. American policy in the Gulf, before and after the Cold War, demonstrated a remarkable continuity. The end of the Cold War did remove an important restraint on the application of American power in the region, but it did not change the definition of those interests.

While oil has been the central reason why the United States cares about the Persian Gulf, the way America defines its oil interest has changed over time, from championing American oil companies to caring about oil as a strategic resource, with little regard for who finds it, produces it, and markets it. Thus, while oil is always present in American calculations about the Gulf, those who argue that "control" of oil resources was a major impetus for recent American policy in the Gulf are off the mark.[1]

America in the Gulf: The Early Years

It is clear that oil drove American interests in the Persian Gulf at the outset of American involvement in the region. Washington pressured Great Britain and France after World War I to allow American oil companies a piece of the Turkish (later Iraq) Petroleum Company (of Gulbenkian fame).[2] American oil men preceded the American government in Saudi Arabia. The fear

---

[1] I expand on the general arguments I make here in more detail in F. Gregory Gause, III, *The International Relations of the Persian Gulf* (Cambridge: Cambridge University Press, 2010).
[2] Daniel Yergin, *The Prize: The Epic Quest for Oil, Money and Power* (New York: Simon and Schuster, 1991), Chapter 10.

of an oil shortage during World War II highlighted the strategic, not simply the commercial, importance of oil for the United States as an emerging world power. But that did not mean that Washington was now uninterested in the fortunes of American oil companies. The friction between American and British oil interests in the region became so intense that it reached the top levels of both governments. Roosevelt and Churchill exchanged telegrams in 1944 in which each pledged that his country was not trying to "horn in" on the oil interests of the other. Roosevelt told Churchill that the United States was not "making sheep's eyes at your oil fields in Iraq or Iran," while Churchill made the same commitment about American interests in Saudi Arabia.[3]

After the war Washington, by granting an exemption from anti-trust legislation, permitted four of the five American "majors" to form the Arabian-American Oil Company (ARAMCO) in order to develop Saudi Arabia's industry. Washington also changed the tax law to encourage the companies to share more of their profits with the Saudi government, with the aim of solidifying their role in the country.[4] In the aftermath of the Mossadegh coup in Iran, Washington made sure that American companies got the chance to buy into the new consortium of companies that would replace Anglo-Iranian (now BP) as the operator of Iran's oil industry.[5]

With the advent of the Cold War, the interest of denying the Soviet Union any influence in the Persian Gulf region joined American commercial interests as a driver of American policy. The first Cold War crisis, in 1946, was over the Soviet reluctance to withdraw from Iran according to the promises made at the Tehran Conference of 1943. American pressure and some adroit Iranian diplomacy convinced Stalin to leave Iranian Azerbaijan and Kurdistan, where the Red Army had set up local Communist governments.[6] The Eisenhower Administration's decision to join the British plot to unseat Iranian Prime Minister Mossadegh (after the Truman Administration had refused)

---

[3] *Ibid.*, p. 401.
[4] *Ibid.*, Chapters 20–22.
[5] *Ibid.*, Chapter 23.
[6] Louise Fawcett, *Iran and the Cold War: The Azerbaijan Crisis of 1946* (Cambridge: Cambridge University Press, 1992).

in 1953 was motivated by its increasing belief that Mossadegh was acting, consciously or not, in the interests of the Soviet Union.[7] The United States might also have been involved in the destabilization of the government of Abd al-Karim Qasim in Iraq in 1963, which it saw as a Soviet ally.[8]

Cold War considerations were certainly central, along with commercial ones, in American Gulf policy during this period. But American policy in the region was not particularly militarized. The United States gave military aid to the Shah's regime and had military training missions there. The same is true in Saudi Arabia.[9] But there were very few American forces in the region. The United States kept a small naval force in Bahrain, usually three ships. Saudi Arabia closed the American air base at Dhahran in 1961, with hardly a murmur of objection from Washington.[10] The United States looked to Great Britain to manage security issues in the region, as the British still had responsibility for their protectorate states. When Iraq threatened the newly independent state of Kuwait in 1961, it was British, not American, forces that rushed to the border to deter the Iraqis.[11] On the whole, the Persian Gulf was a somewhat sleepy corner on the American Cold War map, not nearly as unsettled as the eastern Mediterranean with its Arab-Israeli wars or Southeast Asia with the Vietnam

---

[7] Mark J. Gasiorowski and Malcolm Byrne, eds., *Mohammed Mossadeq and the 1953 Coup in Iran* (Syracuse: Syracuse University Press, 2004); James A. Bill, *The Eagle and the Lion: The Tragedy of American-Iranian Relations* (New Haven, CT: Yale University Press, 1988), Chapter 2.
[8] Roger Morris, "A Tyrant 40 Years in the Making," *New York Times*, 14 March 2003. Morris was a State Department official who served on the National Security Council in the Johnson and Nixon Administrations. Phebe Marr contends that there is "no hard evidence ... one way or the other" about the claim of American involvement in Qasim's overthrow, but adds that "there can be little doubt of U.S. distaste for the left-leaning Qasim regime and its Soviet tilt." Phebe Marr, *The Modern History of Iraq* (2nd ed.) (Boulder, CO: Westview Press, 2004), p. 114.
[9] For excellent accounts of Saudi-American relations in this period, see Robert Vitalis, *America's Kingdom: Mythmaking on the Saudi Oil Frontier* (Stanford, CA: Stanford University Press, 2007) and Nathan J. Citino, *From Arab Nationalism to OPEC: Eisenhower, King Saud and the Making of U.S.-Saudi Relations* (Bloomington, IN: Indiana University Press, 2002).
[10] Nadav Safran, *Saudi Arabia: The Ceaseless Quest for Security* (Cambridge, MA: Harvard University Press, 1985), p. 92.
[11] For an extensive discussion of this episode, see Mustafa A. Alani, *Operation Vantage: British Military Intervention in Kuwait 1961* (Surbiton, UK: LAAM, 1990).

War. It was important in Cold War strategy because of its oil, but the United States did not have to do that much to preserve its interests.

American Gulf Policy from 1970 to 2000

The Persian Gulf arose from its slumber in the 1970s. The period began with a profound change in power relations in the world oil market that made the Gulf producers both fabulously wealthy and newly powerful on the world stage. The region witnessed a major social revolution in the Gulf's largest country, Iran, which fundamentally altered the nature of regional politics. It saw large-scale international wars: the Iran-Iraq War (1980–1988) and the Gulf War (1990–1991). During this period American policy in the region became highly militarized, and the period ended with a string of American military bases established along the Arab littoral. However, the overall strategic goals of American policy did not significantly change. The United States sought to limit the influence of the Soviet Union in the area as part of its Cold War strategy. It worked to prevent any local power — Iran or Iraq — from becoming dominant. Only the means of American policy changed, with a quantum jump in military commitment. Thus, while American interest level in the region shifted as the region's international importance rose with the oil revolution and the Iranian Revolution, the overall American goal of denying any other power a major role in the Gulf was consistent with the previous period.

One element of the American calculation of its interests in the region that did change was the commercial interests of American oil companies. The early 1970s saw the epochal shift of power in the world oil market from the oil companies to the producer countries. In the early 1950s the companies could frustrate Mossadegh's effort to nationalize Anglo-Iranian because they had plenty of oil elsewhere. By 1970 global supply and demand were about in balance, and the producer countries began to take advantage of the changed power realities. Even before the oil embargo of 1973, the countries had forced a substantial (at that time) increase in both prices and in the percentages of profit they took. The embargo, which saw Saudi Arabia order four American oil companies (the Aramco partners Esso, Mobil, Texaco, and Chevron) to stop shipping Saudi oil to the United States and the American companies comply with the Saudi order, symbolized the new power realities. Over the course of the 1970s almost every Middle East producer — pro-American and pro-Soviet, "capitalist" and "socialist" — nationalized its oil industry or, in places where formal nationalization had already occurred, took *de facto* control of the industry.[12]

While all this was happening, the United States government did nothing. It did not try to pressure allies to stop the nationalizations. It did not punish non-allies (such as Iraq and Libya) for doing so. During the oil embargo, it did not react with hostile military acts or efforts to destabilize governments. It pushed friendly oil producers in Riyadh and Tehran to "moderate" the price increases post-1973, but it did not challenge the fact that pricing and production decisions were now in the hands of the producer countries.[13] On the contrary, the United States deepened its relationship with the two Gulf states, Saudi Arabia and Iran, that did the most to create the oil revolution. It did nothing to support American oil companies as they lost control of some of their most valuable assets. In essence, the United States (and the major capitalist countries more generally) accepted without a fight an enormous change in the global energy system, one that helped cause the longest and most serious North American/European recession since the Great Depression and led to one of the largest international transfers of wealth (and from militarily strong states to militarily weak states) in history. Before 1970, the American government acted as the champion for American oil companies in the Gulf. After 1970, it did not.

The oil revolution of the early 1970s vastly increased the strategic importance of the Persian Gulf, but it did not change America's strategic posture in the Gulf. Despite the formal withdrawal of British military protection for the smaller Gulf monarchies (with their independence in 1971), the United States

---

[12] On the epochal changes in the world oil market at this time, see James Bamburg, *British Petroleum and Global Oil, 1950–1975: The Challenge of Nationalism* (Cambridge: Cambridge University Press, 2000), Chapters 18–19; Yergin, *The Prize*, Chapters 24–29; and Dankwart A. Rustow, *Oil and Turmoil: America Faces OPEC and the Middle East* (New York: W. W. Norton, 1982), Chapters 2–4.
[13] Andrew Scott Cooper, "Showdown at Doha: The Secret Oil Deal That Helped Sink the Shah of Iran," *Middle East Journal* 62, 4 (2008) pp. 567–591.

did not seek to "fill the vacuum" by increasing its own military presence in the region. Still enmeshed in Vietnam and facing a public leery of any new military commitments, the Nixon Administration sought to protect American interests in the Gulf by building up the military and political status of its local allies, the Shah's Iran and Saudi Arabia (again, the very countries that had driven the oil revolution) through massive arms sales and an upgraded political status in American global strategy.[14] The "Twin Pillars" of the Gulf would, Washington hoped, take care of American oil and Cold War interests, but the cost was acknowledging their newfound power and autonomy from their superpower patron.

The Twin Pillar policy came crashing down with the Iranian revolution. No longer would Iran be a reliable Cold War ally against the Soviet Union (if a somewhat less reliable oil partner). Now Iran would be a challenge to American interests in the region. The fall of the Shah in 1979, and the subsequent Soviet invasion of Afghanistan later that year, began a process of militarization of American policy in the Gulf that would culminate in the Iraq War of 2003. The change was marked by President Carter's declaration in January 1980 that the United States would oppose with military force any attempt by "any outside force" to dominate the Persian Gulf.[15] The Carter Doctrine made explicit what had been implied in American Cold War strategy up to that point. The Cold War context of the Doctrine is obvious in its reference to an "outside force," clearly the Soviet Union. However, the Doctrine, in the wake of the Iranian revolution and during the Iranian hostage crisis, implied that the United States would also be willing to use force against any regional country that challenged American interests.

The Carter Doctrine began the militarization of American Gulf policy. Yet at the outset, that militarization was halting and uncertain. Washington established a military command for the Gulf region, called the Rapid Deployment Joint Task Force (the forerunner of Central Command), but had precious

---

[14] F. Gregory Gause, "British and American Policies in the Persian Gulf, 1968–1973," *Review of International Studies* 11, 4 (1985): 247–273.
[15] The text of Carter's speech, the State of the Union speech of 23 January 1980, is available online at http://www.jimmycarterlibrary.gov/documents/speeches/su80jec.phtml.

little success in getting Gulf states to accept American bases or "facilities agreements" on their territories. Only Oman was willing to agree, publicly, to giving American forces access to its territory.[16] The United States deployed forces to the region, particularly to Saudi Arabia, on an *ad hoc* basis in response to crises — the fall of the Shah and the beginning of the Iran–Iraq War — but could not get the Saudis or the other Gulf monarchies to agree to host American military forces on a regular basis.[17]

After the initial panic in both Washington and the world oil market over the Iranian revolution and the beginning of the Iran–Iraq War (in September 1980), it did not seem likely that the United States would need to revisit its Gulf strategy in any fundamental way. The Soviet Union hardly benefited from the Iranian revolution, which was almost as hostile to Moscow as it was to Washington. The Iran–Iraq War settled into a violent but desultory pattern in which neither side could defeat the other and try to assert its control over the region. Oil prices actually fell during the fighting, bottoming out at below $10 per barrel during a brief period in 1986. But Cold War dynamics drew the United States into its first major military deployment in the Gulf at the end of the Iran-Iraq War. When Iran began attacking Kuwaiti shipping (in retaliation for Iraqi attacks on Iranian shipping and Kuwaiti support for Iraq), the Kuwaiti government asked the United States to protect its oil tankers by "reflagging" them with the American flag. Washington initially refused, at which point Kuwait asked the Soviet Union to provide that service. Moscow was more than willing, at which point the United States quickly reconsidered. It sent America's largest naval force since the Vietnam War to the Persian Gulf and directly engaged Iranian naval forces, protecting Kuwaiti and Saudi shipping in 1987–1988. The USS Vincennes, in one such engagement in July 1988, mistakenly shot down an Iran Air passenger plane, killing all 290 people on board. Shortly thereafter, Iran accepted the UN cease-fire resolution and ended the war.[18]

---

[16] Joseph A. Kechichian, *Oman and the World* (Santa Monica: RAND, 1995), pp. 150–157.
[17] Safran, *Saudi Arabia*, Chapter 16.
[18] For a discussion of the American naval deployment, see Gause, *International Relations of the Persian Gulf*, pp. 81–85.

The naval deployment of 1987–1988 was the first major American military activity in the Persian Gulf since World War II. But it paled in comparison to what followed shortly thereafter. In response to Saddam Hussein's 1990 invasion of Kuwait, the United States sent approximately half a million of its soldiers, sailors, marines, and air force personnel to the region. At the head of a substantial international coalition and buttressed by the legitimacy of UN Security Council resolutions, it ejected the Iraqi forces from Kuwait and restored al-Sabah rule in the country. However, despite its overwhelming military victory and the presence of such a large force in the area, Washington did not continue the battle to remove Saddam Hussein from power. On the contrary, American forces stood by while Saddam restored his control over southern and central Iraq. The United States, with France and Great Britain, did establish a safe zone in northern and northeastern Iraq that became an autonomous Kurdish zone and is now the Kurdish Regional Government of Iraq. But it did not follow up its victory in the Gulf War with an effort to remake the politics of Iraq or the regional map. Rather, it fought the Gulf War to restore the Gulf status quo, not to change it.[19]

American policy in the Gulf War provides the most important and clearest indicator about how Washington defined its strategic interests in the region during this period. The thought that any other power, either "outside" or local, would become the dominant force in the region was unacceptable to Washington. The United States was willing to go to great lengths to preserve a regional balance of power with itself at the apex. But it was not willing to do much to change regional realities to expand its regional dominance. It took no serious military action against the Iranian revolutionary regime and made no serious effort to restore the monarchy to power (as it did in 1953). When it had Saddam Hussein on the ropes in 1991, it did nothing to stop him from restoring his control over most of the country. Washington could live with a Persian Gulf in which the two major regional states were hostile to the United

---

[19] For their explanations of American policy in the post-war period, emphasizing the need to maintain a stable balance of power in the Gulf, see George H. W. Bush and Brent Scowcroft, *A World Transformed* (New York: Alfred A. Knopf, 1998), p. 489 and James A. Baker, III, *The Politics of Diplomacy* (New York: G.P. Putnam's, 1995), pp. 437–438.

States, as long as that hostility did not lead them to interfere with the oil trade or to try to assert their own control over the area.

The end of the Cold War did not alter American policy in the region. The Gulf War represented the beginning of the end of the Cold War, with the Soviet Union holding America's coat while Washington fought erstwhile Soviet ally Saddam Hussein. Within a year of the end of the Gulf War, the Soviet Union no longer existed. But the end of the Cold War, which had been the strategic context in which so much of America's Gulf policy had been made, did not lead to a rethinking about America's regional interests. On the contrary, the United States vastly increased its military infrastructure in the region. The only real change the end of the Cold War brought was to remove the most important restraint on the use of American military power in the Gulf. During the Cold War, a direct American assault on a Soviet ally would have risked escalation to nuclear war. After it, that serious disincentive was removed.

The experience of the Gulf War ended the previous reticence of the Gulf monarchies to hosting permanent (or semi-permanent) American military forces and bases. In the 1990s the United States established a base in Kuwait, vastly expanded the headquarters of the Fifth Fleet in Bahrain, built an enormous airbase in Qatar, expanded its access to air and naval facilities in the UAE and Oman, and stationed an air wing in Saudi Arabia (to patrol the skies over southern Iraq).[20] Without this military infrastructure, it is doubtful that the United States could have fought the Iraq War in 2003. But in the 1990s this major military buildup was not put to transformative uses. It was meant to protect a status quo that was not perfect from the American point of view, but was more than favorable to American strategic and economic interests. Pressure was put on Saddam Hussein, but not enough to overthrow him. The Islamic Republic of Iran was sanctioned economically and contained militarily, but

---

[20] On the American military buildup in the 1990s, see Rachel Bronson, "Beyond Containment in the Persian Gulf," *Orbis* 45, 2 (2001): 193–209; Anthony H. Cordesman, "Saudi Arabia, the U.S. and the Structure of Gulf Alliances," Center for Strategic and International Studies, 25 February 1999, available online at http://csis.org/publication/saudi-arabia-us-and-structure-gulf-alliances; and Geoffrey Kemp and Robert E. Harkavy, *Strategic Geography and the Changing Middle East* (Washington, D.C.: Brookings Institution Press, 1997), Chapter 7.

no serious efforts were made to change that regime, either.[21] America vastly increased its permanent military footprint in the Persian Gulf in part because it could and in part because it could not rely on its local allies to protect its interests as it could during the days of the Shah. The Iranian Revolution, the Iran-Iraq War, and Saddam's invasion of Kuwait all signaled that the Persian Gulf was an unstable area. With little reason not to, Washington decided it would stabilize it.

Failed Hegemony: The Iraq War and the 2000s

The American commitment to the Persian Gulf status quo ended with the Iraq War of 2003. The origins of that war remain a matter of great political and academic controversy. My contention is that the most important impetus behind the American decision to remove Saddam Hussein's regime and attempt to restructure the Iraqi state was the attacks on New York and Washington that occurred on 11 September 2001. The Bush Administration determined that the deep cause of the 9/11 attacks was the dysfunctional politics of the Middle East, which bred terrorism and anti-Americanism. At a minimum, an attack on Iraq would restore America's deterrent power and put other hostile regimes on notice that there was a price to pay for supporting groups the United States defined as terrorist and for developing weapons of mass destruction (as Washington, incorrectly, contended Iraq was doing). More grandiosely, some in the Administration thought that the installation of a pro-American democracy in Iraq would have a ripple effect throughout the region, pressing both anti-American regimes in Iran and Syria and pro-American regimes in Saudi Arabia (from where Osama bin Laden and most of the 9/11 hijackers hailed) and Egypt toward democratic political reform.[22]

---

[21] In recognition of these limited goals, the Clinton Administration labeled its Gulf policy "dual containment," as in containment of Iraq and Iran. The policy was presented by National Security Advisor Anthony Lake in "Confronting Backlash States," *Foreign Affairs* 73, 2 (March 1994).
[22] I lay out my case for this explanation of American decision-making in the Iraq War and assess alternative explanations in Gause, *The International Relations of the Persian Gulf*, Chapter 6.

While there is debate about why the Iraq War occurred, there can be no debate about what the Bush Administration sought to do in Iraq — to reconfigure Iraqi politics in a deep and profound way. Not only was Saddam Hussein removed from power, but the ruling Baʻth Party was disbanded, the Iraqi army was dissolved, and the Iraqi bureaucracy was fundamentally restructured by prohibiting Baʻth Party members of a certain rank from holding bureaucratic positions.[23] The three foundations of the modern Iraqi state were thoroughly altered as part of a conscious American policy to, in effect, destroy and rebuild the Iraqi polity. The United States did succeed in implementing democratic elections in Iraq, though the democratic governments that have ruled Iraq since 2005 have been characterized by administrative weakness and internal division.

This was a hegemonic project far beyond anything that the United States had ever attempted in the Middle East. Occupying a regional state, changing its government, and fighting a debilitating and extended war to sustain the new government had no precedent in the American experience in the Persian Gulf. It is clear that, at least in the heady early days of its victory over Saddam Hussein, the Bush Administration did not see its transformative regional mission as limited to Iraq. In his State of the Union address in January 2002, President Bush included Iran along with Iraq in the "axis of evil" that the United States had to confront.[24] As the United States became bogged down in the Iraqi insurgency, any hopes of pressuring Iran fell by the wayside. The United States also pressured Saudi Arabia to begin a very modest political reform program that included elections to municipal councils in the country's cities and towns.[25] For the first time in the post-World War II period, American policy in the Gulf was as concerned with altering the domestic political orders of the Gulf states

---

[23] On the American occupation, see Rajiv Chandrasekaran, *Imperial Life in the Emerald City: Inside Iraq's Green Zone* (New York: Alfred A. Knopf, 2007); Thomas Ricks, *Fiasco: The American Military Adventure in Iraq* (New York: Penguin Press, 2006); and George Packer, *The Assassins' Gate: America in Iraq* (New York: Farrar, Straus and Giroux, 2005).

[24] For the text of the 2002 State of the Union address, see http://stateoftheunionaddress.org/2002-george-w-bush.

[25] The Saudi municipal elections were held in February, March, and April 2005. For an indication that American pressure played a role in the Saudi decision to hold the elections, see David B. Ottaway, "U.S.-Saudi Relations Show Signs of Stress," *Washington Post*, 20 April 2004.

as it was with preserving a favorable regional status quo. In fact, it put at risk that regional status quo through its policy in Iraq, allowing Iran to increase its influence in Iraq in a way that would have been unthinkable during Saddam Hussein's regime.[26]

This was an ambitious agenda for regional hegemony. Had the Bush Administration succeeded, it would have rivaled Great Britain of the inter-war period in terms of its control over the Persian Gulf region. Then, Britain had a mandate in Iraq, protectorate treaties with the smaller Gulf states, predominant influence in Iran, and significant influence (later shared with the United States) in Saudi Arabia. Its navy was unchallenged in the Gulf; its air force patrolled the borders of the regional states and put down local rebellions; its ground forces kept the regional peace and preserved friendly governments.[27] The Bush Administration sought the same kind of dominance, not just over the regional power balance but also over the domestic political arrangements of the Gulf states. It found, at a tremendous cost of blood and treasure, that much had changed in the 70 years between Britain's Gulf hegemony and its own effort in that direction. It was hard enough for Britain to sustain its position then; it was impossible for the United States, despite its enormous power, to achieve a comparable standing. Regional states are stronger, and local populations are less willing to accept foreign interventions and are better able to bring force to bear against foreign occupiers.

While the Bush Administration seemed to want to walk in Britain's imperial footsteps in the Persian Gulf, in one way its goals were very different. For Britain, control of and access to Gulf oil was a major imperial goal during the inter-war period. Oil did not play nearly as important a role in American decision-making in the Iraq War of 2003. Of course, oil is part of every American decision taken about its role in the Gulf. Without its vast oil reserves, the United States would not have the military infrastructure it has in the Gulf and would not devote as much time and resources to the region as it does. Hence

---

[26] See, for example, Kenneth Katzman, "Iran-Iraq Relations," Congressional Research Service, 7-5700, 13 August 2010, available online at www.fas.org/sgp/crs/mideast/RS22323.pdf.

[27] For a discussion of inter-war British power in the region, see Elizabeth Monroe, *Britain's Moment in the Middle East, 1914–1956* (Baltimore, MD: Johns Hopkins University Press, 1963).

oil was part of the reason, a necessary cause, of the American decision to go to war in Iraq in 2003.[28]

But oil is not a sufficient explanation of the American war decision.[29] There is little evidence from the public record about post-war oil planning in the deliberations leading to the war. In one of the few briefings President Bush received on post-conflict issues, on 24 February 2003, he supported the proposal to shift control over Iraq's oil industry to a new Iraqi government as soon as possible.[30] If the war had been about control of Iraq's oil resources, the post-war policy of the American occupiers toward the Iraqi oil sector would have been very different. During the Bush Administration's control of Iraq, not a single American oil company was given a contract or a concession.[31] The Iraqi oil sector was not privatized, even though the Coalition Provisional Authority privatized almost every other state economic sector.[32] Iraq stayed in OPEC. There were certainly plans circulated in Washington to undertake these measures, but they were not implemented.[33] Iraqi oil production at the end of the Bush Administration was about where it had been before the war began, about two million barrels per day.[34] If increasing Iraqi oil production was an American policy goal in the war, Washington failed to achieve it.

---

[28] For an extended version of this argument, see Sheila Carapico and Chris Toensing, "The Strategic Logic of the Iraq Blunder," *Middle East Report* 239 (Summer 2006).

[29] Perhaps the strongest argument made for the centrality of oil in the war decision is provided by Michael Klare in *Blood and Oil* (New York: Metropolitan Books, 2004), Chapter 4. My extended critique of Klare's argument can be found in *The International Politics of the Persian Gulf*, pp. 235–237.

[30] Bob Woodward, *Plan of Attack* (New York: Simon and Schuster, 2004), p. 323.

[31] In 2009 two American oil companies, ExxonMobil and Occidental, signed service contracts with the Iraqi government to manage production of Iraqi fields. But they were joined by a number of other companies in signing such deals, including BP, Shell, and China National Petroleum Company. American companies seem to have no advantage in access to Iraq's oil industry. Timothy Williams, "Oil Companies Look to the Future in Iraq," *New York Times*, 1 December 2009.

[32] Rajiv Chandrasekaran, "Economic Overhaul for Iraq, Only Oil Excluded from Foreign Ownership," *Washington Post*, 22 September 2003.

[33] Warren Vieth, "Privatization of Oil Suggested for Iraq," *Los Angeles Times*, 21 February 2003.

[34] U.S. Department of Energy, Energy Information Administration, *Monthly Energy Review*, December 2008, Table 11.1a.

As such, the Iraq War was more than an oil grab; it was the beginning of an ambitious effort to reconstruct the politics of the Persian Gulf region (and ultimately the Middle East as a whole). That hegemonic ambition foundered almost immediately as the Bush Administration discovered that while it might be easy to remove an Arab dictator from office through war, it was much harder to occupy an Arab country and reconstruct its political system. As the costs of the Iraq adventure escalated, the hegemonic dream was set aside. The Bush Administration concentrated on trying to secure Iraq against multiple insurgencies and a brutal sectarian civil war, as it saw Iranian power both in Iraq itself and in the Middle East more generally increase. The stage was set for a return to the less ambitious, more balance of power Gulf policies of the past.

Conclusion: The Obama Administration and America's Persian Gulf Policy

The Obama Administration at its outset seemed more than happy to shelve the hegemonic ambitions of its predecessor and approach the Persian Gulf from a balance of power perspective. The Administration made it clear that it would draw down the American military presence in Iraq, and it has been good to its word. By the end of 2010, fewer than 50,000 American troops remained in the country. At the end of 2011, all American combat forces had been withdrawn. Whether any American forces will return to Iraq seems to hinge more on Iraqi domestic politics than on American strategic plans.[35] The Administration made a very public overture toward the Iranian government, seeking a new relationship based on state-to-state relations. It also was extremely solicitous of King Abdullah, with Obama meeting a number of times with the Saudi monarch in 2009 and 2010. It thus seemed that the president was set to return American policy in the Gulf to the more modest goals of past presidents, who were concerned with the regional balance of power and intent on maintaining American geopolitical dominance there, but

---

[35] Tim Arango and Michael S. Schmidt, "Should U.S. Stay or Go? Views Define Iraqi Factions," *New York Times*, 10 May 2011.

were not terribly concerned about the domestic political orders of the regional states.

While the current Administration has largely followed this more "realist" approach, it remains possible that it will adopt a stance closer to that of its immediate predecessor in the wake of the Arab upheavals of 2011. The massive protests in Iran after the presidential elections of 2009 seemed to put an end to Obama's outreach toward the Iranian government, indicating that domestic politics in Iran still matter to Washington. The popular uprising in Bahrain in 2011 once again placed the Administration in a difficult position, in which its rhetorical support for democracy and human rights clashed with its more modest strategic goals of maintaining America's geopolitical position through good relations with a friendly government. The fact that Saudi Arabia actively supported Bahrain's quashing of the popular demonstrations by sending Saudi troops to the island highlights a potential rift between Washington and Riyadh that goes beyond Bahrain. While Obama has tentatively, and with different emphases in different countries, supported the wave of political upheaval that the Arab world has seen, the Saudis have seen the political changes, particularly in Egypt, as an enormous setback to their interests.

By the end of 2011, it seemed that geopolitics still dominated the Administration's view of the Gulf. Relations with Saudi Arabia had been repaired, and containment of Iranian influence and pressure on Iran's nuclear program remained the major goals in Washington's approach to Iran. However, if the Administration reads the results of the political upheavals in the Arab world as an indication that it has to prioritize domestic political reform in the region, as (in its own way) the Bush Administration did, relations with both Saudi Arabia and with Iran could become more conflictual. The case of Bahrain will be key here. If Washington maintains the pre-2011 status quo in relations with Manama, it will be a clear sign that geopolitics has trumped political reform on the American agenda. If Washington distances itself from Manama, it will signify that the Obama Administration has decided to follow its predecessor's path in making the domestic political arrangements of Persian Gulf states a major element of its regional policy. Though the pre-"Arab Spring" status quo appears to be the Administration's choice, the political crisis in Bahrain is far from over.

Chapter 9

Neither East Nor West? The Gulf in a Post-American World

Alain Gresh

In March 2011 Prince Bandar bin Sultan, former ambassador to Washington and, as of July 2012, Director General of the Saudi Intelligence Agency, visited East and South Asian capitals. He began in China, then traveled to Malaysia and Indonesia, and finally went to Pakistan and India. He was carrying King Abdullah's view on the uprisings taking place in the Middle East, particularly those in Bahrain, Yemen, and Libya. The first stop on the prince's tour was Beijing, where he met with President Hu Jintao and others. The Chinese leaders stressed their country's understanding of and support for the efforts of the member states of the Gulf Cooperation Council (GCC) to preserve peace and stability in the region.[1]

According to Saudi sources,[2] King Abdullah stressed in his envoyed message that he would not allow anyone to attempt to harm the security and stability of any GCC state. He also said that he would not allow any regional or international entity to exploit the ongoing events "to achieve personal interests at the expense of the sons and peoples of the six states." The position of other states regarding the events, he continued, would prove "the real touchstone for the future of Riyadh's relationship with these states at all levels."

---

[1] See the London-based, Saudi-owned Elaph website, 24 March 2011, available online at http://www.elaph.com.
[2] Personal communication, Saudi Arabia, 2011.

Most of the worries of the Saudi leadership concerned its own intervention in Bahrain, where it sent 1,000 troops to help crush the protests in 2011, and the way the king of Bahrain denounced the uprising as the result of "Iranian interference." That the first American reaction to these developments was not positive and that the United States left president Mubarak without support created anger and anxiety in the Saudi leadership as well as among other Gulf leaders.

The visit of Prince Bandar to Asia was a clear sign of this discontent on the part of Saudi leaders. It reflected a deeper interrogation about their future and perhaps also the hope that Asia will represent a new ally in a changing world.

Are We Entering a Post-American World?

A decade ago, the United Sates was considered the world's only superpower. Today, there are more Internet users in China than in the United States, and the United States accounts for only 25 percent of global traffic on the web, compared with more than 50 percent a decade ago. Attempts to revive the Doha round of international trade talks failed, mainly because India and China refused to sacrifice their impoverished farmers to free trade. In 2010, Brazil and Turkey tried to broker an agreement with Iran on its nuclear aspirations, and Turkey, a member of NATO and a strong ally of the United States, began voicing harsh criticism of Israel's policies *vis-à-vis* the Palestinians. Standard & Poor's downgraded the United States' credit rating to a notch below AAA in August 2011, noting that the country's ability to manage its finances is now "less stable, less effective, and less predictable."[3] And the economic crisis set in motion by the United States at the end of 2008 is still in evidence. "The End of Arrogance" was the headline in the German weekly *Der Spiegel* on 30 September 2008, with the subtitle: "America is losing its dominant economic role." Unlike past crises, such as those in Asia and Russia in the 1990s, the current financial storm has also confirmed the marginalization of

---

[3] Zachary A. Goldfarb, "S&P Downgrades U.S. Credit Rating for First Time," *Washington Post*, 6 August 2011, available online at http://www.washingtonpost.com/business/economy/sandp-considering-first-downgrade-of-us-credit-rating/2011/08/05/gIQAqKeIxI_story.html.

international organizations such as the International Monetary Fund (IMF) and the World Bank. Soon after the year 2000, Russia, Thailand, Argentina, Brazil, Bolivia, Serbia, and Indonesia decided to pay back their IMF debts early[4] to be free of the rules imposed by these international bodies.

These diverse facts indicate dramatic changes in international relations — chiefly the end of the absolute domination that the West has enjoyed since the first half of the nineteenth century. It is one of the ironies of history that this shift is occurring less than 20 years after the collapse of the camp led by the Soviet Union and the apparent triumph of liberal economic policies. After the first Gulf War (1990–1991) many observers thought they saw the dawning of the American twenty-first century. 20 years later, another consensus is emerging, closer to reality: we are entering a "post-American world."[5]

What does it mean? Without a doubt the United States will remain the dominant power for many years, and not just militarily. But it will have to take account of emerging centers of power in Beijing, Delhi, Brasilia, and Moscow.

For the first time since decolonization, the countries of the South are able to follow their own political and economic direction and find partners not aligned with the American vision. New relationships are being forged, as demonstrated by the China–Africa summit or the BRICS (Brazil, Russia, India, China, and South Africa) foreign ministers' meeting in New York on 26 September 2010. Countries can plan their own development without having to accept the unfavorable terms of the old "Washington consensus."

The new powers are not only states. Richard Haas, President of the Council on Foreign Relations in New York and a former senior official in the administration of President George H.W. Bush as well as in the State Department, lists other powerful players in his description of a "non-polar world:" the International Energy Agency, the Shanghai Cooperation Organization,[6] the World Health Organization and its regional bodies, Shanghai, and Sao Paulo,

---

[4]Jacques Sapir, *Le nouveau XXIe siècle. Du siècle "américain" au retour des nations* (Paris: Seuil, 2008).
[5]See Fareed Zakaria, *The Post-American World* (New York: Norton, 2008).
[6]Established in 2001, the Shanghai Cooperation Organization (SCO) comprises China, Russia, and the four Central Asian states of Kazakhstan, Kyrgyzstan, Tajikistan, and Uzbekistan. Iran, Mongolia, India, and Pakistan have observer status.

Al Jazeera, and CNN, militias from Hizbullah to the Taliban, drug cartels, and NGOs. "Today's world is increasingly one of distributed, rather than concentrated, power," he concludes.[7] Joseph Nye, co-founder of the theory of neoliberalism, shares Haas's position. Nye writes that "world politics will no longer be the sole province of governments. Individuals and private organizations — ranging from WikiLeaks to corporations to NGOs to terrorists to spontaneous societal movements — are all empowered to play direct roles in world politics."[8]

With multipolarity and so many different development models, it is no longer just the West's economic domination that is being challenged, but also its right to define right and wrong, to lay down international law, and to interfere in other countries' affairs on moral or humanitarian grounds. The former French foreign minister, Hubert Védrine, said the West has lost its monopoly on history, on "the big story." World history, as invented two centuries ago, is the story of the rise and dominance of Europe.[9]

No More Camps

What is most important is that the world is no longer split into two camps as it was during the Cold War; it is not even divided between North and South or East and West. States, which have, despite predictions to the contrary, survived the onslaught of globalization, all want their place in the sun. China, India, Russia, and Brazil are asserting their global ambitions and reject an international order that marginalizes them. Other countries, from Iran to South Africa, Israel, Mexico, and Indonesia, have more limited ambitions but still defend their interests. None of these states is driven by a global ideology, as the Soviet Union was, and none is setting itself up as an alternative model. They have all, more or less, accepted the market economy, though none would

---

[7] Richard Haas, "The Age of Nonpolarity: What Will Follow U.S. Dominance," *Foreign Affairs* 87 (May–June 2008).
[8] Joseph Nye, "Power Shifts," *Time*, 9 May 2011.
[9] Hubert Védrine, "L'option atlantiste/occidentaliste et la politique arabe de la France," *Nouvelles d'Orient* (blog), 9 September 2007, available online at http://blog.mondediplo.net/-Nouvelles-d-Orient-.

consider compromising its national interests. Their main struggle is to control their rare and expensive resources, primarily oil and gas, as well as their agricultural products in order to feed their populations. (Agricultural production, already falling, is further threatened by global warming.) Their second priority is to protect their strategic interests based on their political vision and history: Taiwan and Tibet for China, Kashmir for India and Pakistan, Kosovo for Serbia, and Kurdistan for Turkey.

States now collaborate with others on what they consider their national interest; essentially, states have interests, not friends. If we look at the vote on 2011 UN Security Council resolution for a no-fly zone and air strikes against Muammar el-Qaddafi and his supporters, we see a split that illustrates this phenomenon. Germany, Russia, India, China, and Brazil abstained, while the United States, France, Great Britain, South Africa, Nigeria, and Gabon voted in favor. Here, Third World countries are not necessarily allying together but are acting upon their particular interests — and as such are found in both camps.

The Gulf and China

It is in the context established above that we should view China's relations with the Gulf. The new role of China in the Gulf is first linked with oil. It is clear that oil binds the alliance and has done so for the past decade, ever since oil consumption plateaued in the United States and Europe but took off in China. Saudi Arabia desired a long-term market, and China wanted a supplier. Chinese officials are fluent in diplomatic-speak, often using such phrases when speaking about the alliance as "our common destiny," "the need for coexistence," and "the mutual benefits of cooperation."

But outside the communiqués, the anxieties of an emerging superpower are evident. The plot of a popular 2003 Chinese online novel, *The Battle to Protect the Oil Routes*, involves "imperial powers who fear China" imposing a naval blockade that leads to war.[10] Experts in the Chinese press are concerned about a possible closure of the Malacca Straits, a transit route for tankers that links the

---

[10] Ben Simpfendorfer, *The New Silk Road: How a Rising Arab World Is Turning Away from the West and Rediscovering China* (London: Palgrave Macmillan, 2009).

Indian Ocean with the South China Sea and the Pacific Ocean and that provides the route for oil from the Gulf to China. When the price of oil reached $150 dollars a barrel, the Chinese press suggested it was the result of U.S. malevolence.

China has made commercial agreements with Saudi Arabia to reduce its dependency, and has expanded its reciprocal investments in the oil sector. Saudi Arabia's national oil company, Aramco, working with ExxonMobil and the Chinese company Sinopec, has built an oil refinery with a capacity of 240,000 barrels a day in Fujian Province. In addition, Saudi Basic Industries Corporation (SABIC) and Sinopec have built a huge petrochemical complex in Tianjin, which began operations in 2011. At the same time, Chinese companies have built petrochemical complexes in Saudi Arabia and have been given permission for the first time to begin gas exploration in the Kingdom's Rub al-Khali basin.

China has broken into markets across the Middle East in record time. Trade leapt from $37 billion to $110 billion between 2004 and 2009. Since 2004 regular Sino-Arab forums have taken place and have been attended by politicians, businessmen, and representatives of civil society. China has launched an Arabic version of its news channel CCTV, Xinhua news agency has a presence in Riyadh and many other Arab capitals, and Al Jazeera has an office in Beijing. The press has evoked a renaissance of the Silk Road from the fringes of China to the Mediterranean — the main intercontinental trade route until the fifteenth century. But the Silk Road reached its apogee when Asian empires were at the height of their power and were able to protect the route militarily. That point has not yet been reached.

Beijing's low profile is an asset. Prince Turki al-Faisal, the former head of the Saudi secret service and former ambassador to Washington, where he dealt with post-9/11 anti-Saudi campaigns, explained: "Our relations with China are less complicated than with the United States. Over there, they don't have lobbies influencing policy, and we are not held hostage to their domestic disagreements." Riyadh and Beijing take a similar approach on international issues, including Darfur. They respect national sovereignty and non-interference and share a disdain for the West's human rights diplomacy, perceived as opportunistic and inconsistent.

But there are also hurdles, such as Iran. China has consolidated its relationship with Iran over many years, as Iran is its third biggest supplier of oil, behind Saudi Arabia and Angola. In return, China sells Iran arms. General trade between the two countries reached $30 billion in 2009 and is expected to rise to $50 billion by 2015. Hence Beijing is reluctant to impose more sanctions on Tehran. It took months of negotiations, a public visit by the Saudi foreign minister as well as secret delegations, and a major effort by Washington to get Beijing to vote in favor of the UN Security Council resolution of 9 June 2010 that expanded an arms embargo and tightened restrictions on financial and shipping enterprises related to nuclear "proliferation-sensitive activities."[11] Saudi diplomatic sources have confirmed to this author that Saudi Arabia gave China a guarantee that it would step in if Iran suspended oil deliveries.

Though the United States continues to pressure China to take a more severe stance with Iran, China remains cautious. It is adhering to the last UN resolution, refusing to extend sanctions as the United States and the EU would like, even replacing Western companies in Iran who have disengaged from the country.

Many in the Gulf profess "admiration for China, its civilization, its Great Wall, the way it organized the Olympic games. Many want to learn Chinese. While most people hate the United States, the success of China is in some ways comforting."[12] Thousands of young Saudis and Emiratis study in China, following the Prophet's instruction to "seek knowledge even as far as China." Yet those from the Gulf know the feeling is not mutual. "The Chinese do not admire the Arab world because we are weak, and because part of their image of us comes from the West."[13] Saudi Arabia, like the other Gulf countries, is working hard to improve its image. It was the biggest donor of aid to China after the Sichuan earthquake in 2006 (more than $53 million), a fact well publicized in the Chinese media. Its impressive pavilion at the World Expo

---

[11] UN Security Council Resolution 1929, 9 June 2010, available online at http://www.un.org/News/Press/docs/2010/sc9948.doc.htm.
[12] Personal communication with Chinese official, Saudi Arabia, 2011.
[13] *Ibid.*

in Shanghai in 2010 drew crowds with its display of a huge boat with palms planted on the deck — a garden symbolizing an oasis in the desert.

Gulf leaders know that China cannot give it the same security guarantees that the United States provides, and which it demonstrated after Iraq's invasion of Kuwait in 1990. But what about the future? In December 2008 China announced that it was sending warships to the coast of Somalia in order to protect its oil supply and exports to the Mediterranean via the Suez Canal. And, in March 2010, two Chinese vessels arrived at Abu Dhabi's Port Zayed. As regional media noted, this was the first time since the fifteenth century that Chinese ships had sailed the Indian Ocean. Admiral Zheng He, a Chinese Muslim, had commanded the emperor's fleet between 1405 and 1433, sailing to Hormuz, the Red Sea, and the east coast of Africa. (According to a controversial theory, he circumnavigated Africa and ventured as far as the Antilles.[14]) One Saudi commentator told this author that he wanted to see the return of China's golden age in the hope that it would allow his country to escape the obligatory confrontation with the United States. The visit of Prince Bandar to Asia was one sign of this hope.

A Forgotten Episode

While the Gulf and China were thus in good contact in centuries past, another episode from history (though not so distant) brought Beijing and Riyadh together — and it was one that could have come from a spy novel. In February 1985 the Iran–Iraq war was at its height. Iraqi missiles bombarded Iranian towns and oil installations, and Iran retaliated against tankers in the Gulf. The Tanker War affected Saudi vessels, and Riyadh, which supported Saddam Hussein's regime, was worried. King Fahd approached the then U.S. president, Ronald Reagan, to buy missiles. But Reagan was afraid of Israel's reaction — he had just bypassed Israeli opposition and convinced Congress, with difficulty, to allow the sale of AWACS aircraft to Saudi Arabia — so he turned down the request. "We could ask either Moscow or Beijing," said Rihab Massoud, who worked at the Saudi embassy in Washington at the time and is now

---

[14] See Gavin Menzies, *1421: The Year China Discovered the World* (London: Bantam Press, 2002).

Deputy Assistant Secretary General of the Saudi National Security Council, "but Reagan had described the Soviet Union as the evil empire, so we turned to China, with whom we didn't even have diplomatic relations."[15]

This confidential mission was entrusted to Prince Bandar, who was at the time the Saudi ambassador to Washington. He was able to approach Chinese diplomats discreetly in the American capital, and after many fake economic delegations, genuine military missions, secret meetings in Hong Kong hotels, and long negotiations, the purchase of 50 Dongfeng 3 missiles, known in the West as CSS-2s, with a range of 3,000 km, was agreed upon in December 1986. Chinese ships transported the equipment (to fool the United States they were officially said to be heading for Baghdad), and Saudi personnel acquainted themselves with the new weapons.

In 1988, U.S. satellites discovered the missiles. The press speculated that these weapons, "capable of carrying nuclear warheads," could reach anywhere in the Middle East. The Israeli government threatened to bomb the Saudi bases where the missiles were stocked. The United States, furious at having been kept in the dark, told Saudi Arabia it could dismantle the missiles, send them back to China, or allow U.S. officials to inspect them. The affair reached a crisis point when the U.S. ambassador to Saudi Arabia lodged an official protest with the king, who, in his anger, expelled the ambassador — an unprecedented move.

But the storm died down. In March 1988, China signed the nuclear non-proliferation treaty, and the United States managed to calm Israel. The Saudis did not forget China's support at a crucial moment, and Beijing was grateful that Riyadh had refused to allow the United States to inspect such sensitive weapons. Saudi Arabia and China have discreetly maintained military relations since. The only weapons known to have been purchased from the Chinese since the CSS-2s were guns in 2008, but there have been rumors about CSS-5 and CSS-6 missiles — enough to worry U.S. neoconservatives about a Saudi nuclear weapons program aided by China and another historic ally, Pakistan.[16] Hence

---

[15] Personal communication, Saudi Arabia, 2011.

[16] For more on these conspiracy theories, see Jeff Stein, "Former CIA Analyst Alleges China-Saudi Nuclear Deal," *Washington Post*, 7 June 2010, available online at http://voices.washingtonpost.com/spy-talk/2010/06/former_cia_officer_alleges_chi.html.

this 1985 episode appears to have helped establish a firm foundation for future Gulf–China relations, of which we are currently witnessing the expansion.

We have entered a new world in which the ideological divides no longer play a large role, in which the interest of states is what drives the policy of leaders, and in which one dominant power no longer exists. The relations of two such different countries as Saudi Arabia and China epitomize these changes. We are entering a more complex world that begs for new analytical frameworks in order to be understood.

Chapter 10

U.S. Military Bases in the Gulf and the Dynamics of Redeployment[1]

Degang Sun

The Middle East is a region with some of the most serious ethnic conflicts, religious discords, terrorist attacks, territorial disputes, and various other cross-border problems. Due to its unique location as a corridor of the three continents of Asia, Africa, and Europe, as well as its rich oil and natural gas reserves, the region has remained a hot spot for big powers' competition and rivalry over the past century.

The establishment of overseas military bases is undoubtedly one of the most effective ways for these big powers to project their influence.[2] At present, such countries as the United States, the United Kingdom, France, and Japan

---

[1] This Chapter was jointly supported by the research program of the 2013 National Social Science Foundation of China, "U.S. Military Base Deployment in the Middle East and Islamic Regions and Its Evolution (13CGJ042);" the program for "New Century Excellent Talents in Universities of China" (NCET); the Chinese Ministry of Education research program, "The Western Powers' Military Bases in the Middle East Since the End of the Cold War"(10JJDGJW022); and the academic team of Shanghai International Studies University, China.

[2] For more literature on military bases, please see Alexander Cooley, *Base Politics: Democratic Change and the US Military Overseas* (Ithaca, NY: Cornell University Press, 2008); Mark L. Gillem, *America Town: Building the Outposts of Empire* (Minneapolis, MN: University of Minnesota Press, 2007); Thomas Barnett, *The Pentagon's New Map: War and Peace in the Twenty-first Century* (New York: G.P. Putnam's Sons, 2004).

have established dozens of military bases near the Persian Gulf and the Gulf of Aden. Even India, an emerging developing country, is ambitious enough to consider building a military base in Djibouti (as Japan has), after the base it has established in Tajikistan in recent years. Of 21 countries in and around the Gulf, only three are without any overt foreign military presence (Iran, Azerbaijan, and Turkmenistan). The United States has a foreign military presence in 13 of these countries, the United Kingdom is in nine, and other external powers have a military presence in nine as well. Hence, the external powers have gradually become Gulf powers by means of power projection.[3]

What is the definition of an overseas military base? What is the difference between an overseas military base and an overseas military presence? Despite the divergent understandings of an overseas military base, scholars of international relations seem to have reached a preliminary consensus on the key features of it. According to this definition, it refers to an area on land or on sea beyond the sovereign state's jurisdiction that has a certain number of armed forces, military activities, organized institutions, and facilities.[4] Overseas military bases are by nature the geographical and functional extension of a country's domestic military bases.

The U.S. Readjustment of Its Military Bases in the GCC States after the September 11 Terrorist Attacks

The United States, located far from the chessboard of Eurasia — the universally recognized power center — has overcome its geographical disadvantage and intensified its intervention in the peripheral affairs of Eurasia for the past seven decades via overseas military bases. Through these bases, it projects its

---

[3] J. E. Perterson, "Foreign Military Presence and Its Role in Reinforcing Regional Security: A Double-Edged Sword," in *Arabian Gulf Security: Internal and External Challenges, Emirates Center for Strategic Studies and Research* (Abu Dhabi: Emirates Center for Strategic Studies and Research, 2008), p. 93.
[4] Robert E. Harkavy, *Strategic Basing and the Great Powers, 1200–2000* (New York: Routledge, 2007), pp. 2–9.

military power, exhibits its political resolve to contain potential enemies, and reveals its military commitment to allies. Outside of the Middle East, the United States has four other major military base conglomerations, in Europe, the Asia-Pacific region, North America, and the Caribbean. The U.S. military bases in the GCC countries are part of a grand deployment under the leadership of Central Command.[5] In the twenty-first century, these bases are not static but dynamic. The last two decades can be divided into two periods, with the September 11 terrorist attacks delineating a watershed.

In the 1950s and 1960s, the United Kingdom instead of the United States was the predominant power in the Gulf. It enjoyed supreme military presence, with U.S. influence limited to sporadic and temporary port visits.[6] In 1968, Britain declared that it would withdraw all military forces from east of the Suez Canal and terminate its mandate in the Persian Gulf, which had lasted for over two centuries.[7] In the early 1970s, though the United States was ready to fill the vacuum of power in the region, President Nixon hesitated due to the rise of Arab nationalism after the 1973 Yom Kippur War, and U.S. large-scale military presence in the region halted. As a result, during the Cold War era, U.S. military presence in the Persian Gulf mainly relied on aircraft carriers afloat in nearby waters. The number of permanent U.S. military bases was quite small, and they had more political than military implications. The aircraft carriers were interlinked with the Sixth Fleet in the Mediterranean Sea, with a view to prevent the former Soviet Union from interfering in Gulf regional affairs.

After the outbreak of the Gulf War in 1990, U.S. military presence and bases in the region began to mushroom, centering on Saudi Arabia, the most powerful GCC state flanked by the waters of the Gulf and the Red Sea, along

---

[5] U.S. Central Command's area of responsibility covers the "central" area of the globe and consists of 20 countries, including Afghanistan, Bahrain, Egypt, Iran, Iraq, Jordan, Kazakhstan, Kuwait, Kyrgyzstan, Lebanon, Oman, Pakistan, Qatar, Saudi Arabia, Syria, Tajikistan, Turkmenistan, United Arab Emirates, Uzbekistan, and Yemen.
[6] Ann Williams, *Britain and France in the Middle East and North Africa* (London: Macmillan, 1968), pp. 38–55.
[7] Alvin J. Cottrell and Frank Bray, *Military Forces in the Persian Gulf* (London: SAGE Publications, 1978), pp. 7–8.

with lesser GCC powers.[8] This distribution of influence came to an end after September 11, when the Bush Administration shifted a large amount of U.S. military presence from Saudi to the new host countries of Kuwait, Qatar, and Bahrain. During the Iraq War in 2003, as many as 334,000 troops were stationed in Saudi Arabia. But during this period, U.S.–Saudi relations went through ups and downs, forcing the Bush Administration to seek other spaces for its troops in the Gulf.

Since the Bush years and especially since President Obama entered the White House in 2008, the United States' bases in the GCC states have shifted their immediate task from overthrowing the Saddam Hussein regime and safeguarding the post-war reconstruction in Iraq to confronting Iran and combating Taliban militants on the Afghan–Pakistan border. With this task transformed, the bases have exhibited five new attributes: They are expanding geographically, diminishing in size, approaching their potential enemies, becoming stronger in maneuverability, and becoming gradually interlinked.

First, in terms of geographical "expansion," U.S. military bases as well as military personnel have been distributed more evenly in the area. Despite its abundant oil reserves and unique role in the control of regional sea power, the Saudi government is inherently vulnerable to both internal and external threat. As a terrorist-torn monarchy, internal and external Islamic radical elements frequently challenge its legitimacy of rule. To meet security needs, the Saudi government was pragmatic and heavily depended on U.S. military bases, which they saw as neutralizing these elements. After September 11, Saudi Arabia was again regarded as a hotbed of terrorism, and the United States spread its military bases elsewhere.

On the eve of the Iraq War in 2003, Kuwait was the most resolute country in the GCC in its support of the U.S. military campaign to topple Saddam Hussein. The government not only provided free fuel, but also allowed the military forces to occupy as large as one quarter of the nation's territory for military purposes.[9] In 2008, the United States and Kuwait signed an arms

---

[8] Anthony H. Cordesman and Khalid R. al-Rodhan, *Gulf Military Forces in an Era of Asymmetric Wars* (Washington, D.C.: Praeger Security International, 2007), p. 163.
[9] *Ibid.*, pp. 87–88.

sales agreement of $328 million, and the Bush Administration declared that it would sell Kuwait laser-guided missiles.[10] Since then, the United States has maintained about ten military bases in Kuwait, the largest ones being Camp Buehring and Camp Arifjan. During the Obama Administration, the number of U.S. military troops in the country stood at approximately 5,000, which comprised one of the largest groups overseas.

The United States moved the headquarters of Central Command from Saudi Arabia to Qatar in 2002, and al-Udeid air base, west of Doha, became one of the largest bases abroad. Although Qatar was publicly against the Iraq War, the country's former emir, Shaykh Hamad bin Khalifa al-Thani, reportedly told General Tommy Franks, Commander in Chief of U.S. Central Command, that the United States had an opportunity to "salvage Iraqi people."[11] As Hamad bin Jassim al-Thani, then foreign minister of Qatar put it, "We need the U.S. forces to stay here, and the U.S. needs us too."[12]

Bahrain was made the headquarters and homeport of the Fifth Fleet in the mid-1990s, with a military base as large as 60 acres in Manama.[13] During the Gulf War in 1991, Bahrain offered support and acted as a "bridgehead" in the U.S. military campaign.[14] In February 2003, bilateral relations reached a new height when Bahrain allowed the United States to continue to use its air and navy bases on the eve of the Iraq War.[15] Under Obama, the number of U.S. troops in Bahrain was in the vicinity of 2,000.

The United States also sought to build military bases in Oman, a state that controls the Musandam Peninsula and the waters of the Hormuz Strait after September 11. In 2002, the two countries renewed the Collective Defense Treaty, in which Oman permitted the United States to use the three air bases

---

[10] Robert E. Looney, *Handbook of US-Middle East Relations: Formative Factors and Regional Perspectives* (London and New York: Routledge, 2009), p. 459.
[11] Tommy Franks, *American Soldier* (New York: HarperCollins, 2004), p. 404.
[12] Greg Jaffe, "Desert Maneuvers: Pentagon Boosts US Military Presence in the Gulf," *Wall Street Journal*, 24 June 2002.
[13] Cordesman and al-Rodhan, *Gulf Military Forces in an Era of Asymmetric Wars*, pp. 65–67.
[14] Ed Blanche, "Getting Smart: Gulf States Go for US Wonder Weapons," *The Middle East* 4 (2002): 24.
[15] Han Zhibin, *Bahrain* (Beijing: Social Science Academic Press, 2009), p. 179.

of Seeb, Masirah, and Thumrait.[16] In return, the U.S. government offered $9.4 million in military assistance to Oman in 2009, which amounted to $20.27 million in 2010.[17] Oman also sought to secure congenial trade relations with the United States. On 1 January 2009, the U.S.-Oman Free Trade Agreement took effect.

The United States also built military bases in the UAE in the early twenty-first century. The UAE has since 1971 had a territorial dispute with Iran over the islands of Abu Musa and the Tunbs. Partly due to the GCC's weakness and reluctance to offer military aid to the UAE in regard to the matter, the Emirates pinned high expectations on the United States and allowed it to build military bases in the past decade.[18] In January 2008, President Bush visited the UAE for the first time in American history. UAE President Shaykh Khalifa remarked that the UAE was committed to partnering with the United States in the war on terrorism and maintaining regional and world stability,[19] and in May 2009, President Obama ratified the U.S.–UAE Agreement on the Peaceful Use of Nuclear Energy. On 1 February 2010, Obama declared that the United States would send the UAE arms, including 80 F-16s and Patriot missiles as well as long-range anti-ballistic missiles. The American airbase of al-Dhafra near Abu Dhabi hosts approximately 1,500 U.S. military personnel.[20] Al-Dhafra has a "Special Airborne Operation Center," which functions as a pilot training center.[21] The seaport of Dubai holds several hundred U.S. warships of various kinds, outpacing the rest of the GCC bases.

During this post-September 11 period, the United States steadily withdrew 200 military aircraft and other supporting troops from Saudi Arabia, and only 500 forces remained, mostly for training purpose. The rest of the troops

---

[16] Ed Blanche, "Regional Briefing — Gulf States: Winds of Change," *Jane's Defense Weekly*, 9 February 2005, p. 15.
[17] Kenneth Katzman, "Oman: Reform, Security, and US Policy," *Congressional Research Service*, 29 June 2009.
[18] Cordesman and al-Rodhan, *Gulf Military Forces in an Era of Asymmetric Wars*, p. 284.
[19] Looney, *Handbook of US-Middle East Relations*, p. 387.
[20] David S. Cloud, "U.S. Sees Emirates as Both Ally and, Since 9/11, A Foe," *New York Times*, 23 February 2006.
[21] Michael Sirak, "Interview: U.S. Air Force Lieutenant General Walter Buchanan," *Jane's Defense Weekly*, 29 September 2004, pp. 32–37.

were redeployed to Qatar, Bahrain, Kuwait, Oman, the UAE, and Central Asian countries.

In fact, due to Obama's new campaigns in Afghanistan and Pakistan, a significant number of Saudi forces were dispatched to Central Asia to combat the Taliban and al-Qaʻida.[22] As John Brennan, Obama's senior consultant on anti-terrorism, stated in 2009, "The Obama Administration would be committed to ending the military action in Iraq and reopening a new battle for countering terrorism on the border of Afghanistan and Pakistan to eliminate the remaining terrorists."[23] The scattered Gulf military bases were seen as aiding the United States in confronting multifaceted threats in the region, including the traditional threat of Iran as well as the nontraditional threat of terrorism and social unrest in Iraq and Yemen. By "putting eggs into different baskets," the United States avoided the risk of intimidation by a single host nation if the two countries' relations deteriorated.

Second, the U.S. military bases in the GCC states are decreasing in number and size. According to the U.S. Department of Defense's 2011 *Base Structure Report,* bases can be placed in five categories: Those hosting the army, navy, air force, and marines, as well as the Washington, D.C. command sites, which cover 50 states at home, seven overseas territories, and 39 foreign countries. There are 611 large-scale overseas bases abroad, including 255 army bases, 113 navy bases, 221 air bases, and 22 marine bases, most of them located in Germany (194), Japan (108), and South Korea (82)[24] (See Tables 10.1 and 10.2).

Compared with Pacific and European Command, U.S. Central Command is responsible for a relatively limited area, and its headquarters is in Florida instead of the Middle East. Since the founding of Africa Command in 2007, states in northeast Africa, such as Egypt, Somalia, Djibouti, and Ethiopia, have been excluded from Central Command's area of responsibility. Due to the now smaller geographical area, the number of military bases in

---

[22] Sherifa Zuhur, *Saudi Arabia: Islamic Threat, Political Reform, and the Global War on Terror* (Carlisle Barracks, PA: Strategic Studies Institute, U.S. Army War College, 2005), p. 32.
[23] John Brennan, "A New Approach to Safeguarding Americans," *Foreign Policy*, 6 August 2009.
[24] Office of the Deputy Undersecretary of Defense, *Base Structure Report, Fiscal Year 2012 Baseline* (Washington D.C.: U.S. Department of Defense, 2011), p. 7.

214 Degang Sun

Table 10.1: The U.S. Military Bases At Home and Abroad (2002).

Location	Army Bases	Navy Bases	Air Bases	Marine Bases	Total
Homeland	3,866	431	1,266	49	5,612
Overseas Territories	53	11	23	1	88
Foreign Countries	394	46	283	2	725
Total	4,313	488	1,572	52	6,425

Source: Office of the Deputy Undersecretary of Defense, *Base Structure Report, Fiscal Year 2002 Baseline* (Washington D.C.: U.S. Department of Defense, 2001), p. 3.

Table 10.2: The U.S. Military Bases At Home and Abroad (2011).

Location	Army Bases	Navy Bases	Air Bases	Marine Bases	Total
Homeland	1,536	795	1,534	130	3,995
Overseas Territories	27	50	10	0	87
Foreign Countries	255	113	221	22	611
Total	1,818	958	1,765	152	4,693

Source: Office of the Deputy Undersecretary of Defense, *Base Structure Report, Fiscal Year 2012 Baseline* (Washington D.C.: U.S. Department of Defense, 2011), p. 7.

Table 10.3: The U.S. Military Force in GCC Countries (2000).

Host Nations	Qatar	Bahrain	Saudi Arabia	Kuwait	UAE	Oman	Total
Number of Stationed Troops	52	949	7,053	4,602	402	251	13,309
Main Bases	Air	Navy	Air	Army	Air	Air	

Source: Adapted from Tim Kane, "Global U.S. Troop Deployment, 1950–2005," The Heritage Foundation, 2005, available online at http://www.heritage.org/research/reports/2006/05/global-us-troop-deployment-1950-2005.

GCC countries has shrunk, with a parallel reduction in the number of troops. Since 2008, the number of U.S. troops in GCC member states has been only 11,000 (See Tables 10.3 and 10.4).

Third, U.S. military deployment in the Gulf increasingly approaches potential enemies. These bases are being well maintained. Since September 11,

Table 10.4: The U.S. Military Force in GCC Countries (2008).

Host Nations	Qatar	Bahrain	Saudi Arabia	Kuwait	UAE	Oman	Total
Number of Stationed Troops	3,432	1,496	500	About 5,000	About 546	About 26	About 11,000
Main Bases	Air	Navy	Air	Army	Air	Air	

Source: Richard F. Grimmett, "Instances of Use of United States Armed Forces Abroad, 1798–2009," *Congressional Research Service*, 27 January 2010, pp. 2–3; Jules Dufour, "The Worldwide Network of US Military Bases: The Global Deployment of US Military Personnel," *Global Research*, 1 July 2007, pp. 2-7.

although stationed troops are smaller in number compared with those in Europe and East Asia, U.S. military facilities in the GCC states have been consistently updated, with those strategically placed near Iran, such as Camp as-Sayliyah near Doha, becoming major headquarters of Central Command. Another Qatari base, al-Udeid, is at the forefront of U.S. containment of Iran. The airbase boasts a 14,760-foot-long runway, the longest in the Middle East. Its huge concrete bunkers can house 120 aircraft. Moreover, its construction, with advanced electronic facilities, cost $1.4 billion.[25] In 2010, 34 key construction projects were in process at al-Udeid,[26] and most of them have been finished as of 2012. The Doha seaport is also under construction in order to accommodate U.S. aircraft carriers. Apart from Qatar, American military garrisons in Kuwait, the UAE, and Bahrain have also been updated with improved infrastructure.

Fourth, U.S. military deployment in the GCC states is increasingly mobile. According to the U.S. Department of Defense, overseas military garrisons can be placed in three categories: Main operating bases, forward operating sites, and cooperative security locations. The main operating bases are overseas bases for permanently deployed forces, with robust sea and/or air access. Forward operating sites are facilities that can support sustained operations but

---

[25] Kent E. Calder, *Embattled Garrisons: Comparative Base Politics and American Globalism* (Princeton, NJ: Princeton University Press, 2007), p. 30.
[26] Department of Defense, "United States DOD Contracts for April 16, 2010," *Defense Professionals*, 19 April 2010.

have only a small permanent presence of support or contractor personnel. They occasionally host rotational forces, and many contain pre-positioned equipment. Cooperative Security Sites (CSS) are host nation facilities with little or no permanent U.S. personnel presence, but which may contain pre-positioned equipment and/or logistical arrangements that aid in security cooperation activities and contingency access.[27]

Since 2003, the U.S. government has increased the number of Cooperative Security Sites with a view to make substantial use of host countries' military bases and facilities in case of emergency. For instance, in 2009, U.S. contractor personnel in Oman numbered 26, while in Saudi Arabia and the UAE they numbered only several hundred. Nevertheless, should a crisis erupt, the United States can make use of these host states' military facilities and base infrastructure to aid a quick military deployment. Hence, the CSS system is not only economical but also flexible, and the host country can adjust its scale and number of military bases in accordance with practical need.

Fifth, U.S. military bases and facilities in the GCC states are increasingly interlinked. According to the shifting regional security situation, the U.S. government has integrated all the military facilities and garrisons in the Persian Gulf so that they have formed a network of containment. Bases in the GCC countries are centered in Kuwait, Qatar, and Bahrain, accompanied by sites in Saudi Arabia, Oman, and the UAE. Together, these have forged an "arc of containment" after the outbreak of the Iranian nuclear crisis.[28] Further, during the Obama Administration, bases in GCC countries have coordinated with those in Iraq, Afghanistan, Kyrgyzstan, Tajikistan, and Pakistan so that West Asia, Central Asia, and Pakistan under Central Command can support the counter-terror campaign in Afghanistan and Pakistan while at the same time deterring anti-American forces in the Middle East.[29] These military bases also have close ties with the American military base in Djibouti as well as other

---

[27] C. T. Sandars, *America's Overseas Garrisons: The Leasehold Empire* (New York: Oxford University Press, 2000), p. 301.
[28] David F. Winkler, *Amirs, Admirals and Desert Sailors: Bahrain, the U.S. Navy, and the Arabian Gulf* (Annapolis, MD: Naval Institute Press, 2007), pp. 181–198.
[29] Liu Jinqian, "Analysis of the US Afghanistan-Pakistan Strategy of Anti-terrorism," *Arab World Studies* 29 (2009): 38.

military facilities in East Africa, the designated area of responsibility under Africa Command.

The Dynamics of the U.S. Readjustment of Its Military Bases in the GCC Countries

The dynamics of the United States' readjustment of its military bases in the GCC countries are fourfold. The first dynamic is the change in U.S. national security strategy. As mentioned, after September 11, the United States designated terrorism and the proliferation of weapons of mass destruction (WMD) as its primary threat and regarded the greater Middle East, including Central Asia, West Asia, and part of South Asia, as an "arc of instability."[30] As a result, the Obama Administration shifted its focus of anti-terrorism from Iraq to Central Asia, which gave rise to the readjustment of its military bases in the region.

In late 2009, the National Security Forum in Chicago noted that the future security challenge to the United States will include both sovereign states and non-sovereign entities. The former includes Iran, North Korea, and Venezuela, while the latter includes religious extremists, ethnic radicals, and terrorists. What is more overwhelming, according to the Forum's analysis, is the confluence of the two categories. When they converge, such anti-American coalitions might launch an asymmetrical threat to overseas U.S. facilities.[31] After a riot in Kyrgyzstan broke out on 9 April 2010, the U.S. government was concerned that the new pro-Russian government might close U.S. military bases on its territory. As such, military bases in the GCC seemed more valuable. Thus, the American readjustment of military bases in the GCC might better meet the diversity of security threats to the United States in the region.

Second, the transformation of the United States' military objectives in the Gulf also gave rise to a readjustment of its military bases. After new Iraqi leadership was elected under U.S. supervision, Iran became the United States'

---

[30] Clive Moore, *Happy Isles in Crisis* (Canberra: Asia Pacific Press, 2004), p. 9.
[31] John Allen Williams, "The US Military: Balancing Old and New Challenges of US National Security Strategy 2010," *National Strategy Forum Review* 19 (2009): 1–3.

main target and was regarded as the supreme challenger to U.S. power in the region.

Iran has been happy to feed this idea. For example, from 22 through 26 April 2010, for the commemoration of the 31st anniversary of the founding of the Islamic revolutionary guards, Iran initiated a large military maneuver of joint army, navy, and air forces near the Hormuz Strait, testing homemade cruise missiles. Over 300 warships of various kinds participated in the maneuver, which was regarded as a countermeasure to balance U.S. influence in the region. On 5 May of the same year, Iran initiated another eight-day military maneuver. Due to these dynamics, Kuwait, Qatar, Bahrain, and the UAE, the very neighbors of Iran, became even more important non-NATO allies of the United States in the region.[32]

Third, after September 11, U.S.–Saudi relations worsened, and Saudi Arabia was charged as a covert sponsor of terrorists. Due to this bilateral discord, Saudi Arabia prohibited the United States from using certain military facilities in the country, and U.S. air force command and communication centers were forced to move to Qatar. After the outbreak of the Iraq War, the U.S. air force in Riyadh and Patriot missile troops eventually withdrew from Saudi Arabia, with the remaining small-scale troops only undertaking defensive and training tasks.[33] From a Saudi perspective, the rise of domestic anti-Americanism, an emphasis on diplomatic independence, and the American practice of a "power balance policy" sabotaged U.S.–Saudi special relations. As a result, the United States had to rely elsewhere for new bases, as outlined above.[34]

Finally, U.S. readjustment of its military bases in the GCC resulted from the economic slowdown. The year 2008 witnessed a worldwide financial crisis, with the United States as the epicenter. To aid the national budget, the Bush and Obama Administrations reduced the size and number of military bases in the region. By late 2010, the United States maintained only 50 military bases in Iraq, with less than 50,000 troops in the country. The main operating bases

---

[32] Charles Aldinger, "US Honors Kuwait as Major Non-NATO Ally," *Reuters*, 1 April 2004.
[33] Anthony H. Cordesman, *The Military Balance in the Middle East* (Westport, CT: Praeger, 2004), pp. 312–324.
[34] Charles M. Perry and Toshi Yoshihara, *The U.S.-Japan Alliance: Preparing for Korean Reconciliation & Beyond* (Dulles, VA: Brassey's Inc., 2004), p. 12.

in the GCC were also cut to minimize expenditure. By the end of 2011, the United States had evacuated all combat troops from Iraq.

Implications of the U.S. Readjustment of Its Military Bases in the GCC Countries

Since the 1980s, the GCC countries have tried in vain to maintain regional peace and security. This failure is due to a lack of enforcement power in conflicts such as the Iran–Iraq War, Iraq's invasion of Kuwait, and the Gulf War. After the outbreak of the Gulf War, the Saudi government even disbanded GCC troops in Hafar al-Batin, portending U.S. deployment of armed forces in the Gulf.[35] The last two decades have witnessed a substantial readjustment of this deployment, which has exerted a far-reaching impact on the regional security pattern and does not appear to be lessening, despite an outward appearance of doing so.

This readjustment consolidates U.S. predominance in the Gulf. In recent years, three different notions of the Gulf security order have been at play: the first is a Western-dominated framework advocated by the United States; the second is a Shi'i security framework advocated by Iran; and the third is a Saudi-dominated framework advocated by the Arab countries. It is the first arrangement that still holds water. In 2005, the GCC rapid response force was formally disbanded, and only one headquarters and one air force command system remained in Saudi Arabia. As a result, the GCC internal security mechanism is only symbolic.[36]

On 27 January 2010, President Obama remarked in his State of the Union Address that the United States would deal with Iran by both military and diplomatic means.[37] In February 2010, David Petraeus, commander-in-chief of Central Command, stated that the United States would formally deploy eight Patriot PAC-3 missile companies in Qatar, the UAE, Bahrain,

---

[35]W. Andrew Terrill, *Regional Fears of Western Primacy and the Future of U.S. Middle Eastern Basing Policy* (Carlisle, PA: U.S. Army War College, December 2006), pp. 45, 244.
[36]Cordesman and al-Rodhan, *Gulf Military Forces in An Era of Asymmetric Wars*, p. 11.
[37]Tariq Saeedi, "Pakistan, Iran Set to Face Hot July," *Daily Mail*, 21 April 2010; "Obama's State of the Union Address," *The New York Times*, 28 January 2010.

and Kuwait, with each country having two. These missile defense systems were basically finished by July 2010. And, to foster military integration between the GCC and the United States, the Obama Administration integrated the six countries into its economic orbit, estimating that the U.S.–Greater Middle East Free Trade Area would be built by 2013,[38] though it now appears to have a long way to go due to the complications arising from the outbreak of the Arab uprisings.

Second, the readjustment causes more uncertainty in the region. With the intensification of the Iranian nuclear and oil issues and the renewed deployment of U.S. military bases closer to Iran, GCC countries are hijacked by U.S. foreign policy. The intensification of relations between the United States and Iran or Israel and Iran may make U.S. military bases in the GCC potential Iranian targets. Former Iranian President Mahmoud Ahmadinejad had often appealed to the GCC countries not to allow the United States to set up military bases. On 25 April 2010, Kazem Jalali, a drafter of Iran's National Security and Foreign Policy Commission, said,

> The continued presence of foreign military forces in the region has caused insecurity and instability in our region. Under these conditions, Middle East countries, particularly those in the Persian Gulf, should join one another in a collective security treaty to ensure regional safety.[39]

Though this proposal appears to show Iranian concern, it has yet to receive a positive response from the GCC.

Third, anti-Americanism in the region has intensified due to the readjustment. Since the end of the Second World War, most Muslims have resented the United States and the Soviet Union for their continual deployment of armed forces on Muslim lands.[40] After the Soviet invasion of Afghanistan, a number of Muslim radicals, supported and funded by the United States, launched a "holy war" to force the Soviet forces to retreat. Since the 1990s, al-Qaʻida has

---

[38] Looney, *Handbook of US-Middle East Relations*, p. 430.
[39] "Iran Calls for Collective Security Treaty," *Iran Times*, 26 April 2010.
[40] Kylie Baxter and Shahram Akbarzadeh, *US Foreign Policy in the Middle East: The Roots of Anti-Americanism* (London and New York: Routledge, 2008), p. 3.

initiated a series of attacks, including September 11, in part to put pressure on the United States to close its military bases in Saudi Arabia. More recent terrorist activity includes the 28 August 2009 attack on Muhammad bin Nayef, Saudi Arabia's Interior Minister, by suicide bombers.[41] And on 28 April 2010, the UAE's Supreme Court ordered the arrest of five natives and one Afghan with the charge of financing the Taliban and attempting to set up a terrorist organization in the Gulf.[42] U.S. military bases in the GCC countries are thus politicalized and become a source of anti-Americanism.[43] For instance, Osama bin Laden reiterated time and again that all Muslims in the world reserve the right to launch terrorist attacks against the U.S. military and civil targets because U.S. military bases have spread throughout the holy Islamic land.[44] To lessen domestic resentment and dissatisfaction, the GCC countries began to encourage the United States to use their military facilities as Cooperative Security Sites rather than full-fledged bases in order to reduce the number of U.S. troops in their countries.

Finally, the readjustment is bound to cause more competition among big powers. The Gulf has played host to the Iran–Iraq War from 1980 to 1988, the Gulf War in 1991, the Iraq War in 2003, and the Iranian nuclear crisis since 2006. The area is thus a powder keg, and the establishment and expansion of military presence is the principal way for big powers to project their power and influence. It has been reported that the United States will reestablish the Tenth Fleet in the near future, with five aircraft carriers either permanently stationed in the Persian Gulf or present in the region after a crisis.[45] However, as of 2012, the United States had not yet taken any concrete steps. Also, on 26 May 2009, then French President Nicolas Sarkozy declared that France would build the first permanent military base in Abu Dhabi, with the capacity to

---

[41] Abdullah al-Shihri, "Prince Mohammed bin Nayef, Saudi Prince, Injured in Suicide Attack, Vows To Continue Fight Against Terrorism," *The Huffington Post*, 28 August 2009.
[42] "UAE Jails Five Emiratis on Terrorism Charges," *Maktoob News*, 28 April 2010.
[43] Alexander Cooley, *Base Politics: Democratic Change and the U.S. Military Overseas* (Ithaca, NY: Cornell University Press, 2008), pp. 10–11.
[44] Bradley L. Bowman, "After Iraq: Future U.S. Military Posture in the Middle East," *The Washington Quarterly*, 31, 2 (2008): 84.
[45] Tariq Saeedi, "Pakistan, Iran Set to Face Hot July," *Daily Mail*, 21 April 2010.

house 500 army, navy, and air personnel. This implies that France will play a more essential role in Gulf affairs.[46] The United Kingdom is also considering returning to the Persian Gulf. In 2010, it was in negotiations to reopen a military base in Oman. Moreover, France, the United States, and Japan have built military bases in Djibouti, and Iran is planning to build a navy base at Jask, near the Hormuz Strait.[47] It appears that rivalries among the big powers will be fiercer in the region in the next decade.

Conclusion

Though it may seem that American power is diminishing in the Persian Gulf due to a decrease in the number of U.S. troops and military bases in the GCC, a more strategic plan is actually underway. The United States has redistributed its bases within the GCC itself and has established more of a presence in Central Asia due to its new goals of containing Iran and fighting terrorism in Afghanistan and Pakistan. Its focus, for example, on greater mobility, flexibility, and connectivity among the Central Command bases and troops supports this strategy. In December 2013, Hagel paid a visit to the Gulf and promised that the United States would maintain a 35,000-strong force in the GCC, despite the recent deal with Tehran on Iran's nuclear issue. The military footprint includes 10,000 U.S. army troops with tanks and Apache helicopters, roughly 40 ships at sea including an aircraft carrier battle group, missile defense systems, radar, surveillance drones, and warplanes.[48]

Results of this redeployment of military bases in the Gulf may cause mutual misperception between the United States and Iran, worsen security dilemmas in the region, and stimulate rivalry for military presence in the Gulf among the big powers of the United States, France, Britain, India, Japan, Russia, China, and Iran.

---

[46] "Iran Slams UAE Over French Military Bases," *Tehran Times*, 27 May 2009.
[47] Nazila Fathi, "Iran Opens Naval Base Near Routes for Gulf Oil," *The New York Times*, 28 October 2008.
[48] "US to Maintain 35,000 Troops in Gulf," *The Peninsula*, 8 December 2013.

Index

al-Baharna family 59
al-Khalifa 59–61, 63, 71, 74–76
al-Khalifa, Hamad (King of Bahrain) 63
al-Khalifa, Khalifa (Prime Minister of Bahrain) 59–61, 71, 74–76
al-Khalifa, Salman (Crown Prince of Bahrain) 63, 71
al-Khalili family 59
al-Said, Qaboos 57–59, 61, 62, 75
al-Sultan family 57
al-Urayyid family 59, 60, 72
al-Zawawi family 58
Arab Cooperation Council 150
Arab Gulf 11, 13, 81, 87, 92, 96, 101, 106
Arab League 149, 150, 158
Asia-Pacific Economic Cooperation (APEC) 142, 145, 155–159

Bahrain 11, 20, 22–28, 31–36, 50, 55, 56, 59–64, 67, 69–76, 114, 150, 153, 184, 196, 210–219
Bahrain Chamber of Commerce (BCCI) 60, 72, 74
Bahrainization 69
basic income 44–46
brokerage 109, 113, 121, 131, 136
bureaucracy 114, 126, 128, 129, 131, 135
Bush, George W. 210–212, 218
business elite 14, 55, 56, 59–61, 69, 74, 76

Carter Doctrine 187
cash grants 43, 44
China 4–8, 143, 166, 172–176, 197–206, 207, 222

development plans 13, 14, 16, 20, 21, 26, 27
diversification 22, 24, 25, 52, 55, 61, 64, 74, 143, 156
diwaniyya 109, 131–137
Doha 79, 99, 100, 102, 106, 198, 215
Dubai 100, 104, 106, 212

economic development 15, 16, 18, 20, 56, 75, 142
Economic Development Board (Bahrain) 63, 64

Fakhro family 60, 70
foreign policy
    Iran 161–177, 220
    Western 80

Greater Arab Free Trade Agreement (GAFTA) 150, 156
Gulf Cooperation Council (GCC) 19, 29, 142, 208–210, 212–222
    GCC economies 19, 51
Gulf War 185, 189, 190, 199, 219, 221

hegemony 181, 191, 193
human rights 83, 85, 96, 98, 99, 103, 104, 106, 196, 202

ideology 93, 94, 158, 162, 163, 167–171, 173, 174, 176, 200
instrumentalism 156
interdependence 51, 167
Iran 161–177, 198–200, 203, 204
Iran–Iraq War 185, 188, 191, 204, 219

Iraq War 191, 210, 211, 221
Islam 87–91, 94, 95

kafala 73, 104
Kanoo family 59
Kuwait 11, 20–27, 109, 111–127, 129–136, 204

labor market 30, 36, 44–55, 56, 61, 64, 66, 67, 69–71, 76
Labor Market Regulation Authority (LMRA) 70, 71, 73, 76
legal reform 81, 96, 99–101, 106
liberalization 81, 84, 96, 97, 99, 142, 144, 150, 155–159

military bases 8, 185, 207–222
military presence 187, 195, 208–211, 221, 222
monetary union 146

national interest 162, 163, 166, 168, 201

Obama, Barack 152, 210–213, 216–220
oil 32–40, 56–60, 62, 99, 110, 117, 121, 124, 141, 165, 176, 181–188, 190, 193–195, 201–220
Oman 11, 18, 20–28, 55–59, 61–69, 73–76
Omani Chamber of Commerce 58, 67
Omanization 23, 61, 65–69
open regionalism 155, 157

patronage 29, 31, 32, 36, 38–40, 52, 135
Persian Gulf 1, 61, 166, 181–196, 208, 209, 216, 220–222
planning 14–21, 24, 26, 165, 194
political Islam 162, 168, 169, 171–174

post-American world 198, 199, 201, 203, 205
public sector employment 44

Qatar 11, 20–26, 79–82, 86, 87, 96–104, 106, 107, 150, 190, 210, 219

Rajab family 59
regionalism 142, 147–149, 155–157
religion and politics 173
rent distribution 45, 109, 124
rentier states 30, 31, 42, 44, 45, 52, 110, 131
rentierism 136
rule of law 79–88, 90–99, 101–103, 106, 144, 147, 158

Saudi Arabia 11, 14, 18, 20–28, 31, 34–41, 43, 45, 47, 48, 52, 197, 201–206
shari'a 7, 87, 88, 94, 95, 97, 101, 106, 147
Silk Road 201, 202
soft institutionalization 156
Sohar 62, 68, 69, 75
subsidies 31, 32, 34, 36, 45, 47, 52, 124, 130

Trade and Investment Partnership Initiative in the Middle East and North Africa (TIPI-MENA) 152, 153
Twin Pillar Policy 187

United Arab Emirates (UAE) 11, 12, 86, 97, 101, 107, 146, 170, 212–222

wasta 7, 125, 127–129, 131–135

Zubair family 58